EXCITER FISHING

EXCITER FISHING

Fred Olson

Winchester Press

Library of Congress Cataloging in Publication Data

Olson, Fred.
  Exciter fishing.

  Includes index.
  1. Fishing. I. Title.
SH441.045   799.1'7'55   77-26891
ISBN 0-87691-233-1

98765432

Published by Winchester Press
205 East 42nd Street
New York, N.Y. 10017

Printed in the United States of America

WINCHESTER is a Trademark of Olin Corporation used by
Winchester Press, Inc. under authority and control of
the Trademark Proprietor.

Book Design by Marcy J. Katz

Contents

ACKNOWLEDGMENTS

Clyde Allison, Motion Picture Producer, Michigan Department of Natural Resources (D.N.R.)

Frank Amato, Editor, *Salmon Trout Steelheader*

Rupert E. Andrews, Director, Sport Fish Division, Alaska Department of Fish and Game

Robert H. Armstrong, Regional Research Supervisor, Sport Fish Division, Alaska Department of Fish and Game

Robert Baade, Fisheries Biologist, Sport Fish Division, Alaska Department of Fish and Game

Jim Bedford, Assistant Director, Michigan D.N.R. Water Quality Control Lab

Dave Borgeson, Inland Fisheries Chief, Michigan D.N.R.

Etienne Corbeil, Director, Fish and Game Branch, Quebec Department of Tourism

Lud Frankenberger, Anadromous Fisheries Specialist, Fisheries Division, Michigan D.N.R.

Delano R. Graff, Chief, Division of Fisheries, Pennsylvania Fish Commission

Joseph L. Janisch, Fisheries Specialist, Division of Fish and Wildlife, Indiana D.N.R.

Ernest R. Jefferies, Fish Culture Supervisor, Oregon Department of Fish and Wildlife

Paul T. Jensen, Chief, Anadromous Fisheries Branch, California Department of Fish and Game

Clayton Lakes, Fish Management Supervisor, Ohio D.N.R.

Dennis P. Lee, Fisheries Biologist, California Department of Fish and Game

Jim Lichatowich, Fisheries Biologist, Oregon Department of Fish and Wildlife

Stan Lievense, Natural Resources Manager, The Michigan Travel Bureau

K. H. Loftus, Director, Fisheries Branch, Ontario Ministry of Natural Resources

Jim Martin, Research Biologist, Oregon Department of Fish and Wildlife

Cliff Millenbach, Chief, Fishery Management Division, Washington Game Department

David W. Narver, Anadromous Fisheries Coordinator, British Columbia Fish and Wildlife Branch

Mrs. Marion Olson, the Author's Wife and Partner

William A. Pearce, Supervisor, Great Lakes Fisheries Section, New York Department of Environmental Conservation

Ronald J. Poff, Supervisor, Boundary Waters and Great Lakes, Wisconsin D.N.R.

Camille Pomerleau, Research Biologist, Quebec Ministere Du Tourisme, De La Chasse Et De La Peche

Richard B. Sternberg, Research Biologist, Cold Water Fisheries, Minnesota D.N.R.

Harry Wight, Fishery Biologist, Division of Fisheries, Illinois Department of Conservation

PHOTO ACKNOWLEDGMENTS

The cover illustration shot by Gilbert Clark, Michigan Travel Bureau photographer, shows Stan Lievense, Michigan Travel Bureau Natural Resources Manager, with a fresh-run coho in spawning dress.

Figure drawings are by Steve Olson, Kent State architecture student, and Mrs. Marion Olson.

The black and white picture of the author on the inside jacket flap was shot by Robert Denk.

Unless otherwise indicated, individual photos used in the text are by the author.

Introduction

This book is about fishing for the salmon, trout, and char called chinook, coho, pinks, steelhead, sea trout (browns), cutthroat, Atlantic salmon, Dolly Vardens, arctic char, and coaster brooks during their spawning run. (At some points chum and sockeye are also discussed.) These fish are cousins and are called migratory salmonids. They all belong to the same subfamily, Salmoninae.

Migratory salmonids share a common behavior pattern that is the basis of exciter fishing principles. They fast while they're on their spawning run, although some break their fast frequently, others occasionally, and still others, never.

The fish are difficult to talk about for several reasons. In the first place, many of them are not correctly named. Atlantic salmon are not salmon, they are trout. Brook trout are not trout, they are char. In addition, each of the trout and char has two strains—anadromous and nonanadromous. Rainbows and steelhead, for example, are the same species, but rainbows are nonanadromous; steelhead are anadromous. All Pacific salmon die after spawning, but all trout and char can live through spawning stress. Finally, most of these fish have many popular names. Chinook, for example, are called kings, tye, and springs.

The best way to make sense of all this is to call them by their Latin names. But fishermen are not biologists or Latin scholars.

Therefore I shall arrange the popular names into the order taxonomists use. They place salmon, trout, and char in the salmon-trout subfamily called Salmoninae under the "salmon" family called Salmonidae. Salmon-trout are one of three sub-families. The other two are grayling and whitefish. They are all "salmon"—hence all are called salmonids.

There are five Pacific salmon, five trout, and four (some biologists list five) char in the salmon-trout subfamily. They are:

Pacific Salmon

*Pink (humpback), *Oncorhynchus gorbuscha* (Walbaum)
*Sockeye (blueback), *Oncorhynchus nerka* (Walbaum)
 Kokanee, *Oncorhynchus nerka kennerlyi* (Suckley) is a
   dwarfed, landlocked form of sockeye
*Chinook (king), *Oncorhynchus tshawytscha* (Walbaum)
*Chum (dog), *Oncorhynchus keta* (Walbaum)
*Coho (silver), *Oncorhynchus kisutch* (Walbaum)

Trout

*Cutthroat, *Salmo clarki* Richardson
*Atlantic "salmon," *Salmo salar* Linnaeus
*Brown trout (sea trout), *Salmo trutta* Linnaeus
 Golden trout, *Salmo aguabonita* Jordan
*Rainbow trout (steelhead), *Salmo gairdneri* Richardson

Char

 Lake trout, *Salvelinus namaycush* (Walbaum)
 Ciscowet, *Salvelinus siscowet* (Agassiz) (sometimes regarded
   as a form of lake trout)
*Arctic char, *Salvelinus alpinus* (Linnaeus)
*Eastern brook trout (coaster brooks), *Salvelinus fontinalis*
   (Mitchill)
*Dolly Varden, *Salvelinus malma* (Walbaum)

The asterisk indicates the various species described in this work. I give the popular name I'll use (for Pacifics a second popular name), and the Latin name of each species. (If the popular name I've listed here puzzles you, check to see if your favorite name is listed in the life history section.) Golden trout, lake trout, and ciscowet are not discussed in this book because they do not migrate from big water into streams to spawn.

The reason taxonomists can run all the salmon, trout, and char into one corral is that they all have the same brands and earmarks—each species is characterized by adipose fins and an axillary process at the base of each pelvic fin. In addition, they are fine-scaled fishes having well-developed teeth and coarse, stubby gill rakers.

The salmonids marked by an asterisk are popularly called migratory. This inexact word is used in place of a biological term, anadromous. To further complicate matters, the word anadromous changed meaning when Pacific salmon were successfully introduced into the Great Lakes.

The classic meaning of anadromous is spawning in fresh water, feeding in salt water. There are two major migrations involved: from the stream of birth to a feeding region in an ocean (Atlantic, Pacific, or Arctic), and from the feeding region to the birth stream to spawn. Many biologists once believed that anadromous fish could not live unless they spent some time in salt water. They called Pacific salmon "obligatory anadromous." But introduction of the fish into the Great Lakes shows that they can live in an entirely freshwater habitat. They continue to make the two major migrations—from their freshwater birth stream to a freshwater (Great Lakes) feeding region, and from the feeding region to their birth stream to spawn. Today we know that the feeding region of salmonids can be either salt or fresh. All that's needed is forage fish that are abundant in the Great Lakes and the oceans.

In order to understand clearly about the fish marked with asterisks, there's another thing we need to know about the word anadromous. All Pacific salmon make the major migrations. They are all anadromous. But trout and char have two strains, anadromous and nonanadromous. Nonanadromous trout and char elect not to go down to Big Water to feed. They omit that migration. In streams that have no barrier to downstream migration they live their lives within the stream. They can be transplanted to other streams tributary to Big Water having no barriers to downstream migration and they stay within the stream. In this sense, they're "cows" that require no pasture fence. They will save their own lives if transplanted to warmwater streams tributary to southern Great Lakes by running to the cooler lake when stream temperatures heat up. But, in most instances, they have to be forced out of the "pasture." When nonanadromous fish spawn, they run farther up in their streams to spawn in headwaters. (Of course, that's a migration, and it's one of the reasons it's inexact to call anadromous fish "migratory.") Nonanadromous fish do not grow as large as anadromous fish; they don't have the forage fish to get fat on. Rainbows and steelhead are examples of anadromous and nonanadromous strains of the same species. Rainbows stay within a stream; steelhead migrate. Both anadromous and nonanadromous cutthroat live in streams tributary to the Pacific.

In order to migrate from salt water to fresh water, anadromous fish have to have special equipment. They can live in salt water without becoming dehydrated, and in fresh water without becoming waterlogged. This is called osmoregulation.

Some Atlantic salmon are landlocked. This does not make them nonanadromous. In their attempts to get to sea, landlocked Atlantics have run onto dry land when their lakes have overflowed.

The listing earlier in this Introduction left out the Asian Pacific salmon that swim west of the North American continental shelf. On the taxonomic key they belong with the American Pacifics.

EXCITER
FISHING

Eggs in
Silk Stockings

I first got hooked on migratory salmonid fishing because of something that happened to me on the way to church one Sunday morning in the spring of 1960. I was en route to preach when I saw a friend (I'll call him Sulo Maki) carrying a steelhead—28 inches of bright silver, with jade green back, pewter sides, pearl white belly, the lateral line joining the small, gaping pink mouth to the steel tail. The sun shone through the tail fin tissue illuminating black dots. I feel in love with that fish. I wanted to take it into the pulpit to hold it up before the congregation. The fish, after all, is a Christian symbol!

We were too poor to buy a fly rod, line, and reel, so my wife proposed getting the equipment with Green Stamps.

A few weeks later, with a whippy rod and a Zebco 606 closed-face reel equipped with 6-pound-test line, I approached the Misery River weir with Sulo. It was daybreak. We could hear the Lake Superior surf pounding as we got out of the car, and the air was misty with fog and spray. We went along the path to the electric lamprey weir. In those days of lamprey predation on Great Lakes fish, it was the upper limits for steelhead fishing.

"The run is sparse," Sulo said. The steelheads were coming in with round scars where the lamprey had sucked their body fluids. "A guy caught one with the lamprey still on it," Sulo said.

Sulo rigged a dropper about 6 inches long and put a light weight on that. At the line end he tied a small hook and threaded the point through a silk stocking bag.

A sandbar split the stream into two channels. I was told to "stand like a statue and run your spawn bag through that current." The idea was to cast just about at my own feet, let the spawn bag drift through, pick it up, and cast again.

There was light in the sky, but not much on the water between the stream banks. A fog rose off the stream. I could barely see the channel between the sandbars. Perhaps the fish couldn't see me. I was disturbed by being so close to their water, but I didn't want to question my teacher.

"The steelies hang around here trying to make up their minds whether to go through the weir," he said. "If one comes through he *might* take real light. Just a tap." Sulo touched a finger tip against the back of my hand. "Like that," he said. "That's the touch of dynamite. Feel for them with line in your fingers." He gave a demonstration cast, then watched me attempt the plunk and short-drift method.

Sulo went downstream to another good spot leaving me alone. I could hear the wild Lake Superior surf pounding against the shore, and my heart pounding within my chest. An hour later I was wondering whether I had understood the instructions. I'd made about ten thousand casts, and caught nothing. The sun had burned through the lake mist; I saw the stream, shallow and clear at my feet.

"Getting pretty light," Sulo said from the bank. We went downstream to a hole under a log. Sulo showed me where to cast. My left hand fingers felt a vibration in the line. I raised the rod tip and the line surged away from me running against the drag for 50 feet. The fish rose from the water showering the tag alder bushes with spray. I saw a silvery torpedo shape, an eye, a curled tail, and a tinge of pink; then the water curled around the falling body, and the line went slack. A horrible sense of frustration sank into my heart.

"What did I do wrong?" I cried out.

I had wanted to be initiated with dignity, and to win honors I hadn't earned. Then Sulo gave me a crushing blow.

"That whippy rod and that light line will never work," he said. He got a spool of 20-pound line from his car. "It's not right for that reel, but nothing else will hold them," he said.

A friend of Sulo's came from downstream with an 8-pounder and gutted it beside the water.

"Let's see what it's been eating," Sulo said.

"They don't eat," his friend said. And, indeed, the stomach was empty and shrunken. I began to wonder.

The spawn bags puzzled me. I had never seen one before. It was just dawning on me that the fish were on a spawning run, and it took two or three years for me to understand fully that the streams we waded in were "wombs" for eggs.

The first place I saw steelhead eggs milked was at the mouth of the Big Elm. The creek makes a small, clear pool about 20 feet across in the Lake Superior agate and gravel. The inlet waters tumble from a small drop into the pool. The outlet is cut through the gravel windrow thrown up against the creek flow by wave action. Sometimes fish "kick" their way through the shallow outlet, their dorsal fins out of the water.

A student from Michigan Technological College caught a female steelhead in the pool at daybreak. Splashing gravel and spray in the air, it ran the outlet into the Big Lake. The fisherman fought it while running along the shore. The surf was heavy—perhaps the surf pressure on its head kept the fish from making a long run into the lake, a tactic that invariably defeats the fisherman. At any rate, this fish ran parallel to the shore, the line cutting through the wave foam. Fish and fisherman worked their way nearly half-way to the mouth of the Big Elm. When the student beached the fish, I saw silver scales chipped into the air from the fish's tail flailing against the beach gravel. Then round, orange, gelatinous eggs flowed luminous in the sunlight from the fish's vent.

"She's ripe!" he exclaimed. The tone of his voice said, "I've found gold!"

The Tech student took a plastic bag from his jacket pocket and knelt, expectantly alert to the treasure that gushed in a

When the author started steelheading he didn't know that they over-winter. After catching on, he started catching fish. Here he holds a steelhead and a stream-resident brown taken in Michigan's Little Manistee during a snowstorm.

golden stream as he pressed the fish's belly milking downward with his hand. At the last of the stream a little blood came out, which he aimed onto the sand.

"Now we'll catch fish," the student said. He got some squares of silk stocking out of his jacket pocket and a spool of red thread. Working on a large, flat rock, he tied up a half-dozen baglets—each with a thimbleful of orange eggs. Seeing my puzzled look, he pushed the rock toward me.

The silk was curious. It had sequins sewed on it. They glittered in the sunlight. While I tied up a half-dozen eggs, he told me how he'd thought of using sequins. Last year, while tying up spawn bags, he'd been called to the phone, and his dog came along and gulped up all the spawn. He'd decided to use small, orange, glass marbles for substitutes. Dissatisfied and uncertain, he'd added sequined silk.

"Caught a female full of spawn on glass marbles," he said.

I didn't know what to make of the story. It was the first exciter lure I'd heard of. I did use those six sequined spawn bags. I caught nothing with them.

2

Nighttime Statue Fishing

The Little Elm and the Big Elm are so small you can jump across them in many places. The Misery isn't too wide, but there are deep holes. I was sure the fish could see me. I blamed that for my failures.

"At daybreak and at dusk they can't see you," Sulo said.

He took me to the Falls River in L'Anse. The Falls, another short-run narrow stream, makes a long glide from a pool beneath a rock ledge to empty into Keweenaw Bay. Plunkers fish the pool. Above it there's a rapids. We waded into the rapids at dusk. Light still reflected from the water, but the trees on the far bank were shrouded in darkness. There were knee-deep pockets between the rocks, but in most places the water was ankle deep making it seem silly to be encapsulated in chest waders. I found a channel that looked like a highway for a migrating fish. There was a large rock between my waders and the channel. Extending my rod length over the rock I began to plunk and short-drift. Sulo was below me—only 15 feet or so. I didn't trust this water; I was sure the fish could see me in the dark.

"Watch the water," Sulo said.

Then I saw a fish squiggle its tail against a rock; half out of the water it slid into my channel and swam over my spinner.

Then a fish struck my ankle, and in the gloom a fish's body struck a rock so hard that it made an underwater "glomp" sound. The fish were all around me, working their way through the rapids.

My hands shook, and an eerie feeling of anxiety came over me. What would I do if I got one on? "Stumble after it through the rocks," Sulo said. Then he yelled and a fish splashed twice under his rod tip. "Got off! Rubbed my line on a rock," Sulo said.

For an hour I stood in the same spot, like a statue, casting maybe 12 feet, "plunking" in the water, letting the line vibrate through my fingers, then casting again. The moon came out showing Sulo in shadowy silhouette.

I moved up a few feet. Sulo took my spot. A fish took; Sulo stumbled downstream after it. In five minutes I heard the slap of limbs on Sulo's waders as he moved along the bank.

"Got him," he said. "Maybe eight pounds."

I got my flashlight from the car while Sulo cleaned the fish. There was nothing in the stomach.

"Could they be rooting in the rocks for crawdads?" I asked.

"They're running upstream," Sulo said. "We just hit a little migration. Maybe ten, twelve fish. When I was a kid there'd be hundreds of them."

Statue fishermen do not probe the waters for fish in their lies. They drift the scant few feet of a migratory route that fish follow on their way upstream. It's ideal for small streams where the waters are too thin to afford many lies. The method works best under cover of darkness or when a rising stream is silted or muddied.

ANOTHER FAILURE

I found out about a different method—rolling the line along the bottom through riffles and holes. An old man told me about it. "They do it that way out in California," he said. It was his version of drift fishing. But he didn't rig with a dropper; instead he had a universal swivel between the line and the leader so the spawn bag could roll along the stream bottom contour without twisting the line. Along the leader he put several small round weights so that it stretched full length across the stream bottom.

Perhaps "California" caught some fish that way. I could not. Three frustrating trips later I gave the method up without understanding what was wrong. When resting in lies, fish don't hold on the bottom. Unless they have bottom business, such as digging redds or crouching to spawn, their attention is directed toward a zone about 6 to 18 inches above bottom. A leader that's too long or too short can pass over or under a fish's exciter zone. The lure must pass through the mouth plane and along the lateral line. I was rolling my spawn bag under the fish.

It was a horribly frustrating method. The line, laid flat out, caught every snag it came to, and I was constantly breaking off and tying in new leader. I became troubled and grumpy. The beautiful steelhead, the fish of my dreams, seemed like an elusive fantasy. I stumbled along the stream with a bleeding ego.

I returned to statue fishing, and one evening I drifted a spinner into a fish's mouth. He leaped twice—landing the second time on the bank across the stream from me. I jumped over the stream and drew the fish farther up the bank through the woods. I can still hear the thrash of that fish's tail in the leaves.

The fish weighed a few ounces over 9 pounds. My first steelhead! It had a trace of pink along the lateral line, and an old lamprey scar on its side. I put the fish on the kitchen sink for my wife to admire, and accepted more credit than I deserved.

This fish had a spawn bag with a gold hook in its stomach.

The next day I got a fish on in the weir pool just below the trap in the Little Elm. The fish, cutting an arc around the outside perimeter of the pool, bent my whippy rod around my body and broke off. I was heartbroken. I needed better equipment, so I began to save money to buy a fly rod.

I did buy better equipment—a St. Croix rod, a Pflueger 1498 Medalist reel, and a number seven Scientific Anglers line. I went to the Misery with high hopes, and came back with my tail dragging. I went to the Big Huron where I could see in-

This 9-pound steelhead from Michigan's Little Manistee was taken on a Blue Tail Fly. The fish is wearing dark red and brown over-wintering colors. The author is wearing his favorite down jacket.

migrating steelhead, and I caught nothing. In deep frustration I went to the library, and checked out some books. I read the books, and kept on fishing. Through experience, book learning, and conversations with fishing biologists, I learned how to fish for migratory salmonids. In the following chapters I share that knowledge.

3

Which Fish Did I Catch?

HOW TO TELL THE SPECIES APART

Because several salmonid species can be in a stream at the same time, fishermen need easy ways to tell them apart. It's not unusual to have coho, steelhead, and chinook running together. Steelhead and cutthroat may run together. In New England and some Great Lakes, Atlantics and browns are in the same stream at the same time: in Quebec, Atlantics, arctic char, and coaster brooks may run together. From quick checks, fishermen can identify fish well enough to conform with the fishing laws and orient themselves. Biologists using toxonomic keys study more complicated variables. (Good quick identifications established by the Michigan Department of Natural Resources appear on pages 236-238. Unfortunately, cutthroat and arctic char are not included.)

Telling fish apart with fisherman's quick checks can be easy if a little language is learned first. The location of the opercle, the axillary process, and several fins needs to be known. We also need to know about vomerine bones, anal rays, and gill rakers.

What are gill rakers? When a gasping fish opens its gill covers, we see red filaments full of blood vessels. The filaments are the major tissue in a set of gills. Each gill is boomerang-shaped

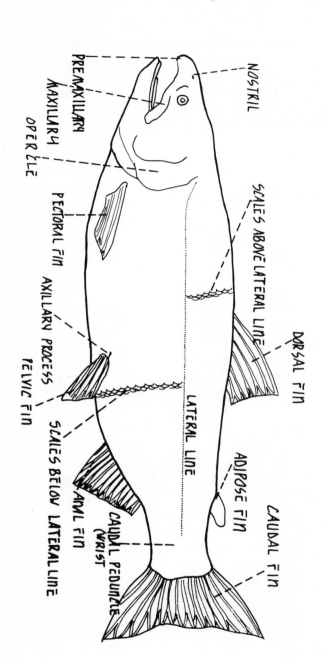

SALMONID BODY

PREMAXILLARY

MAXILLARY

OPERCLE

PECTORAL FIN

AXILLARY PROCESS

PELVIC FIN

SCALES BELOW LATERAL LINE

NOSTRIL

SCALES ABOVE LATERAL LINE

DORSAL FIN

LATERAL LINE

ADIPOSE FIN

ANAL FIN

CAUDAL PEDUNCLE (WRIST)

CAUDAL FIN

with three parts: the filaments at the leading edge of the boomerang, the gill rakers at the inside edge, and the gill arch that supports both. The filaments point in one direction, the gill rakers in the opposite direction. Water contains sticks, leaves, and other debris. The rakers are the sieve that strains these foreign bodies out. Counting gill rakers is one way biologists differentiate species.

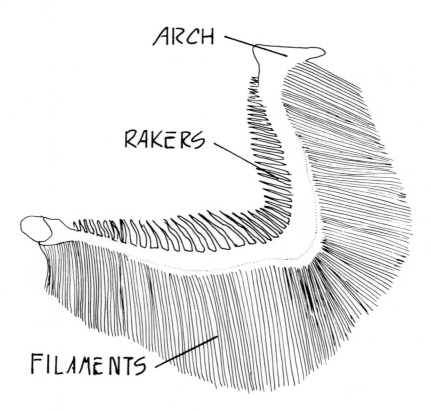

ARCH

RAKERS

FILAMENTS

SALMONID GILL

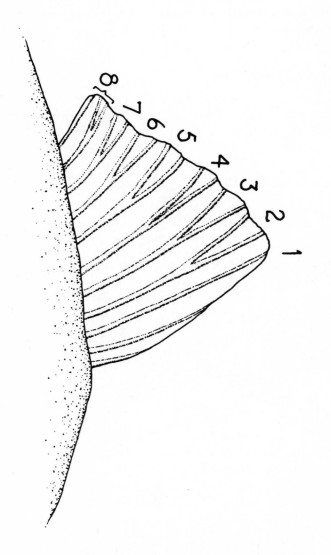

DORSAL FIN RAY COUNT

Fins are membranous structures supported by rays or spines. Rays may be soft or hard. Soft rays have many joints and may be split at the outer end. The rays at the front of a fin, called rudimentary rays, are usually soft, not divided, and short. Biologists don't usually include rudimentary rays in ray counts. But the long unbranched ray often found at the front of dorsal and anal fins is usually counted. The last ray in dorsal and anal fins may be split almost to the base, and can mistakenly be counted as two. For these reasons ray counting isn't an exact science.

The vomerine bone is shaped like a boat having a pointed stern and bow. The bone can be seen in the inside upper jaw at the center and extending about halfway to the gills. The bones on either side of the vomer are called palatines. People grow teeth on their jaws only, but fish can have them on nearly every, or any, inside mouth bone. For this reason, the place teeth grow and their pattern is often a species-distinguishing characteristic.

QUICK CHECKS FOR TELLING SPECIES APART

Trout and char have twelve or less fully developed rays in the anal fin; Pacific salmon have thirteen or more. Don Fry, in *Anadromous Fishes of California*, reports rare specimens of rainbows with thirteen rays.

Cutthroat are not always smaller than steelhead. Usually they can be distinguished from steelies by their yellow-orange or red-colored undermandible ("cutthroat marks") but fresh-run cutthroat may be silvery or pale. In that case put a finger on the fish's tongue. Both steelies and cutts (and all trout) have small teeth at the tip, but cutthroat have a second group farther back at the base of the tongue. They're called hyoid teeth. Rainbows (remember steelhead are rainbows) don't have them.

Anadromous browns (sea trout) can be confused with both Atlantics and steelhead. Sea-run browns turn pale and silvery, and may lose their red spots entirely while the black spots become much less conspicuous. If there are both black and red spots present, the fish is a brown. In England, sea trout and Atlantics may run in the same stream at the same time. The

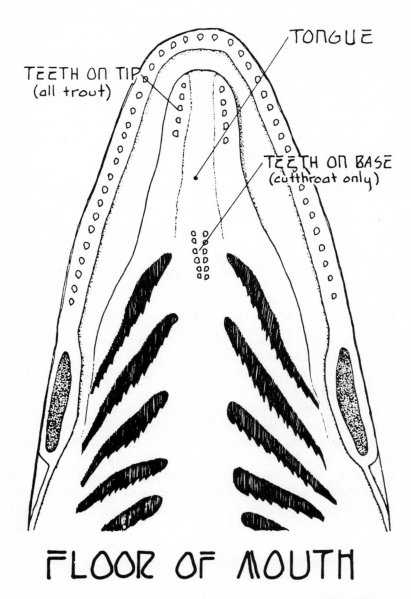

TONGUE

TEETH ON TIP
(all trout)

TEETH ON BASE
(cutthroat only)

FLOOR OF MOUTH

When the "throat marks" fade on cutthroat they can't always be told from small steelhead. Cutthroat are the *only* trout that have teeth on the base of the tongue. Feel with your fingers on the tongue.

quick check there is to count the rows of scales between the adipose fin and the lateral line. The Atlantic usually has thirteen or fewer rows; the brown fourteen or more. The Atlantic has x-shaped spots. Cecil Heacox says in *The Compleat Brown Trout,* "The brown's most reliable identification character—distinguishing it from brooks, rainbows and landlocked salmon—are the well-developed vomerine teeth on the raised shaft of bone in the center of the mouth, arranged in distinctive double-zigzag rows."

Trout and char often exist in the same water so it's good to be able to tell them apart. Char have rounder bodies, smaller scales, and, in the Dolly Varden and brooks, either pink or red

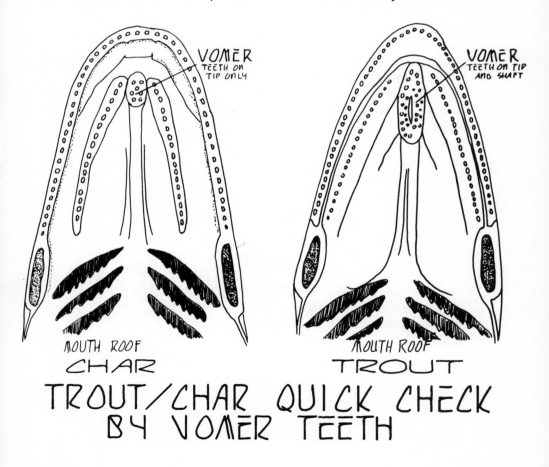

VOMER
TEETH ON TIP ONLY

VOMER
TEETH ON TIP AND SHAFT

MOUTH ROOF
CHAR

MOUTH ROOF
TROUT

TROUT/CHAR QUICK CHECK
BY VOMER TEETH

spots. For more complete identification, check the vomerine bone. In trout the vomer extends from the palatine bone nearly halfway to the gill arches and has teeth the full length. The char's vomerine bone has teeth only at the front, and the back of the bone is sunken and not visible.

Because coho and chinook may run at the same time in the same river, a quick check that distinguishes one from the other is helpful. Coho have white gums around the teeth, while the gums of a chinook's mouth are all dark-colored. Coho are sometimes called silver salmon. The gums of silver salmon have a silver lining.

It isn't always easy to tell male from female fish because their genitals are mostly inside their bodies and none of them have breasts or Adam's apples. They do have ovipores that become swollen and distented during spawning, but these are not marked "male" or "female." Male fish extrude white sperm or milt; female fish orange eggs called ova. In most species male fish, during spawning, develop kypes, a prolonged, hooked bottom jaw with a fitting socket in the prolonged, upper jaw. Female fish develop pregnant bellies before spawning; flabby bellies afterwards. If you see a fish moving gravel to make a redd, it's probably female. If you see a fish aggressively chasing other fish or butting the female in the side, it's probably a male.

NAMES OF LIFE STAGES

It is also important to learn the various stages in a fish's life, each of which has a name. The standard names are those given to the life stages of Atlantics. They came into the language first, and because Atlantic salmon fishing ideas have dominated the migratory salmonid writings they are the most often used. Migratory salmonid fishermen can use them in their streamside diaries.

Alevins—Hatched fish that have the nourishing yolk sac still attached.
Fry or fingerlings—Their yolk sac has absorbed. The fish is about 1 inch long.
Parr—The distinction between fry and parr is based upon a

gradation in size. Parr are bigger than fry. In effect, they are the length of the hatchery manager's finger. Parr have parr marks that in some species may last into adult life.

Smolt—Silvering fish with enlarged thyroids, and salt cell screens in their gills.

Hen—Female fish.

Cock—Male fish.

Grilse—A small, sexually mature fish on its first in-migration.

Kelt—A fish that has spawned, and will out-migrate.

Well-mended kelt—A well-recovered, spawned-out fish. It may be a fish that spawned immediately after running in and never lost all of its silvering and vitality.

Baggot or rawner—A female that didn't lay its eggs.

Grilse is a word that is often used as a synonym for small Atlantics, but it also means a sexually mature fish. Grilse run to spawn carrying both roe and milt. Most of them are male. They are young, mature fish returning from the sea to spawn for the first time when between three and three-and-a-half years of age. They may weigh from 4 to 12 pounds.

Biologists who set grilse age by years can be more accurate because they can count the scale rings. Where fish management requires verification of grilse populations by stream section, this method is preferable. At camps where weight instead of age is the criteria, the term has a more general meaning.

All the anadromous juvenile species featured in this book except pinks and chum smolt before running down to sea. The external sign of smolting is silvering from guanine deposits in the layer of cells covering the scales over the lower body. There are two other physiological changes—enlargement of the thyroid gland, and growth of excretory salt cells in the gills.

The term "well-mended kelt" causes confusion. Fishermen hunt for fighting fish that have a prestigious, silvery look. From their point of view, well-mended should mean muscular recovery and guanine deposits. Hungry diners don't like the taste of kelts because they lack the flavors that are in the juices and fats of healthy fish. The problem is that a fisherman may catch a kelt that has silvered enough to look prestigious, and has a full enough stomach to look well rounded and well fed, but may not be mended well enough to taste good. Few kelts are mended enough to be flavorsome fish, except those that ran directly upstream, spawned, and started feeding during an immediately started return trip to sea.

For several reasons, not all of the terms listed here are used with great uniformity for the wide range of anadromous salmon, trout, and char. For example, the word "juvenile" often replaces both the words "fry" and "parr." For some species and for some hatchery situations, juvenile may be a more accurate term. There are no kelts among Pacifics because they die. Pinks do not have parr marks. So the total uniformity that the terms might seem to offer isn't possible among these extremely variable species. Still the terms are used so often that one must keep their exact meanings clearly in mind.

4

How to Live and Die Under Water

The worm fisherman has a rudimentary knowledge of the behavior of feeding fish. He knows that if you don't spook them they'll take a cleverly offered, baited hook. The migratory salmonid fisherman must have a more complex knowledge of fish behavior, because many of the species he fishes for are not feeding.

Fishes are vertebrate animals having fins and gills. Their jointed backbones are more flexible than man's. The inter-vertebral connections filled with a jelly are fluid ball-and-socket joints. Their streamlined bodies are driven through water by long layers of muscles—the white muscles are power-stroke muscles, and the pink muscles probably assist in cruising. In the body cavity vital organs adopted to a water-foil shape are suspended in a hammock that stretches and contracts in harmony with the graceful movements of their muscled bodies.

Salmonids react, metabolate, and spawn under continuous conditions of yaw, pitch, and roll in water of various pressures, degrees of visibility, and depths. They struggle with a fluid instead of a gas for oxygen.

Many fish, including salmonids, have swim bladders that help them overcome gravity by making their density nearly equal to that of the water in which they swim. The swim bladder, located in the abdominal cavity beneath the backbone, is a balloon filled with gas that the fish releases from its bloodstream. When a fish swims into deeper water, the increase in outside pressure triggers removal of gas from the swim bladder, increasing its density. Swimming into shallower water of decreased outside pressure triggers an increase in swim bladder size, decreasing the fish's density; the organism automatically adjusts to the change in pressure. When a bird flies, much muscular effort is expended to overcome gravity and maintain altitude. Fish with swim bladders achieve weightlessness that allows all muscular effort to be devoted to propulsion.

The lateral line, a unique sensory organ, called the organ of sixth sense, functions in harmonious concert with the total organism to achieve underwater orientation and perception. In salmonids it runs parallel to the long axis of the body from brain to tail on both sides. It gives the side view of salmonids an imbalanced bilateral symmetry because the belly curves more deeply below it than does the backbone above it.

Pacific salmon and steelhead could be imported from the Pacific drainage to the Great Lakes because they can live in a saltwater/freshwater habitat or an entirely freshwater habitat. In their native Pacific slope habitat they are born in fresh water, go down to salt water to feed, and return to freshwater streams to spawn. In other words, they are anadromous. They are capable of osmoregulation in both salt water and fresh water. In their Great Lakes region of adoption these species are capable of juvenile growth, feeding, and spawning entirely in fresh water. They do not need to osmoregulate in fresh water during some of their life cycle and in salt water during another part of their life cycle to maintain functional unity. Furthermore, they do not forget to run into their stream of birth (or imprinted stream) after having fed in fresh water for the time normal to their species. As long as they can drop down to a sea that has an adequate supply of forage fish, their life cycle can be normal in the Great Lakes habitat.

Osmosis follows the law that when two salt solutions of unequal strength are separated by a membrane, water passes from the weaker solution to the stronger. Gills are a porous membrane, and in salt water, fish lose water to the sea; in fresh water, fish absorb water. In salt water fish drink continually. Salt cells in their gills screen some of the salt effect. Kidney secretion further regulates body fluid balance. The blood of fishes is of higher salinity than fresh water, which in streams and lakes seeps into their bodies threatening water-logging. Fish in fresh water urinate frequently and never drink.

The skin of a salmonid has two major layers. The outer layer is the scales. The inner layer is sometimes called the skin, but is more accurately referred to as the dermis. The scales of anadromous salmonids change color, but are never shed. Because they do not shed their scales, their growth rings and spawning scars record their bodily history chronologically. The tip edge of each scale is set into the dermis at a 45-degree angle. The angle makes it possible to scrape them out of their pocket in the dermis. When we scale fish we remove the armor layer of the skin. Scales that are killed or knocked out of place by injuries regenerate. They are not useful for scale-reading.

Each scale is a thin, shingling disk of bone, and the exposed part is covered with a thin layer of cells, which could be referred to as a third layer of skin. It is the outer layer, and it can change from transparent to silver.

Trout scales have year bands called annuli that are somewhat similar to those seen on tree stumps, except that on scales the annual bands are each composed of several rings or ridges called circuli. When a salmonid leaves its birth stream and goes to sea, its faster growth there causes widely spaced rings. When a salmonid over-winters in a stream while waiting to spawn, its slower growth causes thinly spaced rings. The first set of rings around the core of the scale is often thinly spaced; the next set, reflecting the fish's first sea-feeding period, is usually widely spaced; the following set, reflecting a return to the stream for spawning, may be thinly spaced. The biologist looking at these rings under a low-power microscope or a hand lens separates them into sets of rings instead of counting each ring as a tree life expert does.

Scales of migratories that have spawned and run back to Big Water, and returned to spawn again, bear a spawning mark. It is an erosion resulting from calcium deficiency during the

The center is called the focus. To determine age, count the rings in sets called annuli. Note erosion marks indicating spawning.

fasting period that migratories adopt during their spawning runs. The spawning mark starts at the scale shoulder (the outer area where there are no rings) and usually spreads in an irregular triangular shape. It's possible to count them and learn how many times a salmonid has spawned.

Salmonid scales reveal the age of the fish, the number of times it has fed in the sea, and the number of times it has spawned.

Anadromous fish change their colors. When they go to sea, they become bright fish because they assume sea camouflage. When they run back into their birth streams to spawn, they become dark fish because they assume stream camouflage and adopt mating colors. Changing color is a part of getting ready for sea, for mating, and, for Pacifics, for death.

The change from stream colors to sea colors occurs for juveniles that are out-migrating to the sea to feed. They smolt. Most of them become greenish on the back and nearly all of them become silvery on the sides and belly. The silvery color mirrors the surrounding colors of the water and the bottom. Their enemies do not see the salmonid's silhouette; instead they see the mirrored water and sea bottom. It's somewhat like hiding behind a mirror. These beautiful sea colors, so highly prized by fishermen, become a liability in the stream and the fish change colors when they return to streams to spawn. This color change also includes a display of spawning colors. The colors are more gaudy than nonanadromous cousins find necessary to adopt for hiding from stream enemies. Pacific salmon move from combination spawning-camouflage colors to mourning colors—the black skin of death. Fish that don't die after spawning put on new, silvery sea clothes when they return to Big Water.

In anadromous salmonids these color changes occur in two places—in the cells covering the scales and in the cells in the dermis. When fish go to sea the cells covering the scales take up guanine deposits; when they run back into the birth stream the process reverses. Steelhead have melanophores in their dermises. A melanophore is a black or brown pigment cell containing melanin. The major colors in fishes' dermises come from cells called chromatophores. Hues are mixed by arrangement of three chromatophores—black-yellow, yellow-black, and orange-blue. The changes in an anadromous fish's color occur because of changes in both the dermis and the epidermis.

When fish smolt, and when they return to sea after spawning, they get silvery sea clothes. The silvering is done by guanine deposits (guanine is a purine constituent of certain acids that are soluble in water) in the scales covering the cheeks, opercule, and sides. In anadromous brook trout the dorsal surface may become pale green; in steelhead, steel-blue. This silvering hides the pigment in the skin, parr marks, crosshatches, or other skin markings. In the stream as guanine fades, pigmentation changes also occur.

Spawning colors transcend stream camouflage, a habitat adaptation, into the realm of sexual signaling. These colors are highly variable. A species may adopt one spawning color in one area and another color in another area. Spawning male coho in Michigan usually have red sides—sometimes a wide, brick-red stripe—but in Ohio streams they have little, if any, red on their sides.

Another fish color occurs among spawned-out kelts. They become anemic-looking and lose color because of a loss of vitality. They may have sores that are slow to heal. Of course, they're thin and lacking in swimming power. The kelt, if it mends, will become silver-colored on the way downstream to the sea.

The term "dark fish" is indeed rather vague. It may refer to an over-wintering fish that has lost its silvering and adopted some stage of camouflage. (In steelhead there may be several color changes.) It may refer to fish such as Toutle River chinook stocks that immediately lose their silvering and adopt a green or bronze camouflage. It may refer to this same chinook whose camouflage gradually gives way to black dying skin. Or it may refer to a spawned-out kelt whose spawning colors gave way because of the anemic, washed-out state of exhaustion.

Because bright fish are usually fresh from the sea they have fighting vitality. Landing them is a contest that the migratory fisherman welcomes, and he displays bright fish as prestige trophies that bear witness to his skill at playing against worthy antagonists. A dark fish is lacking in fighting vigor, and it is not a trophy. In rivers having in-migrating bright fish and out-migrating kelts, the bright fish get away and the kelts come in like tame dogs on leashes. A dark fish is not a photographic trophy, and it is not good eating. Dark salmon don't taste good because their cells are dying. Dark Atlantic and steelhead kelts don't taste good because their cells are not well nourished. They've been fasting, swimming, and mating instead of fattening themselves for the fisherman's skillet.

Unfortunately, not all Pacific salmon come in from the sea in bright colors. Some stocks lose their sea colors as they approach the river mouth and come into the streams nearly ready to drop their eggs and die. Fishermen who catch these stocks, and they exist in the Great Lakes plantings, should not be harshly judged by Pacific Coast fishermen where the fish are much brighter. Some of the bronze and green-colored fish displayed by Great Lakes fishermen have leapt three or four times and run out a lot of backing before they were beached. So one region's dark fish may be another region's bright fish. Furthermore, kelts across the Atlantic and steelhead ranges often fight harder than an inspection of their pictured skin may indicate.

Fishermen who are aware of the color changes from bright to dark made by the species in the rivers they know can tell a great deal about the progress of a run by the colors of the fish. If the fish are all bright and the stream has had only one major freshet, then the run has not gone on very long. If some of the fish are bright and some have stream camouflage, there have been several successive waves of in-migrating fish. If there are dying black chinook wobbling around upside down in the current and bronze chinook in the shallows, the run has gone on for some time, but will continue longer. If there are bright fish at the river mouth and dark fish on the spawning gravel, another run will reach spawning gravel before long. These are some of the deductions that fishermen may make from inspecting fish color.

All Pacific salmon die after spawning. Their deaths are not due to the functional failure of a vital organ. The gonads and fallopian tubes do not become diseased because of spawning stress and cause death. Everything—blood, organs, tissues, the whole body in all cells—ages at one time. The skin darkens as the fish approaches death.

Darkening skin results from the release of melanin from pigment cells. This can be normal or abnormal depending on life cycle and species. Rapid and marked melanogensis is a normal sign of death among postspawning Pacifics. But pronounced melanogenesis among prespawning Atlantics, for example, is a sign of illness.

Fish have paired and unpaired fins. The paired fins corresponding roughly to arms and legs are pectoral and pelvic. In salmonids (bony fishes) the pectoral fins push out to brake forward motion. When one is pushed out it acts as a pivot to assist turning. The pelvic fins can also brake, and they compensate for the lifting action that raises decelerating fish in the water.

The anal and dorsal fins act as keels. The adipose fins of migratory salmonid are rudimentary fatty lumps that no longer have rays, and, like a human's appendix, are evolutionary sheddings.

The tail or caudal fin is the rudder-paddle that aids the swimming muscles. A fish can swim after its tail fin is amputated. Locomotion is mainly produced by muscular waves of curvature that pass toward the tail with increasing amplitude. The white muscles of steelhead and Atlantics produce immediate muscular waves of outstanding amplitude.

Fish eyes can see in water, regardless if it is murky or clear. Their eyes, high on the sides of their heads, give them a wide monocular (one-eyed) range, and a short field of binocular vision where the fields of monocular vision overlap. Monocular vision doesn't give a sense of perspective, but the small field of binocular vision provides an adequate amount.

Fish take lures, food, and other objects into their mouths by expanding their cheeks and gill covers to create suction. As they suck inward they open their gill covers to let the waterborne object flow toward the stomach opening. A fish using the speed of its body to strike a lure or food bites instead of sucks. Objects lodged between bottom rocks, such as nymphs, are dislodged by sucking or rooting and taken into open mouths as they float toward the oral suction and onward in the water stream through the gills. In some instances the gill rakers stop the food, which is then transferred to the gullet lining and swallowed. Most taking of food involves a transfer of body position so that the open mouth and gill covers are lined up with objects or food floating in the current. That is one reason why so many takes are felt as light taps. Another reason takes are so light is that fish may close their mouths tentatively (the gills are open), then react against the object by closing their gills and opening their mouths to expel the object.

Objects that aren't taken with an onrush of the body and a snapping of the teeth are tested for palatability by a casual mouthing, and ejected quickly by shutting the gills. This process is stream-flow testing. There is a side glimpse of a floating object in one monocular field, a turning to get binocular perspective, a positioning of the body on the floating object (the fish may let itself float down in the current ahead of the object), and an opening of mouth and gill covers to let the object float into the mouth. Suction may be applied to increase the speed and direction of the current carrying the fly, lure, egg, or bit of trash selected. Trout feeding on aquatic insects are especially adept at stream-flow tasting.

There is another taking method that is extremely important to fishermen of migratory salmonid that is based on lateral line perception which will be discussed below.

Fish do see color, and for specific situations the color of lures is crucial. Flies, streamers, and exciter lures work best when they have the right color mix. Although much about color vision in fish is not fully understood, it is more important to fish in shallow water than to those in waters that are so deep that no color is apparent.

Fish hear, but not all of their hearing is sensed through their inner ears. Some sound is sensed as pressure changes picked up by the lateral line.

Fish have an extremely keen sense of smell. (Lamprey can smell the presence of fish if the odor is presented in a cupful of water in which the other fish have swam.) They are quickly panicked by human odors, and fishermen should not put their hands into the water or urinate into the water. Fish's sense of smell attracts them to eggs, and this is particularly important to fishermen of migratory salmonid.

Fish do not think about sound, color, or smell, but rather *sense* through affective instinctual sets. For human odors, the affective instinctual set is panic and flight. After that's over with, there's apparently no mental preoccupation with the odor. After adjusting to the new odor, they may swim right back to the human and get caught. The lie from which they were panicked may be attractive to them because there's better aeration or because there's a potential mate under nearby cover.

Fish have two lateral lines, one on each side. They are canals covered by special scales each having a pore or pores opening into the tube that is filled with a slimy fluid and lined with tiny sense organs and sensing cells with nerves making connections to the ear. The lateral line is thought to be an extension of the ear. The sensory endings of a branch of the cranial nerve lie in it. One can see the pores in this canal where it extends along the head.

Lateral line functions provide a sixth sense, working uniquely on the specialized problems of underwater perception. Although biologists know a lot about the structure of the organ, they don't know much about what kind of data it transmits to fish.

Apparently the major function of the lateral line is the perception of disturbances in water made by moving objects. Blinded fish can be conditioned to locate moving glass rods if their lateral line is functional. The lateral line is not used to detect the flow of water from currents or swimming. Disconnecting the line doesn't affect a fish's ability to swim. It will still keep station against current provided that it can see. Blinded fish put into a current are swept to the bottom where they get information about the current from touch receptors. Because station keeping within the currents is such a unique and important part of the orientation in the water medium, biologists often erroneously thought the lateral line filled that need.

The lateral line helps fish find their way around obstacles in the dark. Experiments with blind fish show that they can find their way around by sense of touch. Fish don't bump into the aquarium sides, but birds do bump into windows. A fish in water may pass from one well-lighted zone to another, from sunlight to shadow, from shallow to deep, never "stumbling" against rocks, logs, or other fish.

Fish can locate lures with only their lateral line—without using either their sense of sight or their sense of smell. In *Functional Design in Fishes,* Alexander states: "A wriggling worm on a muddy bottom might be impossible to see if its movement stirred up the mud, but the lateral line system could locate it." He also explains that a fish can locate the ripples an insect makes on the surface with its lateral line. It may be that some Atlantic salmon rise to twitched surface flies because their lateral lines are more sensitive to ripples than the lateral lines of other migratory salmonids. When a fisherman's lure and line land in the water, a series of expanding concentric ripples are activated. The ripples are sensed by the neuromasts in the lateral line.

For fishermen, the mouth is the most important part of a fish. It is through the mouth that the fish communicates a take, and it is with the mouth that a fish actually takes a hook. Lure and fly presentation is to the mouth. The fish's mouth is the major entry to two other trap doors—the buccal cavity (which is the opening to the opercular cavity and the gullet) and the opercular cavity (the cavity between the gill covers). That's really three trap doors—mouth, a set of gill covers, and the gullet. Fish can open each of these trap doors or a combination of them together.

Trap door opening is vital. The fish takes some water in with its food, and lets it out by opening the gill covers; then it opens the gullet door and swallows. Fish create suction by expanding the buccal and opercular cavities, and that suction starts objects off the stream floor or guides currents that objects float upon into the mouth instead of onto the chin.

Breathing is done by opening and shutting trap doors. The mouth is open, the gill covers are open, the gullet door is closed.

Taking is done in many ways. First there's the approach to the object to be taken. Swim up, open the mouth, and surround the floating object with the mouth. That can be done slowly for a dead mouse or with speed when striking a baitfish. Positioning the body in the current line that an object is floating within and then opening the mouth and gills to let the object flow in is another approach to an object. Finally there may be no approach at all. The object may simply float to the waiting fish. I call this the inert approach.

After a fish has approached an object it remains to be seen whether the object will float in or be stopped by water resistance at the mouth. Some objects, such as baitfish, have to be stopped by teeth action (chomping). Objects that don't just float in, or ones that may be lying on the bottom (perhaps between or under rocks), need some guiding suction. The fish may suck food into the mouth by enlarging its buccal and opercular cavities. The suction may start an inert object from the bottom surface, or may guide a floating object. Combinations of positioning, closing the mouth, allowing dead float, and sucking are the usual ways of taking. And for each take a combination of trap doors is opened and closed.

Fish do something extremely important to lures and other floating objects that I call "taste-spitting." They can close their gill covers as an object they don't like floats in and expel it by spitting with the same muscles that suck, thus rejecting many things that are not digestible.

A fish may not see every object it takes. The lateral line information or the scent of the object may be enough to establish contact and tell the mouth to open. Double checking occurs when the object is in the mouth. If it doesn't feel right, it can be spit out. So, fish often just lie there taking objects in and spitting them out. Still, a fish stomach may contain an odd assortment of objects, including pine needles, pieces of bark, or floating detrital matter. Fish swallow many mistakes in spite of "taste-spitting."

Your lure is often the floating object examined in the taste-spitting action. This explains why steelhead take so lightly. Pacific Coast fishermen who are aware of taste-spitting tie a length of yarn on their lures. It catches on the fish's teeth, giving the fisherman more time to set the hook. The bright-colored yarn also adds excitement to the lure. Fluorescent-dyed yarn is usually the most exciting.

After a fish has chosen the proper approach to an object and has decided whether to apply suction it completes the take. The approach may have been at high speed to set the mouth and teeth into a baitfish. The next step is to let the gill covers be open long enough to get rid of surplus water. Then it lets go of the baitfish and gets it into gullet position. Next it lets the bait-fish float in by opening the proper gates, gets rid of the excess water, and opens the gullet gate. The approach may have been made by positioning the mouth in the current line and by dropping downstream until alignment of object and body allows the current to carry it into the mouth. At that point object guidance by suction may or may not be necessary. The proper gates will be opened and shut. The approach may have been made by swimming beneath a fly on the surface or by swimming to a nymph struggling to the surface. In these approaches selective trout fishermen see rise forms resulting from air bubbles and fish positioning. Migratory salmonid fishermen do not see rise forms because take positioning of most fasting salmonids occurs below the surface.

Most often, these fishermen encounter the inert approach. The fish on a spawning run aren't really actively feeding, but they're lying beneath objects that continuously float by, or to, them. They can hardly resist opening their mouths and gills to take objects that will float right in. And they can react by spitting the object right back out. This helps explain why we miss so many fish.

5

The Spawning-Run Calendar

The migration of salmonids from their feeding grounds in Big Water to the spawning gravel in their streams of birth has many wonderful aspects. They travel great sea distances to the mouth of their home stream; they may travel several hundred miles up their stream of birth to the gravel where they were born. They are capable of traveling about 8 miles or more per day through rapids, over falls, through pollution, and over all kinds of man-made obstacles. About 98 percent of them recognize their stream of birth. They don't need to energize by feeding along the way.

Because entry into the streams, migration upstream, and the beginnings and endings of spawning follow a predictable pattern, fishermen can develop a spawning-run calendar. The spawning-run calendar for each stream gives the same kind of information to the migratory salmonid fisherman as the aquatic insect-hatch calendar gives to the selective trout fisherman. A spawning-run calendar makes it possible for the fisherman to meet fish at nearly the same time each year.

The spawning-run calendar begins with in-migration time instead of hatch time because in-migration is the beginning of stream fishing. Biologists tell us that fish recognize their birth stream through their sense of smell. There are also other factors that help bring them home, including the coincidence of sexual maturation (in many species triggered by photoperiods, or periods of lightness and darkness affecting growth and maturity) at times when ocean feeding currents bring them near their birth stream mouth. The length of the day stimulates gonadal development. There may be other factors (e.g., temperature), but the length of time that light shines is extremely important.

The season of in-migration varies. We think of fall as the traditional time because many Atlantics, steelhead, and Pacifics make fall runs. But all of these fish also make spring and winter in-migrations. Great Lakes fishermen begin their spawning-run calendars in the fall because all of the Pacifics planted in the Great Lakes are fall spawners, and some steelhead begin in-migration in the fall, but on the Pacific Slope, in-migration calendars are more complicated. In England, Atlantics migrate in spring, late summer, and summer-fall.

So runs have beginnings in fall, winter, and spring. The beginnings usually require the coincidence of most of the following factors: photoperiod, water-discharge rate, water volume, and water temperature.

Fish feel more stimulated to enter streams on a discharge surge when there's better navigability over shoals and rocks. In streams having a strong discharge rate with navigable water, fish's exploratory entrances into the stream are reassuring and they'll continue upstream at varying rates of speed and for varying distances. A freshet will increase their determination to swim onward.

These are cold-water fish that in the southern fringes of their native range enter some warm-water streams. When the water temperature is about 70° they'll be injured or die. So the fish prefer entering streams when the water temperature is comfortable. In-migration through a surge of water that is followed by a dry spell that warms the stream can result in fish mortality. This can be a problem in the southern limits of the Pacific range or in the southern Great Lakes.

Factors that bring fish in should coincide in a logical manner. When a ripe fish that has experienced the temperature and light conditions that cause sexual maturity comes to a stream with a naturally deep channel and good rate of flow or comes to a stream in freshet, it will swim right in. If the rate of flow continues and the stream continues to cool, the fish is going upstream; but if the freshet should subside while the fish is laying in the mouth, and the water temperatures should rise, the fish may run back to Big Water.

This is all rather complicated, but a good freshet cures poor rates of flow, volume, and temperature. On the Pacific Slope, the fall freshets come on a general weather front. In the Great Lakes, in local rains. Either way, the run will have its beginning.

It's important to understand that in-migration may soon be followed by spawning and death, as in the case of Toutle River stock chinook in Michigan's Muskegon, or by over-wintering, as in the case of September steelhead that run in with the Muskegon chinook, anadromous brooks in James Bay, or Dolly Vardens in southeast Alaska.

A run can be fished to at various places in the stream from the mouth upstream to the tributaries. At each place the fish may be in a different physiological stage. We fish to bright fish that may still have some hunger urges at the river mouth. We fish to these same fish farther upstream in holes where they lay waiting for another freshet to carry them even farther upstream. By this time they may have entered into a fast. We fish to them where they lay near gravel waiting to spawn. They are even less likely to feed at that time. We may, where it is legal, fish to them on their redds, and if they are species that survive to spawn again, we may fish to them during their out-migration when they are relatively listless kelts. If these are fish that over-summer or over-winter before spawning, we may fish to them at times of semihibernation in water that is warm or very cold. Finally among some species we may fish to the juveniles, or use juvenile fly imitations to fish to adults. So a spawning-run calendar includes the place where we meet the fish and an awareness of its condition at that stage.

Fish prefer cooling freshets for travel within the streams. They will travel through astonishingly low water, but low, *warm* water blocks them. So it's important to keep track of the rainfall along your stream. In the West streams may be blocked at their mouths by tidal bars. Many western streams run low and warm during the summer months and high and cool during the rainy season. If the high, cool season is delayed, the fish will hold at the mouths or other schooling places. Western summer steelhead and cutthroat may come in on adequate freshets, but the freshets that bring winter steelhead may be delayed. Low water can occur in midwinter, so good timing for summer runs and early fall runs doesn't necessarily mean good timing for winter runs.

After the freshets bring the runs, it's often beneficial to wait until the waters recede so that the water will be clear enough for the fish to see lures and low enough for the fisherman to see currents and lies. For these reasons the migratory salmonid fisherman must know the condition of his home stream for the full season of all the runs he fishes.

The spawning-run calendars between pages 41 and 42 are based on biologists' reports. They do not have much personal information or many references to specific drifts and riffles. They are the foundation upon which a fisherman can base his own personal fishing calendar. I try to keep my own streamside diary, and to merge the general biologists' salmonid calendar with my own observations. Many other migratory salmonid fishermen that I know do this.

A private stream diary kept for the annual runs of all species using a stream could establish a spawning-migration calendar. The following information should be gathered:

1. Average in-migration time.
2. Average migration time to best fishing drifts.
3. Peak of in-migration.
4. Beginning of spawning.
5. End of in-migration.
6. End of spawning.
7. Out-migration time for kelts.
8. Time fry are observed moving away from redds.
9. Out-migration time for juveniles.

A good way to get this data is to join with several fishing buddies and compare notes. If a standardized streamside daily report can be agreed upon and mimeographed, that makes recording easier and more objective.

A fisherman cannot make a spawning-migration calendar unless he understands how many year classes of a species are associated with each stream. Somehow we all think that the coho that threw the hook on the first jump will be back next year for us to catch again. Even when the stench of dying coho is so bad along the riverbank that I have to go a half mile up the hill to eat my lunch, I still use that kind of reasoning. But this year's class of fish will never be back again, and if there weren't two more year classes of fish out in the Big Lake feeding, there'd be a gap in the runs—that is, years when there will be no fish at all.

A stream that has annual coho runs has three different populations associated with the stream. A stream that has annual chinook runs has many different populations associated with it. These populations or year classes are hard to explain unless one has a pattern example in mind. The following three tables present a typical pattern example. They are the pattern that Michigan followed in the three successive plantings that established its coho runs.

COHO PLANTING CYCLE

First Planting—Class I

1. Stocked spring 1966
   at 18 months of age.
2. Went to sea immediately.
3. Fed in lake, summer of 1966.
4. Run of Jacks, fall of 1966.
5. Fed in lake, summer of 1967.
6. *Returned to spawn, fall of 1967*.
7. First eggs hatched, February 1968.
8. Went to sea, spring of 1969.
9. Fed in lake, summer of 1969.
10. Run of Jacks, fall of 1969.
11. Fed in lake, summer of 1970.
12. *Spawned in stream, fall 1970*.

Second Planting—Class II

1. Stocked spring 1967
   at 18 months of age.
2. Went to sea immediately.
3. Fed in lake, summer of 1967.
4. Run of Jacks, fall of 1967.
5. Fed in lake, summer of 1968.
6. *Returned to spawn, fall of 1968.*
7. First eggs hatched, spring of 1969.
8. Went to sea, spring of 1970.
9. Fed in lake, summer of 1970.
10. Run of Jacks, fall of 1970.
11. Fed in lake, summer of 1971.
12. *Spawned in stream, fall of 1971.*

Third Planting—Class III

1. Stocked spring 1968 in first year of life
   at 18 months of age.
2. Went to sea immediately.
3. Fed in lake, summer of 1968.
4. Run of Jacks, fall of 1968.
5. Fed in lake, summer of 1969.
6. *Returned to spawn, fall of 1969.*
7. First eggs hatched, spring of 1970.
8. Went to sea, spring of 1971.
9. Fed in lake, summer of 1971.
10. Run of Jacks, fall of 1971.
11. Fed in lake, summer of 1972.
12. *Spawned in stream, fall of 1972.*

When these three tables are placed side by side, it becomes obvious that a three-year planting cycle is required to establish runs every year. A stream that has a coho run each year has three different year classes associated with it. A hatch cycle (from the hatch time of egg A until the hatch time of eggs spawned by offspring of egg A) is three years. Jacks will cross with adults, so the year classes are not genetically isolated.

Other conclusions can be drawn. It becomes clear what kind of population would develop if an oil tanker turns over on a highway bridge upstream from the spawning gravel and wipes out one age class. It also becomes clear that where there are multiple species in a stream, for example, the Skagit, there are many age classes associated with that stream.

Each year we wait for the fish in their running season, without knowing exactly when the weather conditions will encourage the fish to swim into the stream, but we know that as long as the river flows without obstructions the fish will come.

The spawning gravel stream sections are peculiar hosts to the fish. Female fish do not have wombs where fertilized eggs are nurtured for a gestation period. The streams are their wombs. This preserves body streamlining, so essential for maneuvering in the water. Adding a distended womb that swells large enough to hold several thousand fry to the milt and roe load would ruin the streamlining. It really is more simple to swim into the womb than to carry it around.

The spawning gravels are not only wombs, they are also nurseries for hatched fry. All salmonid fry are fed by their birth stream, some for longer periods than others.

The lower sections of streams are highways for the spawning gravel-wombs. Roderick Haig-Brown said that the major purpose of the streams tributary to the Pacific Ocean is to be mother and father to the migratory fish. Consequently, we should modify the attitude that causes an increasing Pacific Slope and Great Lakes population to totally expropriate streams for purposes that do not procreate fish.

6

Courting, Sexual Signaling, and Mating

In his book *The Salmon,* J. W. Jones lists terms that he and others have used to describe salmonid matings. I shall expand the definitions.

Cutting—A female task. She makes an egg nest in the stream bed.

Bed—A single depression or egg nest. There'll be several in each redd.

Redd—An area in the stream bed where gravel has been scoured clean by females cutting a series of egg nests— one for each of the orgasms by which she spawns several thousand eggs.

Feeling—Testing the base of the egg nest with the anal fin, and sometimes with caudal and pelvic fins, to determine proper depth and correct receptiveness for eggs.

False Orgasm—An incomplete orgasm. The male following the female's sign crouches with her. They open their mouths, but the female extrudes nothing. The male may release some sperm before stopping.

Spawning Sequence—The events leading to one orgasm and one egg covering.

Thousands of chinook spawn annually in Michigan's Muskegon River north of Grand Rapids. It is a wild scene each fall. The gravel riffles in the spawning rivers look like they had been showered by direct mortar hits. They are pockmarked with light-colored depressions (redds) made by the bellies and tails of enormous fish designing beds for their eggs. Some redds become so deep that fishermen stumble in them. In each redd the female searches the gravel swimming with her back arched, her head turned downwards, her eyes searching for gravel that meets her satisfaction. The green-sided female dribbles eggs and dips her body deeper into the gravel while the male showers her eggs with milky clouds of sperm. When we look through polarized glasses we can actually see fish extruding eggs and sperm. Each male is accompanied by a gang of jealous attendants who vie with him and each other for front spawning position. The males, weighing up to 40 pounds, churn the water with powerful tails and swim menacingly toward each other creating a turmoil of writhing bodies.

The fish can be located easily by the sound of splashing water and by the miniature water geysers thrown into the air by the fish that continually chase each other over the spawning gravel. The chasing fish may be paired or unpaired. (Pairing triggers subsequent spawning actions. Females won't make redds unless at least one potential mate is present. If the males are taken from a completed redd, the female won't lay eggs.) If the sound has one source, walk along the bank to that point. You'll see a female attended by a gaggle of males of many sizes. The female will turn on her side to churn gravel; the males will dart at each other sometimes with opened jaws. They are struggling for a dominance that may be decided finally by sexual readiness rather than by size. When the female lies steady, finning in place, the males will range behind her in the order of the established dominance. I call it the mating rest position— female to the fore; first dominant male slightly behind her, and, perhaps, pressing nearly against her; the next dominant male slightly behind the "boss" male; the next five to six males in a restless, writhing group that sorts itself out by continual charges and buttings. Or, for a time, they may all lie quiet.

But when the female turns on her side to cut away a little more gravel for her egg nest, the suitors will charge each other, swimming over and under each other.

The female may also engage in aggressiveness. If another female comes to move gravel in her egg nest she certainly will charge, but in the main the female accepts the rubbings and buttings of several males while completing the nest. There's time during the nest building for the males to get themselves fairly well sorted out. As the nest is nearly completed the gaggle of suitors is slowly reduced to two or three, and the dominance of one male becomes apparent. (It may not be the first boss male; it may be a fish of lesser size than the first boss, but one will be dominant.) However, some intrusions are bound to occur. Among Atlantics, small parr will be sexually mature, and they will dart under the boss male's body to have an orgasm while being showered with sperm from above.

The male fish continue to strive with each other up to the moment that the female makes her final measurement of the pit in the gravel with her anal fin. A mating salmonid completes her final measurement of the egg nest by squatting just a little longer with measuring fin held against the rocks, and opens her mouth. Then her mate comes alongside, opens his mouth, and, quivering with her, extrudes a white cloud of sperm around her orange eggs. Then the intruders may rush in and spray the nest with their supplementary sperm. When his orgasm is completed the boss male instantly charges the intruders, and the female begins to cover the eggs. The sound of agitated waters is heard again over the egg nest.

Fish watch each other for meaningful signs. That they exchange signs is clear from the fact that males stop releasing sperm when the female has a false orgasm. In their close communion other signs are clearly exchanged. They stimulate each other with quivering and body pressing. Male redfish touch their snouts to the female's body near the adipose fin or the pectorals, quiver, and erect their dorsal fins. Several other species have been observed quivering, rubbing their bellies over their mate's dorsal fins, and touching their snouts to their mate's pelvic fin region. A male brook trout has been observed trying to guide a female to the spawning gravel. To do this he swam close beside her and slightly ahead on the downstream side trying to turn her toward the redd area.

Defending and intruding males also exchange signals. Defending land-locked sockeye (sometimes called redfish) may swim out to meet aggressive intruders with their dorsal fin hoisted. If the intruder doesn't retreat, the defender will turn him and swim alongside trying to escort him away from the redd. If the intruder escapes escort and dashes back to the female, the defender will attempt escort again. In most species, a mad dash at the intruder results in his retreat, and the defender will give chase for several feet.

The fish hanging around the nest are definitely attendant males. Feeding fish rarely hang downstream from the nest and may get a few waste eggs that wash out of the nest. But very few eggs escape. The current in the bottom of the egg nest is reduced, the eggs have some adhesive on them that not only causes them to stick to nest rocks, but also coats them with sand that helps them sink.

Activated by the water the millions of living spermatozoa swim with great rapidity in every direction. They find the single, tiny pore, a micropyle, in the egg shell, swim in, and nature shuts the door. In a few minutes the egg cell hardens in the water and the eggs become about one third larger.

Now that the spermatozoa have found homes, the female begins to cover her eggs. (Arctic char may lay eggs several times in one pit before covering.) Covering is done by cutting upstream. The current will wash stones into the egg nest until they are neatly mounded over it. Further covering will occur as stones wash out of the next egg nest that the female will dig a few feet above the completed nest. Eastern brook trout cover atypically. They position their tail at the basin edges of the nest. Their head is outside the nest rim. Using the edges of their caudal and anal fins they roll gravel into the nest, and with a sinuous, weaving motion, they let their body sweep the nest on a circular axis. In other words, the head circles a perimeter outside the nest rim while the tail moves rocks around a circle at the inner rim.

These fish are now fairly tame. A person can wade up to them. By taking the following precautions, you can actually put your hand out and stroke a king chinook's tail: approach very slowly and cautiously from the rear, moving always behind the fish in the cover of its "blind spot"; the wader's feet should be very quiet in the gravel; no shadows should be cast. When the fish does see you, you will get water splashed in your face from the powerful tail. You can stand like a heron within a few feet of spawning fish and through polarized glasses watch every move they make.

Why are these fish so heedless? I believe there are three reasons. First, to spawn in shallow water they must abandon many of their instinctual fears. Second, they are in heat. Third, they are watching each other, they are not watching for shadows, human scents, and sounds of footsteps in the gravel.

It would be wrong to say that these fish cannot be spooked, because they will become nervous if persistently disturbed. Still, they will return to their redd again and again, and, if necessary, they will spawn in the night when there are no people to spook them. In Petersburg Creek, southeast Alaska, cutthroat spawn only at night. In Oregon, the species may spawn in the daytime or at night.

And the people will come at night with lights to see them. For these reasons many spawning redds in Michigan are protected by rulings of the Department of Natural Resources, particularly steelhead spawning redds. But in Michigan there are so many miles of thin water running over beautiful spawning gravel that fishing can be legal in some of these areas without disrupting a full harvest of all the natural reproduction a stream can support.

Body-Form Changes and Terminology

Salmonids undergo a number of changes in body form at spawning time. For example, body-form changes in Pacific salmon males include elongation of the jaws, the growth of canine-like teeth, and an increase in body depth by ridging of the back. Pinks get a pronounced hump between their dorsal fin and their upper jaw.

As salmonid jaws elongate they grow knobs or hooks called kypes. Usually the term refers to hooks on the lower jaw. In male coho the upper jaw may become quite hooked. In some species the hook on the lower jaw fits into a notch in the upper jaw. In others the knobbing and hooking may prevent the fish from closing its jaws. The jaws of females elongate only slightly and rarely get hooks. All of the trout and char described in this book get changes in their jaws and head at spawning time. Cutthroat kypes are not as pronounced as in other trout. Atlantic kypes may be very noticeable. Arctic char and Dolly Varden kypes may also be significantly large.

Some species get nuptial tubercles, which are little horny excrescences that become evident before spawning and disappear afterwards. Changes in pigmentation and shedding of guanine deposits are also body-form changes.

"Crouch" and "anchoring" are terms that distinguish a species differentiation in orgasm. Arctic char engage in a swimming orgasm while other salmonids hold still. The term crouch describes the orgasmic position taken by most salmonid females after measuring proves satisfactory. It continues the signal to the male to fertilize the eggs that immediately begin to flow. When a female is in the measuring or "feeling" position, she is nearly into the crouch. Her oviduct is well into the nest, her anal fin is touching the egg target, and all she need do to complete the crouch is arch her back and open her mouth. This puts her body into correct anatomical alignment for squeezing eggs out of the body cavity. The position is a dead-stop position.

Arctic char don't hold the dead-stop position. When the female makes her final measurement or "feeling" with her anal fin, she holds still just a little longer than she would if the measurement indicated that the nest is not complete. That pause, called "anchoring," is the signal for the male to swim forward. Then the pair swimming side by side extrude milt and ova over the nest.

An egg nest is a gravel container for percolating (a cool form of incubation) fertilized eggs. If eggs fall into silt they spoil. They need a cooling flow of water. That's why brook trout like to build redds over springs. Other species place redds at lower ends of pools and above swift riffles where water seeps through the gravel. The process of agitating and hydraulically moving the gravel removes from the stones the moss and the loose, fine sand and grit that could clog the spaces between the stones and block the flow of water over the eggs. Fish prefer to make redds in gravel having stone sizes that can't be easily compacted. While the sizes of stones vary widely, pea-size and walnut-size stones certainly are preferable for the lining of the egg nest. These stone sizes roll and tumble most easily, both for ease of cutting and for egg safety. A fish working with flat stones would, no doubt, squash a lot of eggs! Although the current inside a redd pit is so reduced that the eggs are not swept out of the nest at extrusion, it is not so reduced as to obviate the cooling trickle needed by the eggs for percolation.

Steelhead redds of 12 feet by 5 feet have been observed in a water depth of 5 inches; cutthroat redds of 2 feet by 1½ feet have been seen in a water depth of 5 to 7 inches. Chinook redds can be bathtub size and so deep that you can nearly break a leg if you step into them. It is obvious that the sizes of redds vary as widely as bottom and water conditions.

Females don't flip the stones out of the stream bottom with their tails. If they did, they'd be flinging stones onto the bank. The stones and gravel are moved by a combination of plunger-like pressure (down against the stones; upward from the stones) and hydraulic washing from the current. A similar hole can be made by moving one's hand rapidly up and down over gravel without actually picking up or pushing any of the rocks.

Each egg nest often has hatchings of several males, and because of superimposition of other egg nests, a school of fry may include the eggs of several females. This benefits the species.

In the successive runs of other species, a month or even six months later more nests may be superimposed upon the nests of the first species. In the Muskegon, spring spawning nests are imposed upon chinook's fall spawnings. The successive usage of certain gravel areas by different species can be most disruptive to the hatching of the earlier eggs, and the last species to use a redd area may be the stream's dominant species.

SALMONID CUTTING

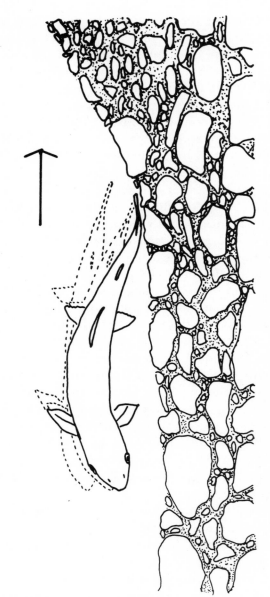

Salmonids do not dig redds by flipping or brushing stones with their tails. Instead, they create a suction through plunger movements of their body. Stones dislodged through plunger action are washed downstream by the current that swirls along the fish's body contours. The female positions her head upstream and contorts her body as the dotted lines show.

7

Fasting for Sex

Exciter fishing methods are based on the theory that fishermen should treat salmon, trout, and char on their spawning runs as though they are fasting. They will not all be fasting, but the unifying biological fact that relates to hooking them is their capability for fasting. Trout rise to flies because they are hungry. Selective trout fishermen imitate the insects, which are trout food. So the theory of tying and presenting exact imitations to rising trout is based on their feeding habits. Exciter fishing is the exact opposite of selective trout fishing.

Ancient Pacific Slope Indians knew that Pacifics won't take a hook. The Romans knew that Atlantics seldom feed. Our European language-givers influenced fishing literature by phrasing this question: "Why do they take?" Fully phrased the question is: "Why do they take if they aren't hungry?"

Without a knowledge of lateral lines, fish-taking methods, and other biological aspects of spawning, the question cannot be answered.

Steelhead fishermen, often using Atlantic salmon flies, have phrased the question differently: "Do they feed?" For steelheaders in cold Great Lakes waters examining stomachs that are usually empty the answer may come too easily: "They don't feed." For Pacific Slope steelheaders in relatively warm water the answer is: "They sometimes feed." For fishermen in the Dolly Varden and cutthroat range who sometimes fish for steelhead the question may be answered: "They often feed."

So the two questions phrased on river banks—"Why do they take?" and "Do they feed?"—are not, in my opinion, productive. Neither allows for a general behavior pattern based upon proven biological facts from which one may draw variations by species and habitat adaptation. Neither lets the fisherman frame a general reference around the bewildering adaptations of chinook, cutthroat, steelhead, Dolly Varden, arctic char, browns, Atlantics, coho, pinks, chums, kokanee, and sockeye across their world range.

In my opinion, the question *Do they fast?* is the one that best frees us to study all the data we've observed about these species, and allows us to develop a productive fishing method that will work for all of them. After studying the data, I find that they all have the capability to fast, and that many of them break their fasts.

Fishermen are likely to present lures to salmonids during their fasting periods. The major activity of these fish during their spawning run is breathing, swimming, and mating. They come into streams to swim to spawning grounds, make redds, and lay eggs. It is not a period of growth or metabolization of food. Every major activity of these fish is devoted to the complex stages of the spawning run.

Trout, salmon, and char can live for long periods without feeding. They live on fat stored in their muscle tissue. Considerable research has been done on the metabolism of Pacific salmon to prove this. Less research has been done on trout and char, but the point has been established. One of the early research projects was done by Charles W. Greene on chinooks. He found that salmon fat furnished the food during the migration fast. The fat can be transferred from one part of the body to another, and much fat is transferred from the pink and dark muscles. "The fat never wholly disappears even in dying salmon," Greene concludes.

Although migrating salmonids use enormous amounts of energy swimming for long distances over and under obstacles, in other instances, they use very little stored fat. Both summer and winter steelhead that are waiting to spawn in over-wintering or over-summering periods have little to do while waiting. Dolly Varden, browns, brooks, and arctic char that have spawned and are over-wintering also have little reason to expend body energies. These are resting times—times when the salmon-trout do not need to draw heavily on their fat reserves. Furthermore, many of these fish are resting in cold water, which arrests metabolism. Even the indigenous fish that don't have spawning duties rest and have empty stomachs. They don't need to eat when cold-water temperatures reduce metabolism.

There's a third time when spawning fish do not need to draw heavily on stored fat. The fish go into semihibernation during some periods of their spawning sojourn in tributary streams. It's clear that a cold fish whose metabolic process stopped when the stream cooled is in a state of semihibernation. Apparently the same thing happens to salmon and trout that have entered their spawning stream during spring and summer periods of relatively warm water, for summer steelhead and spring chinook also give up food for sex. They are more active, however. They may break their fast more often, but their stomachs are usually empty. A summer steelhead may rise to one or two flies in a hatch, but it usually won't rise to many more. Sexually mature prespawners held in hatchery tanks for long periods of time will not feed. Fish that have ripened and been milked and continue in the hatchery tank can be taught to feed. These examples indicate semihibernation that is rooted in spawning migration needs, and is not solely linked to the cold-water temperature that over-wintering fish experience. After studying the data, I find that all migratory salmonids have the capacity to fast, and that many of them break their fasts to maintain body nurture.

Fasting is beneficial to the survival of the subfamily Salmoninae for several reasons: it turns the stream into a safe nursery; it allows the fish to concentrate on one biological purpose; and because there's relatively little food in many headwaters, it allows the fish to survive through spawning.

Migratory salmonids leave their birth streams to find a better food supply. They come back because the stream is good egg-laying water. Of course there are differences among the species in dependence upon the stream of birth for food. Some fish, such as cutthroat and Dolly Varden, hang around the estuary of their native stream and make more frequent runs into them than other species. Pacific salmon and Atlantics usually range farther from their stream of birth and are seldom dependent upon it for food. Steelhead may make feeding trips into their birth stream or into other streams along their feeding route in the ocean or the Great Lakes. But for all the salmonids, their birth stream is a nursery.

No biologist I've ever encountered had records of salmon, trout, and char that failed to spawn because they starved to death on the way to gravel. And no ecology organization has had to haul fish food to the starving, over-wintering steelhead.

The feeding-fasting problem has encouraged bizarre ideas: that Atlantic salmon take flies into their mouths and squeeze the juices out to get nutrients, perhaps vitamins; that Atlantics feed on local butterfly species; that flies accidentally duplicate unknown ocean creatures that steelhead, Pacifics, and Atlantics feed on during their sea-stay. These and other theories arise in minds fevered by the persistent refusal of Atlantics to take during an expensive fishing trip. Bizarre ideas may soothe our troubled feelings, and make a scanty rationality yield a needed sense of momentary order, but they don't produce good fishing methods.

The only evidence that will establish the degree of fasting among specific salmonid species is that drawn from the field data of biologists and fishermen. Among the experts, the general opinion is that most salmonids don't feed, but this is a sweeping generalization. The species should be considered individually.

Pacific Salmon

Because of fat reserves Pacific salmon don't need to feed. Their bodies carry enough stored fats and oils to sustain them through the migration and the spawning act. Moreover, be-cause they die after spawning, they don't have demanding nutritional needs that their stored fat may not have met. It's rather unanimous among biologists and fishermen alike— Pacifics go on a migrating fast without any break more than 99 percent of the time.

Atlantics

Atlantics are trout, and they may live through the stress of spawning and go back to sea. They may break their fast once in a while.

Fasting Atlantic salmon lose as much as 25 percent of their muscle weight. When the stomachs of large numbers of salmon caught in fresh water have been examined, they have been found to be empty or with only slight traces of sea food in them.

In *Atlantic Salmon*, Lee Wulff explains: "The arguments that the salmon empty their stomachs, ejecting the contents when hooked or their digestive processes are so fast nothing can hope to be found in them, do not hold true. In the first place, anglers who have caught thousands of salmon, many of them in clear water from a vantage spot, would have seen the salmon eject food, and this has not been the case. Secondly, if the processes are so rapid, then nothing would be found in salmon taken in salt or brackish water which is not the case."

During the seven days I fished for Atlantics in 1976 on the George River in Quebec, I examined the stomachs of most of the ninety-seven fish taken, and asked the guides to examine the rest as they cleaned them. They were all empty.

British biologist G. Herbert Nall believes that Atlantic salmon do some feeding. In his *Life of the Sea Trout* he says: "But though Salmon may occasionally feed in fresh water, their feeding is not regular; nor do they digest, absorb, and utilize the material, so as to nourish the body adequately. No such feeding is necessary. They live on their accumulated stores of fat." He reports seeing Atlantics taking surface insects in the Lyon, a tributary of the Tay.

Steelhead Trout

The probability of steelhead breaking their fast seems to be somewhat higher than for Atlantics, although they do not commonly eat during their spawning migration in fresh water. Examinations of stomachs of steelhead from various streams support this view. From 1969 through 1975, Jim Bedford, assistant director of Michigan's Water Quality Control Laboratory, caught 296 steelhead. Only two mature fish had food in their stomachs.

Neil Shea, superintendent of the Pennsylvania Fish Commission Hatchery at Fairview, near the state's Lake Erie tributary streams, said that all the steelhead in those streams that he has examined had empty stomachs, even though their sex organs were mature. He said that the steelhead stop feeding when they enter the streams.

One biologist who found that steelhead do some feeding in their spawning streams is Paul R. Needham. In *Trout Streams*, Needham said: "The stomach of sea-run steelhead usually contain some stonefly or mayfly nymphs, caddis larvae, or other typical aquatic foods. In contrast, the Pacific salmon, on their upstream migrations, appear to take little or no food. The necessity for salmon to feed while in fresh water is, of course, less since all die after spawning. Steelheads, on the other hand, if they survive to spawn again must retain sufficient strength to make the return trip to the ocean."

The scientists do not totally agree because their data are taken from different streams running at different temperatures in different regions. But there is evidence that steelhead in some habitats do some feeding.

Most fishermen I have talked with indicated that the majority of steelheads they caught had nothing at all in their stomachs or occasionally would contain a sedge, dragonfly, bee, or yellowjacket. My own field records made from examining stomachs from relatively cold Great Lakes streams include only a few instances of steelhead feeding.

The data from both biologists and fishermen show that steelhead occasionally feed, but do not feed much. Several observers believe that some feeding is necessary in order for the steelhead to live through the stress of spawning.

Cutthroat Trout

Among fishermen with whom I've talked the general consensus is that cutthroat trout feed much more than steelhead. Some fishermen feel that they feed right through their spawning run.

Cutthroat fasting is hard to evaluate because there are many stages of immature fish among the sexually mature fish and they all look alike. One can tell, of course, by examining the sex organs, but not all fishermen conduct such complete autopsies. All the other fish are feeding, and it may be that fasting fish are overlooked in the frenzy of catching nonfasting fish. Some observers insist that cutthroat feed during spawning. Therefore, I would rate the sexually mature cutthroat as a trout that probably feeds considerably more than steelhead. Furthermore, they will take lures much more readily than steelhead.

Sea Trout (Browns)

My theory that salmon, trout, and char have the inherent physiological ability to fast and to interrupt their fasting during their spawning run is substantiated by evidence gathered by G. H. Nall in *The Life of the Sea Trout*. He discovered that both the sexually mature and whitling stages of sea trout go into periods of fasting that he calls resting periods. "The life of the Sea-trout . . . is in fact a series of alternating phases, first feeding and growth, than abstinence and cessation of growth." The whitling stage is an extra life-stage step unique to brown trout.

The behavior of "resting fish" substantiates the theory that members of the salmon-trout subfamily have the ability to fast. Nall says that mature sea trout do some feeding during their spawning runs, but not enough to maintain body weight. I have caught anadromous browns in midwinter in Michigan's Betsie River, and they all had empty stomachs. Jim Bedford's field records show that the browns he has caught have had empty stomachs. Most of them were over-wintering fish in cold water.

The conclusion seems to be that browns probably fast as much as steelhead.

Dolly Varden Char

Many fishery biologists contend that Dolly Varden do not stop feeding during their spawning run, and that they will feed anytime food is available. Other biologists report that Dolly Varden do not feed during July and August. Dollys at Old Tom Creek on Prince of Wales Island have been observed breaking their fast to take salmon eggs and then returning to fasting. A study of nonanadromous Dolly Varden made by the Idaho Department of Fish and Game shows that the species is capable of fasting. This study indicates that very little feeding occurs during the extended migration period, and that the fish exist on fats stored during the sojourn in the lake.

I believe that although Dolly Varden in some areas (southeast Alaska, for example) do not do much fasting, the trait is inherent in that member of the salmon-trout subfamily. Dolly Varden in southeast Alaska over-winter in lakes of lake-stream systems. They reduce their feeding during that time partially because of cold water, but they do some feeding. Dollys may not feed during the physiological stress of changing from salt to fresh water or vice versa. Neither do they feed after spawning when running from spawning streams through salt water to over-wintering quarters in lake-stream systems.

Fasting in Dolly Varden may be masked as in cutthroat by the horde of nonspawners that mix with the sexually mature fish. At spawning time there may be four groups of fish in some streams that are definitely feeding. There are the indigenous (stream-resident), nonanadromous fish; nonconsecutive spawners; mature fish that elected to stay in the stream instead of migrating back to sea; and fish that are too young to go down to sea. In any case, the actual *fishing truth* is that Dolly Varden take avidly, and the exciter fishing method may not be any more effective than a good fishing-lure method for taking them.

Brook Trout Char

Various studies indicate that fasting is a part of the life of brook trout; however, the studies do not indicate that the species fasts as much as some steelheads.

H. C. White has made a three-year study of anadromous brook trout in the Moser River in Nova Scotia. In regard to fasting, he concludes that brook trout feed sparingly in the river prior to spawning, stop feeding while in-migrating at the river's mouth, then feed sparingly throughout the winter in fresh water. Although he does not say so, it is possible that brooks, like Dolly Varden, decrease feeding during the bodily adjustment period to fresh water.

Arctic Char

There is evidence that arctic char stop feeding before spawning, but weather conditions during their spawning time do not make observations easy. As is the case with Dolly Varden and cutthroat, observations of sexually mature fish that will spawn in their season is difficult because many stages of arctic char are mixed together. In the fall all of the arctics in-migrate to escape the arctic sea winter; thus, both sexually mature fish and fish that are not ready to spawn come in silver colored from the sea. It is important to remember that arctic char over-wintering in streams are in extremely cold water. Therefore metabolism is low, and conditions inducing semihibernation are high.

The arctic char is difficult to observe and the species may vary in its fasting habits; nevertheless, the ability to fast during spawning times is a part of that species' adaptation.

When arctic char are fasting, exciter methods work for them as they do for other species. There are frequent fasting periods that occur for three reasons: cold-water temperatures, in-migration to barren waters, and spawning.

By now it should be obvious that each member of the species differs in the amount of fasting it does, and the habitat adaptation of each species and of each individual fish makes fasting highly variable. This means that fishing is always a challenge, because fish are always perplexing!

Fishermen should not gloss over the distinctions between Pacific salmon and anadromous trout. Each species exhibits distinctive traits during its spawning run. There are three links, however, between the species that make them homogeneous: they belong to the same subfamily, they share a common fasting syndrome, and trout (and perhaps char) could evolve toward a more sophisticated spawning behavior. Where Pacific salmon and steelhead occur in the same range (Pacific Slope and Great Lakes), they act very differently from each other.

Pacific Slope and Great Lakes fishermen usually think of Pacific salmon that are well settled into their spawning runs as nonfeeders. They approach steelhead as occasional feeders. So the seasoned fishermen do not get confused about the distinctions between Pacifics and steelhead. But Great Lakes fishermen may become confused if and when an Atlantic fishery develops in the Great Lakes. If that happens, fishermen will have a trout that—like the Pacifics—seldom, if ever, feeds.

The distinction may also be difficult for fishermen who fish steelhead in the cold metabolism-reducing waters of the Great Lakes in late fall and winter. To them, steelhead are trout and they seldom feed. If the Great Lakes fisherman has had experience with Atlantics (a steadfast faster), he may think that all trout seldom break their fast.

Trout have the ability to survive spawning stress. A small percentage do. Sometimes they need to break their fasts in order to nurture their bodies. There are times when the nurture needs of steelhead trout intersect with metabolic catalysts (water temperature, aeration) to trigger feeding. If the need is there and the new environmental conditions accelerate metabolic processes, then the steelhead on a spawning run can break its fast, feed a little, then return to fasting.

From one point of view, Pacific salmon have a sophisticated way of handling procreation. Nothing interferes. The whole body of the fish is devoted to one activity—delivering the eggs to the gravel. Death is a sacrifice to that high state of biological efficiency. Atlantics have also achieved that high efficiency, but make a lesser sacrifice. Steelhead have evolved a little further; cutthroat not so far.

Spawn is a natural food that attracts fish that are not on spawning migrations. It's understandable that ovum can be located easily by fish. Salmonid eggs have amino acid components, and fish have a high olfactory response to amino acids. Through their sense of smell, which is a monitoring of water through the mouth and the nostrils, they can find fish eggs.

Spawn is not taken avidly by any fasting fish. I've seen steelhead ignore both dangled spawn bags and eggs dislodged from nearby redds by females covering their spawnings. But ova are taken often enough and found often enough in stomachs of salmonids on spawning migrations to make one wonder why they will interrupt fasting to take ova.

It may be that ovum taking is related to spawning needs. In addition to metabolic hunger there are two other possible reasons why fasting fish take eggs during the spawning migration: scent and argenine hunger.

Since other animals locate females in heat by scent, probably fish pair in the same manner. If so, smelling for ova and for degrees of ripeness in ova may be a major task of male anadromous salmon, trout, or char. The females may also be aware of this odor. Smelling of themselves may help them know when to dig redds. At any rate, females get an intimate awareness of their eggs while observing their redds, covering them with gravel, and digging successive redds. I would guess that both milt and ovum odors are guides to fish behavior, and fishermen should expect some behavior reaction of the fish to milt and ovum.

Argenine hunger is another explanation for anadromous trout, char, and salmon taking ova during their spawning run. Fish are dependent not only upon protein for nurture, but also need a correct amino acid content in the protein. All animals can synthesize certain amino acids, but fail in synthesizing others. The ones they can't generate in their own bodies have to be gained as supplements through feeding. Experiments with nutrition in chinook show that they don't do well in synthesizing the amino acid called argenine. They do generate some argenine, but not enough for good nutrition. These facts demonstrate the need in one salmonid for argenine. Argenine occurs in rainbow eggs.

In most spawning runs there are feeding fish present with the in-migrating, sexually maturing, fasting fish. These include out-migrating kelts that may occasionally feed; nonconsecutive spawners that are running in but won't spawn during the migration season; fish that are running into the stream on a feeding journey; and anadromous fish that stayed in the stream instead of out-migrating after their last spawning season. The metabolic reasons some of the fish have for feeding can confuse our fasting theory. Everyone catches a few of these fish. They're hungry, they may have the same coloration as sexually mature fish, and they cause us to go home saying that the fish aren't fasting.

Nonconsecutive spawners are fish that skip a year in giving eggs or milt, but run in from the sea with the fish that are sexually maturing. They'll feed except during periods of adjustment to changes from salt water to fresh water. Apparently they never occur among Alaskan or Washington steelhead.

Some anadromous species have some members that stay in the stream for a season's vacation from saltwater feeding. Arctic char are an example. Usually these fish will look like stream-resident fish, and the fishermen will treat them as resident fish. Unless you have a downstream trap and an in-migrating mark on the fish, it's impossible to tell that they're anadromous. So if you catch a large resident fish, look wise and say: "It must be vacationing anadromous fish." Under certain circumstances this could save you a fine for violating fishing regulations.

I'm sure that some steelhead in the short-run Upper Peninsula streams make feeding journeys at random times into the tributary streams. I've caught them in midsummer in bright colors in the Otter, the Big Elm, and the Misery. I don't think they were summer-run steelhead. If they make feeding journeys in summer, they can make them in fall and winter. A fish that may be of a class that runs in to spawn just ahead of the spring-spawning period might make a fall-feeding journey and run back to the lake for a lake-feeding sojourn. I'd expect such fish to travel in schools, but I've never caught more than one on any fishing trip.

In this book I'm trying to present a method that will work in many regions for many species. The migratory fisherman should be able to use the exciter fishing theory to fish for steelhead in Ohio's Chagrin, Atlantics in Quebec's George, Pacifics in California's Klamath, and cutthroat in Alaska's Petersburg Creek. The theory should help to account for the difference in behavior of each species in each different climate. It should make it possible to use only a few rods, one fly reel, one spinning reel, and the same set (different weights) of flies, spinners, and spoons for each species and fishing situation.

The exciter fishing theory should not force a fisherman to overgeneralize and lock dogmatically into one point of view and one way of presenting to these extremely variable fish. Exciter fishing is a frame of reference, a way of looking at the behavior of a large number of species. Within that frame of reference there must be room for many ways of presenting to fish and many fly and lure patterns. Exciter fishing is a consistent method of fishing based upon a behavior pattern (fasting) inconsistently manifested by a subfamily of fish.

The contents of this chapter are meant to prepare the mind for the stream. Once you're in the stream, react to the ways the fish are reacting. Welcome feeding fish just as the selective trout fisherman welcomes nonfeeders that hit because of excitement. If you're in relatively warm water inhabited by Dolly Varden and cutthroat, fish your lures as though they are hungry. Don't be like a dry-fly fisherman who thinks he'll lose status if he fishes wet flies. You're in the stream to battle hooked fish, and you don't hook fish with theories. You hook them by applying general biological facts and years of experience to the exacting variables that the fish in front of you is experiencing within just a few feet of water. The specific experiences of the fish to which you're presenting at the moment of presentation are the only relevant fishing variables. Generalizations should not prevent your immediate observation of that fish. The migratory salmonid fisherman will always be aware that there's a new challenge and a new problem to be solved because of the behavior of the fish in the next drift.

8

Exciter Stimuli

The fact that fish with empty stomachs frequently take lures is sufficient proof of the theory that there is a set of stimuli for taking other than hunger. But this theory does not reveal the various stimuli, their cause, and the lures that can exploit them. It may help our thinking to say that all taking results from a set of subdrives. Hunger is often the most important, but territorial defense, following, or a combination of sensations arising from sight, hearing, scent, and lateral line reactions may result in a take. I call the responses that cause fasting fish to bite lures *exciter takes*. Exciter takes are the opposite of the rises made by selectively feeding trout. They occur because of nonfeeding responses rooted in the physiological nature of fish.

I call the sensing part of a fish's anatomy the *exciter zone*. Lures should be presented to the entire length of the exciter zone. The spoon, spinner, or fly should float at mouth height into the area of binocular vision, hit the fish on the teeth, continue floating past one eye (an area of monocular vision), and continue along the sensing lateral line. The lures should float at current speed. If the lure makes a sound and a disturbance in the water, it will also arouse the hearing and have an added appeal to the lateral line of the sensing fish. If a lure has odor it is *possible* that it will further stimulate a fish.

The exciter stimuli that I've been able to identify so far are sighting, taste-spitting, smelling, hearing, lateral line sensing, following, exercising, territorial defense, the female pick up, and the spawn take. I'll describe them one by one.

Sighting

I want to be certain that my fish have a visual reaction to my flies. The fish that I imagine is lying in the stream with no particular reason to scan the waters for food. Its eyes must remain open. It sees everything within its line of sight, but not with much response. By conditioning, it will respond quickly to an enemy, an intruding alligator, for example. But in its fasting condition it is looking without seeing. So I want my lure to be gaudy to catch the fish's attention.

There are certain advantages to getting the fish's visual attention. It may shift itself slightly in the stream to line up with the float of the lure. I may not be presenting exactly to the fish's teeth, but it may align itself correctly. That's an instinctual response of fish to many floating objects. "Sighting" the lure may cause the fish to become aggressive and charge, giving me a glimpse of its presence.

I would like for my imagined fish to see my lure twice, once in its binocular vision area where the two monocular eyes converge their line of sight, and once in its monocular line of sight when the lure floats close by one eye after leaving the mouth area. The closer the monocular sighting is to the eye, the happier I am, for making the fish uneasy about its eye safety is another way of stimulating a response.

Taste-Spitting

I seek to take advantage of the fact that fish continually take floating objects into their mouths and spit them out. As I explained earlier, I call this "taste-spitting." The relatively lethargic fasting fish will still open its mouth to take objects. It is opening this major trap door to the gills all the time anyhow. A fish respirates by opening trap doors to keep the pumps that separate oxygen from water operating. A small lure floated

THE EXCITER ZONE

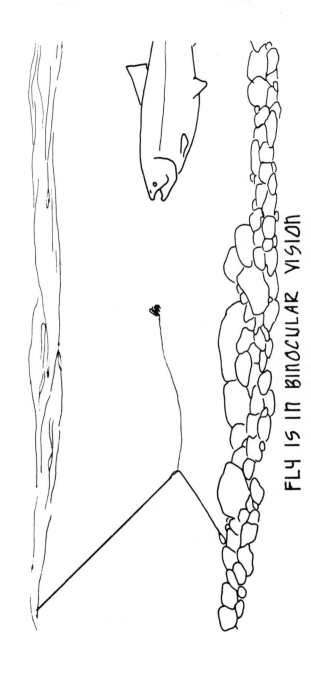

FLY IS IN BINOCULAR VISION

Length of exciter zone. Draw an imaginary line through the fish's open mouth parallel to the lateral line from mouth to tail. Extend that line from the mouth to the point where monocular vision becomes binocular. This lure is now entering the zone.

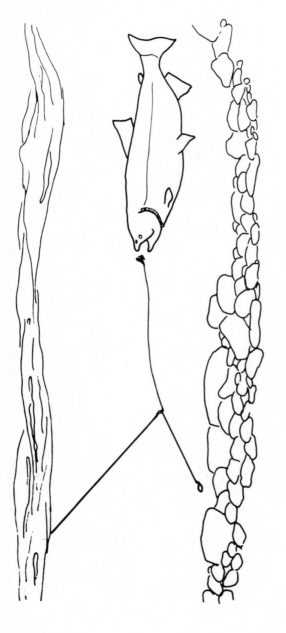

FLY IS IN RANGE OF MOUTH

Breadth of exciter zone. The exciter zone extends on either side of the fish as far as the effective sight of monocular vision, and effective sensing of the lateral line. Although the zone is relatively wide and long, effective excitement in spawning fish occurs tight against it. Here the lure presents to the major metabolating gate, which in fish, as in man, is often open!

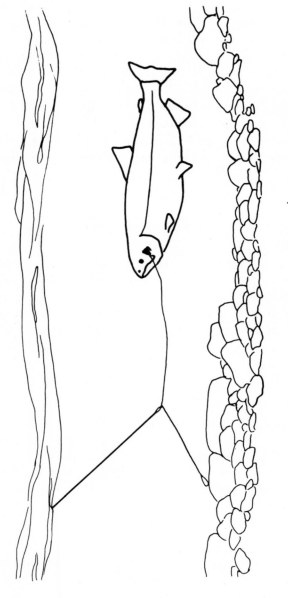

FLY IN MONOCULAR VISION, EARS | NOSE RANGE

Major exciter area. Here the lure can stimulate eyes, nose, ears, and mouth. Takes in this zones require some body turn, and may be harder than when the fish is in binocular vision or in range of mouth.

right to the teeth just at the intake moment of respiration is likely to be accepted into the mouth for a short time.

Don't be too disappointed if your fish spits out the lure you presented before you set the hook. If you felt the fish at all, think about its reaction. It's irritating to have a raspy object fall into your mouth when you're only trying to breathe. If the fish "saw" the lure at all, and if it can retain any set for that sighting, it may add a tinge of anger to the next taking.

I try to use rather small hooks, particularly for blind, drift fishing. A small lure is more likely to be accepted into the mouth, and a light lure is more likely to be held in the mouth long enough for me to feel the take. My hooks are often size six or eight.

Smelling

I don't know much about fish's noses. I do know that fish are attracted to amino acids, and spawn has amino acid component. Therefore, I consider scented flies to be a reasonable development. The only problem is that I've never seen a scented fly work well; nevertheless, I sometimes give myself a sense of confidence by occasionally carrying my flies in a jar of fresh spawn. I don't know that it does any good, but it doesn't do any harm either. At this point, it's strictly a fisherman's superstition, as far as I'm concerned.

Hearing

Fish certainly do hear things, and I want them to hear my spinners. I often give my fly a little pull in the water as it goes through the spot that I imagine to be the fish's exciter zone. I think that this not only appeals to the fish's visual response, but also makes a noise to which it may respond. Spinners appeal to hearing.

Lateral Line Sensing

A fish can find a lure that it can't see by using its lateral line sensing ability. Furthermore, the lateral line is a long sensitive zone that increases the length of the exciter zone

FLY IS FLANKING LATERAL LINE

End zone. Here the lure continues to excite the lateral line, and may enter rear binocular vision. As the rig travels the zone scent and sound are carried to the fish's sensors.

from mouth to tail, the entire length of the fish. For these reasons I want my lure to travel the full length of the fish's body if possible.

Following

Fish, like cats and fox, have a tendency to follow. A cat will follow a pulled string. Fish have a response like that. I often see salmonids following my lure. Muskies also do this. Many of the strikes we get are from following fish, so I do everything that I can do to keep my lure floating at current speed as it swings up to my rod tip pivot. If possible I begin a pull on the line at the point when the line stops in its natural current flow. If that pull can carry the lure in a continuous "follow-the-string" movement, I feel that I'm exciting the fish that I imagine is following. Some of my strikes occur during this pull.

Exercising

Fish seem to take exercise periods. Atlantics leap, for example. In late February and March, steelhead in the Pere Marquette go water skiing. They come out of the water and skate on their tails for maximum distances of about 20 yards. These fish do not leap into the air and return to the water under them. They take a vertical position as they come out of the water, and their momentum carries them forward in that position—tails on the water surface. Many fish "porpoise" or roll on the surface.

I can explain these antics by making a parallel to my Siamese cat. In midwinter in the cold Great Lakes climate she goes into semihibernation before the radiator. In the evening she races up and down the stairs. I believe she does this running to re-establish muscle tone dulled by the enforced inactivity. She seldom races in summer when she's busy lurking in the bushes to catch bugs.

In my opinion, migratory salmonids cramped by lying in small streams after being in Big Water also desire to establish muscle tone by exercising. I guess that this is the reason they leap, roll, and water ski. At such times they are more alert, and they're more likely to take. It is almost impossible to catch up with a violently exercising fish and get the lure to its exciter zone, but in the preperiod or afterwards the fish may take more readily than usual.

Territorial Defense

Aggressive defense against an intruder into one's territory needs no explanation. Many of the biting-type takes that I get, though not hard takes, result from the natural tendency of all fish to defend the space they occupy.

The Female Pick Up

One day my fly became entangled on my rig weight, and the two lay on the redd bottom under a cutting female. She noticed the lure and picked it up. I set the hook. I mentioned this incident to Tom Wasson, an Ohio fisheries biologist, and he explained that bluegills pick up objects that are thrown into their redd and drop them outside the depression. It's an instinctual redd-tidying action. I call this the female pick up. The fly I happened to be using had an egg shape in the pattern, so I've always used such patterns when trying to elicit this take. It doesn't always work, however.

The Spawn Take

Earlier I hypothesized that argenine hunger may explain why fasting fish are attracted to spawn. It certainly is a fact that they like to take objects shaped and colored like eggs. A deadly method of fishing is to float a single egg fly through a fish's exciter zone. Putting a Glo-Go just above the single egg fly increases the excitement. Two other lures that combine exciter colors with egg shapes are equally effective. They are Dave Whitlock's Two-Egg Sperm Fly, and my Blue Tail Fly (which doesn't always have a blue tail).

While discussing sight a few paragraphs back, I did not mention that Atlantic salmon (in some streams) and summer steelhead will rise to a skittered fly. When these flies are presented on the water surface, they are not in the usual exciter zone. The trout seem to like to rise to them.

I've seldom had a steelhead or an Atlantic rise to a floating fly dead drift. I don't know what causes Atlantics and steelhead to rise. It may be entirely sight; it may be a lateral line response. Fish do respond, apparently, as much to the ripples a struggling insect makes as to a visual sighting of the insect. If the lateral line is involved there may be a better way of exciting a take than twitching a winged imitation. Perhaps that's the reason cigar-shaped bombers work so well. It may be that both sight and lateral line stimuli cause the fish to respond. Perhaps that's the reason that the Exotic Bomber I tied of fluorescent deer hair seemed to work well on Atlantics in the George River. At any rate, rising responses to skittered flies is a response to stimuli at a distance from the exciter zone. Perhaps the exciter zone for summer steelhead and some Atlantics is higher. (Atlantics in some streams will not rise. Summer steelhead seem to rise better in thinner water.)

How do I know that the fish are experiencing the exciter stimuli? I know because I often fish to sighted fish in thin water. The two places where I can sight my fish are on redds and in drifts that have shallow water. Some Pacific Slope fishermen unused to Michigan's many miles of spawning gravel in shallow water have a bad reaction to redd fishing. They consider it to be a threat to the natural reproduction of the species.

In Michigan and in several other Great Lakes States it is legal to fish redds and it is not a threat to natural reproduction. The Michigan Department of Natural Resources is well aware of the need for natural reproduction, and enough miles of tributary streams are set aside to provide as many fry of a species as the stream can support. As far as I am concerned, it would be perfectly acceptable to make all redds catch-and-release areas, or to restrict all fishing on all redds. It is just as enjoyable to fish the drifts as the redds, but, as I have seen the fish and their reactions, I want to share my data.

Many Pacific Slope fishermen working in deep water are catching fish on redds that they cannot see. This is also legal.

It is easier to see the reactions of fish on redds than in thin-water drifts, which give only fleeting and occasional glimpses of the fish. Often you can see them as shapes in the water, but you can't see their jaws open or their bodies twitch as you can in redds. A redd is a basin open to light that reflects off the cleaned basin bottom. This improves vision. Another aid to vision is that the water flowing over the basin is relatively placid unless an aggressive defender lashes its tail. Furthermore, the fish on a redd will usually let the fisherman get closer than fish on a drift will tolerate. So, disregarding the moral issue, redds are good zones for observing fish behavior.

Another factor helpful to my experimental design is that fish on redds are the most likely to be fasting. Furthermore, at least 50 percent of the fishing time I spent trying to figure this theory out was to chinook, a species least likely to feed at any point in a spawning run. So one testing of this theory was certainly to fasting fish.

Usually the first float through a redd will be above the imaginary exciter zone line drawn through the fish's mouth and parallel to its eye and lateral line. This first float comes into the area of binocular vision and moves on over the fish to drop behind its tail. There isn't enough weight to get the fly into the right float plane. When this happens the fish often makes an involuntary upward movement of the forepart of its body. It's a partial rise form that indicates to me that it actually "saw" my fly. When the fly floats right up to its jaws, I have seen the fish take it into its mouths and drop it again before I could set the hook. I've never seen the lure actually ejected on a spitting stream as I understand small sticks are ejected. But they'll drop a lure quickly enough, and, as nearly as I can see, they drop with gill covers shut in the ex-pelling position. When a fly moves past the vision of one eye, the fish will often turn its head or quiver. A take at this point is what I call the turned-head take. A fly that gets a response after it has passed the gill covers and is exciting a lateral line stimulus causes a fish to pivot its entire body or quiver. This is a turning, open-mouthed take. The following chart gives a fuller explanation.

I have not included the conditioned response variable as a stimulus in my theory. By "conditioned response" I mean the

Observed Fish Reactions to Exciter Flies

Part of Exciter Zone Stimulated	Take Form Triggered	Fish Body Movement
Binocular vision	Partial rise.	Upward flinch of forepart of body.
	Alignment of mouth to lure in current float. (Seldom occurs in fasting fish.)	Fish moves body and mouth to side or upwards or downwards. May drop downstream with lure while aligning.
Mouth	May allow lure to float into mouth. May absently chomp onto lure and hold in mouth.	Opens mouth wider; flares gills.
Monocular vision	Head and forebody turn to lure.	Turns head, quivers, or flinches.
Lateral line	Half to full turn of body to lure.	Body quivers or flinches. Pivots whole body toward lure.

Note: Often the lure causes an avoidance reaction, and the fish simply gets out of the way. Several avoidance reactions may result in spooking to cover.

theory that fish "remember" feeding on aquatic life during parr days, and that this is the reason they take during their spawning run. They are, the theory holds, still conditioned to take lures that remind them of parr food. The theory does not square rationally with fasting. A fasting fish loses its conditioning for feeding; it has lost all hunger motives.

Fish lack sufficient memory power to be conditioned for very long. Even if a fish breaks its fast to feed after returning from the ocean, I seriously doubt that conditioning would last long enough to create any effect. Fish may "remember" a pattern for a short time. The axiom: "Last night's spinner is this morning's fly" simply means that the last fly seen at night will be taken if there is not another intervening hatch. For example, there's a Hendrickson spinner fall at dusk; we fish until the fish stop feeding. The fish see nothing further to eat. Leaving the same Hendrickson spinner pattern on our lines, we go out and continue to catch fish in the early morning light. The fish seem to remember the spinner, and may take it readily. That's a conditioned response. But the memory pattern lasted only a few hours, and they won't take the spinner pattern if there's been an intervening hatch. So the axiom doesn't prove that fish have the capability for long-remembered conditioning. This means that fish that break their fast, or species that don't fast much, probably are not taking because of conditioned response imprinted during parr days. They don't remember parr days.

Let me make it clear that I understand the implications of postulating two kinds of taking—hunger taking by feeding fish, and exciter taking by fasting fish. The implication is that I can divide my fish into two groups—but I cannot. Some fasting fish will feed; some feeding fish will fast. On the stream it isn't possible to ask a fish which it is. So practical fishermen on drifts and holes never take the legalistic stance that they are fishing to only fasting fish that always have an exciter response. The species are too variable to allow that kind of certainty.

9

Exciter Lures
and Other Patterns

EXCITER LURES

The term "exciter lure" is probably not new. Certainly the term "attractor fly" is an old term that has a generally understood meaning. It is a lure that attracts a fish by appealing to reactions other than hunger. I chose the word "exciter" because at one time it was used in physiology to mean an afferent nerve increasing activity in the part that it supplies. This is what I want to do—increase activity in the body of a fish that may be fasting by stimulating a part of the fish.

Jim Bedford and Stan Lievense, both super fishermen and good biologists, use the term "exciter lure" in their conversations, and I have learned from them. Although neither of them has any responsibility for the way I define the term in this chapter, I am grateful to them for insights and creative dialogue.

The exciter fishing method can improve our selection of flies above the level of random chance. It reduces the number of flies needed by directing the fisherman's attention to fish behavior under field conditions. On the drifts our flies must arouse a lethargic fish by floating through its exciter zone. We are considering water conditions, bottom contour, and our remembrance of fish behavior for the particular stream we're fishing. Within that frame of reference we are prepared to ask ourselves what take we desire to arouse. For example, when I'm snow fishing, it's clear that the fish are predisposed to fasting because they are on a spawning run and because the near-freezing water temperature has reduced all metabolic function. The only take I can arouse is territorial defense. Flies don't do well in arousing territorial defense among hibernating fish, so I shouldn't use any fly at all. Spinners are the order of the day. When the water is crystal clear and the fish are spooky, it's clear that the usual injunction—use hot colors with a lot of flash—should be revised. So I use smaller, darker flies. In such cases I know that I won't move the fish very far, and I have to present right to their teeth to evoke a take. I have to sense my takes very sharply and be prepared to set correctly and with good timing.

My ideal migratory salmonid fasts often and may break its fast. I am concerned about the challenge of catching it during its fast. In addition to fasting the fish is often resting in water that causes it to semihibernate. The fish is lethargic, having few reasons to take. I desire to stimulate the fish, to excite it. Some of my exciting is directed to specific parts of the anatomy that I understand from a biological point of view and from observing fish in their water. An exciter lure stimulates fish to take.

My Blue Tail Fly is the only exciter lure that has been developed entirely with exciter principles in mind. Dave Whitlock's Two-Egg Sperm Fly (my favorite) is an exact imitation of eggs, sperm, and placenta and meets all the criteria of an exciter fly. Drift bobbers are exciter lures. Developed with current drifts and spawn imitations in mind, they've evolved into lures that combine movement with fluorescent color to attract fish. They are effective lures that drift the exciter zone. Spinners, spoons, bombers, and hairwing flies have all been borrowed from related fishing fields and adopted to my theory.

Exciter lures are somewhat different from attractor flies. An exciter lure sharply challenges a lethargic fish. An attractor lure seeks any fish. An exciter lure is a little hotter than an attractor lure. A Bomber, for example, is a cigar-shaped bass-type lure tied with natural deer hair. An Exotic Bomber, the exciter counterpart, uses fluorescent deer hair, a tinsel head, and (where legal) a propeller head. The Exotic Bomber is reaching out to stimulate more nerves in a fasting fish. It screams at the fish instead of talking.

Successful exciter fishing, like selective trout fishing, is dependent upon proper presentation. Present to the exciter zone. In deep water drifts imagine the bottom and imagine a fish in a specific bottom position. Drift that specific distance by feel for an imagined fish. Use small lures and the smallest possible line weight. Remember that larger lures, big weights, and large spinner blades may spook fish. Remember that fresh-run fish have a greater tendency to avoid tree limbs, rocks, nets, and your rig than sojourning fish. (An avoiding fish need not spook from the drift. It can move a quarter of an inch from your rig with one flick of a pectoral fin.) A lure that matches the taking mood of a migrating (fasting) fish must be presented to the proper zone without arousing instinctive avoidance.

Exciter lures have hot colors, bright flash, motion, and drift-ability. Many of them imitate eggs. The spinners make an aquatic racket. Any fly that incorporates at least four fluorescent colors and one tinsel is a good fly for anadromous salmon, trout, and char. A fly that has these qualifications and rides the current at exciter zone level is a "perfect" fly.

Of course this statement is not a summation of all the exciter lure possibilities. The "perfect" fly may be overpowered for certain waters or a nuisance to cast or tie. But if you're fishless for two or three days, try reanalyzing your exciters. It's better to scare the fish into the next drift than to stand for hours floating a friendly fly past their dreaming eyes!

Both drift bobbers and spoons may be dressed with flies. The drift bobber may also be fished with bare hooks or with a spawn dressing. These lures ride the currents to deliver hooks to the fish's exciter zones. In shallow to medium-depth water, spoons can often be used without weight. The drift bobbers usually float above a weighted rig.

I use Spring Spoons manufactured by Best Tackle Company in Unionville, Michigan. Herter's also sells a thin spoon that works called Featherweight Thin Spoon. Such spoons are fly-rod weight having split rings at each end. They are made of extremely thin-gauge metal and range from 2 to 4 inches in length. I use the 4-inch size. Because they are thin-gauge and light metal, exciter spoons work through the miniature eddies and pockets of moving water to gain depth quickly. They give good action and present the attached fly in a relatively flat, sweeping plane. The lure moves through the exciter zone in a stimulating manner.

I paint my spoons weird, hot colors and add spots of several colors. The Blue Tail Fly is my usual dressing, but any hot-colored fly is all right. The lure works best in thin to medium-depth drifts. If the water is tumbling or moving swiftly, the lure may work better.

It's a matter of opinion as to whether the drift requires a spoon, a drift bobber, or only a fly. I carry all three.

The Glo-Go from Poulsen Quality Flies, Portland, Oregon, is the drift bobber I usually use. Spin-N-Glo (from Yakimo Bait Company), Oakie Drifters (distributed by Luhr Jensen), and Lil Corkie are all good lures. Oakie Drifters do not move. Glo-Go and Spin-N-Glo have fins that cause them to rotate. Because Glo-Go fins are molded into the full length of the lure body, they seem to give better wear.

All the drift bobbers look a little like spawn. I've been told that Oakie Drifters were among the first marketed. They are molded plastic spawn bag imitations. They do not spin; neither does spawn. The spinning bobbers add movement as a third appeal to exciter stimuli.

A fly carefully designed to appeal to a selective trout's hunger for a certain aquatic insect is a hunger fly for only the short season and range of that insect. At all other times, and in streams outside the insect's range, the imitating fly is an exciter fly. For that reason any fly can become an exciter fly; but certain fly styles make better exciter flies than others. It would be pointless to tie a no-hackle fly for salmonid fishing. Flies tied in the style of an Adams are equally impractical. All of the hairwing Atlantic salmon flies make good exciter flies; most of the streamer patterns work well.

Two-Egg Sperm Fly

Dave Whitlock's pattern for the Two-Egg Sperm Fly is as follows:

Hook: Black or gold wire.
Head: Fluorescent orange.
Wings: White whisp or maribou feather tied equal to hook length.
Throat: Bright red tied DeFeo style.
Eggs: Fluorescent orange or red.
Waist: Gold or silver Mylar. I often substitute green floss.
Tail: Whisp of golden pheasant crest. Tie equal to length of wing. I do not tie a tail.

The eggs are tied fore and aft with the tinsel or green floss between them. The fly has a dumbbell shape. Whitlock, whose proportions are always artistic, positions the two eggs fairly close together with just a touch of tinsel between them. Mine have a real "hand grip" between the eggs because I like a lot of the fluorescent green I substitute for gold or silver Mylar.

Spawning fish do see a lot of orange eggs and milky sperm. I'm not sure how much bloody placenta or egg sack tissue is extruded during natural spawning, but these are the colors of the fish's season.

Dave Whitlock created the fly in 1968 for a friend to use for Alaskan salmon and rainbows. He began by tying a Babine Special variation, adding a gold or silver Mylar waist and the thin white maribou wing. The fly was immediately popular because it works.

Of course the eggs look like eggs, and the fact that most anadromous salmonids will take single egg patterns indicates clearly that they look like eggs to the fish. I doubt that the wing looks like sperm or the throat like bloody, disintegrating placenta. Still the colors are right, and these are the colors that spawning fish see. I don't think the fly is successful only because of imitation; I think the fly works because it combines eggs that appeal to a postulated argenine hunger with five hot colors. It might be possible to rule out egg imitation because I often tie them of sewing materials that are interwoven with tinsel. Salmon eggs don't have silver and gold sparkle.

The Blue Tail Fly

The Blue Tail Fly is purposely tied to combine at least four different fluorescent colors at random with one orange egg shape. Because the colors are selected at random, the tails are not always blue. Here's how to tie the fly.

1. On a bench, lay out at least four colors of fluorescent hair, three colors of fluorescent chenille, including orange, and both silver and gold tinsel.
2. Find a hook of the size you like, but not too heavy, and put it into the vise.
3. Wrap gold or silver at the butt.
4. Tie in any color tail, and put that hair aside. You've used that color.
5. Tie in a strip of tinsel. Use opposite color of the butt.
6. Grab any color of chenille, wrap it forward a short distance and put that chenille aside.
7. Add a wrap or two of any other clashing chenille, and rib tinsel over that.
8. Select second color of fluorescent hair for beard and tie.
9. Make wings of the remaining two fluorescent hair colors.
10. Add an egg-shaped orange chenille head. Tie off without making a thread head.

The Blue Tail Fly is tied to illustrate the axiom that any fly will work for fasting fish providing that it combines at least four fluorescent hair colors and three fluorescent chenille colors with two tinsel colors. The purpose behind the fly is not the ordering of imitative variables into artistic proportion. The purpose is to scream at the fish. It works well.

Ernest Schwiebert writes beautiful prose about hairwing flies. They're used for Atlantics, and they work well for all of the anadromous salmonids. They are dignified flies having their origins in Canadian guide flies and Newfoundland patterns dressed with calf tail. They introduced simplification into the kaleidoscopic combinations of exotic feathers and furs in Victorian English salmon patterns. I do not tie them at random. Remembering Schwiebert's description, I try to follow the beauty of the patterns.

Use any of the hairwing patterns Schwiebert recommends with confidence. Because they are small and light, fish will hold them in their mouths longer than more prickly patterns. They are translucent, they follow junior eddies and currents in the water, and their hair glitters with tiny bubbles. I prefer those with a touch of green as does Carl Richards, who thinks that any pattern is a good pattern for anadromous salmon and trout if it has a touch of fluorescent green.

Jim Bedford, the dean of the Michigan snow fishermen, silver-plates spinner parts and dresses them with red beads, red tubing, and fluorescent yellow or red tape. He taught me to do the silver plating at home with a dry cell battery and a chemical solution. Silvering adds flash to the spinners.

I use spinners for two reasons. First, when ice forms in line guides it's easier to cast with spinning rods. Second, spinners evoke a better territorial defense reaction than flies. During Michigan winters in temperatures ranging from 20°F above to 20°F below with water temperatures nearing 32°F, the fish are definitely fasting and semihibernating. Even the indigenous fish have empty stomachs. The rainbows and the few coho that are still around respond with fairly hard, direct hits. They are annoyed by the flash and water agitation of the spinner blade. The spinners aren't drifted to them, they are cast into cover, and brought back fairly quickly without much attention to sinking. I believe the fish are protecting their space in the stream.

I've followed Jim Bedford along miles of cold, midwinter Michigan streams using flies and a fly rod while he used silver spinners. He catches fish; I do not. To me that proves that flies are not effective for extreme cold-water fishing conditions. Even a correctly drifted fly that hits the fish right in the teeth is likely to be ignored when the water is that cold. So I think in terms of evoking territorial defense takes from cover with the best territorial stimulator I know—silver spinners!

Chinook on their way upstream will lie in holes where they remain unresponsive. Roderick Haig-Brown discovered that a lure worked slowly across the bottom will take them. The Stanley Streamer made by Grizzly Tackle Company in Vancouver, Washington, is ideal for this purpose. Originally conceived to put the aquatic wiggle into flies, the Stanley Streamer does a better job of imitating insects swimming than any fly on the market. It has great possibilities on the fly tyer's bench, and Grizzly plans to manufacture separate plastic wiggle devices so tyers can create their own imitations. The fly fits into exciter fishing because it has that slow, purposive movement that brings out the cat-chasing-the-string syndrome in steelhead and salmon. Slow-moving, wobbling spoons will also take chinook out of the bottom of holes, but they cannot be cast from fly rods. Stanley streamers are fly-rod weight.

Exotic Bombers are jazzed-up versions of the plain bombers used to twitch steelhead and Atlantics to the surface. I've tried them for chinook and coho without success. I don't know what cutthroat and Dolly Varden would think of small Exotic Bombers. They might work well; I certainly plan to try them. When tying Exotic Bombers pack fluorescent-dyed deer hair into the body to create a hot pattern.

Haig-Brown used two lures for salmon and trout—the Devon Minnow and Superior spoons—that aren't popular any more. They both rank in my mind as excellent exciter lures.

The Devon Minnow is a quick-sinking, bottom hugger. The body revolves. Hardy brought a 3-inch, blue and silver, antikink Devon Minnow about 1926. I do not know whether it is still on the market. The lure quickly descends to the fish's exciter zone and charges through it making aquatic noises and rotating silver and blue flashes at it. Fish reacted well when the lure was popular, and it killed many large trout and salmon.

Haig-Brown carried spoons in cloth-protective jackets. Their trademark was Superior, and commercial trollers called them "washboards." Made of copper, silver, and brass, they were number six measuring 4½ inches long and 1½ inches wide. They were mounted with flat-sided Allcock single hooks. Haig-Brown described using them to take stubborn chinook lying near the bottom of holes. I don't know much more about them.

I've mentioned these two historic lures used by the father of modern anadromous salmonid fishing to demonstrate the true status of spoons and spinners. They both came over to America from England where they were used along with flies on storied Atlantic salmon streams fished by royalty. Spoons and spinners are dignified lures with which to dress expensive lines. It's all right to wear a suit and necktie while fishing them.

Another lure I like isn't exactly an exciter lure, but I'm excited about using it because I hate to float from drift to drift without having something productive hanging out the drift boat. This lure, which I call the Transportation Fly, is the Tadpolly. Tadpollys have a nice aquatic wiggle and they run deep enough to take steelhead. Flatfish don't run deep enough unless assisted by weights that have to be fussed with. Hotshots were used before the Tadpolly came on the market. When you're moving downstream on a Pacific salmon or steelhead stream, hold your boat back with gentle oar strokes and keep your Tadpolly wiggling.

MORE FLIES

I'd like to mention a few more flies, only some of which fit the exciter fly criterion I've already established in this chapter. Some of these flies come from the field of exact imitation and act as attractor or exciter flies. Some of them are too dark or too pale to excite salmonids except in thin water under hot sunshine.

These fly categories are Great Lakes steelhead flies, flies for adult salmonids originated by Haig-Brown, and fly patterns that incorporate egg shapes. (Flies that imitate salmonid fry will be discussed in the next section of this chapter.) They are by-product fishing flies that come out of the migratory salmonid

fisherman's knowledge, to be used for stream fish when salmonids aren't present or to be used at estuaries.

Two excellent reference works on anadromous salmonid
flies are Trey Combs' *Steelhead Fly Fishing and Flies* and Joseph
Bates, Jr.'s *Atlantic Salmon Flies and Fishing.* Enos Bradner's
book *Northwest Angling* also lists some superb flies.

I've made many long-distance phone calls and written dozens
of letters in an effort to establish the original creators of some
of these important salmonid patterns. Despite this effort, I
may err. Locating the creator of fly patterns and citing the
exact pattern recipe can be difficult. Fly patterns are not copy-
righted, and many add new effects. Flies evolve from bench
to bench and may change radically to meet the needs of
fishermen and fish of various regions.

Silver Brown (No 6 or 8 low-water hook)

Roderick Haig-Brown's Silver Brown is recommended for
cutthroat—especially maturing fish during August and September—summer steelhead, and coho.

Tail: Indian crow breast feather (small, whole feather).
Body: Flat silver tinsel.
Hackle: Dark-red game cock.
Wings: Slender strips of golden pheasant center tail. (In
  some versions the strips enclose orange bear hair.)

Silver Lady (No 6 low-water hook or larger)

Haig-Brown's Silver Lady is recommended for summer steelhead and cutthroat.

Tail: Small matching golden pheasant tippet feathers. (In
  some versions pink or orange feathers are used.)
Body: Flat silver.
Hackle: Badger.
Wings: Four strands of bronze peacock herl, teal strips, badger hackles laid along these, topping over all. A second
  wing version uses two blue hackles, good sides out, paired

strips of golden pheasant center tail, barred summer duck topping over all. A third wing version uses pale blue combined with a light barred feather such as teal, wood duck, or light mallard.

Cheeks: Pale blue chatterer. (Trey Combs substitutes Blue Goose.)

The Steelhead Bee

Haig-Brown used a steelhead pattern he called the Steelhead Bee. He created the fly after finding bees in the stomachs of a few fish that were almost empty.

Tail: Fox squirrel. Tie slightly longer than shank.

Body: Dark-brown floss divided by a single bar of yellow silk making three equal bars—brown, yellow, brown.

Hackle: Natural red, sparsely tied.

Wings: Fox squirrel, set slightly forward and well divided. Tie longer than the hook shank and bushy.

The flies that incorporate egg shapes into their patterns are:
Poodle Dog—by Robert Wesson.
Silly Stilly—by Warren Erholm.
Nite Owl—by Lloyd Silvius.
Silvius Demon—by Lloyd Silvius.
Royal Coachman—of English origin.
Lady Godiva—by Ralph Olson.
Orange Wing—by Ralph Olson; it's a Godiva alternate.
Double Flame Egg—by Victor Moore.
Optic—adopted to steelhead flies by Jim Pray.

The Double Flame Egg

Tail: White hackle fibers, tied sparsely.

Body: Fluorescent flame chenille tied in two sections like eggs.

Waist: The section between the eggs. A single turn of white hackle.

Hackle: One turn of white.

Great Lakes steelhead flies have not been much publicized, and there are many among them that are excellent candidates for exciter flies. Dave Borgeson is the creator of many Michigan steelhead and salmon patterns. Dave returned from California to work for the Michigan Department of Natural Resources in 1966. He began using modifications of western steelhead fly-fishing techniques to great advantage on his favorite western Michigan streams at a time when only a handful of Great Lakes fishermen had tried flies. As word got out that steelhead could be taken on flies, the demand for the techniques and patterns grew rapidly. Designation of the Pere Marquette flies-only section near Baldwin for year-round fishing in 1972 accelerated development of Michigen salmon and steelhead fly fishing. Dave, who'd worked out specific patterns for Michigan streams, released five creations—Betsey (Betsie) Special, Little Manistee, Platte Special, Orange P.M. (Pere Marquette) Special, and his favorite, the Red P.M. Special.

Betsey Special

Tag: Silver tinsel.
Tail: Red calf tail.
Body: Rear two-thirds black chenille and front one-third red chenille.
Wings: Black calf tail.
Throat: Black calf tail.
Head: Black thread.

Little Manistee

Tag: Silver tinsel.
Tail: Hot orange calf tail.
Body: Rear two-thirds pink chenille; front one-third black chenille.
Wings: One-half hot orange and one-half yellow. Top with the orange.
Throat: Hot orange calf tail.
Head: Red thread.

Platte Special

Tag: Silver tinsel.
Tail: Red calf tail.
Body: Black chenille.
Ribbing: Silver tinsel.
Wings: Yellow calf tail.
Throat: Yellow calf tail.
Head: Red thread.

Orange P.M. Special

Tag: Silver tinsel.
Tail: Hot orange calf.
Body: Rear two-thirds hot orange chenille; front one-third black chenille.
Wings: One-half hot orange; one-half yellow. Top with orange.
Throat: Hot orange calf tail.
Head: Red thread.

Red P.M. Special

Same as Orange P.M. Special except that rear two-thirds of body is red.

Notice that the Betsey Special, P.M. Specials, and the Little Manistee all have two colored bodies, and they all use black in one section. The leading principle in all of these flies is sharp contrast and hot colors. They have a kinship with the criterion I've set for my exciter fly patterns.

George Richey, owner of Richey's Custom Flies in Clio, Michigan, created two patterns that he ties on Mustad number six and eight 36890 hooks. The Black Polar Bear is his favorite.

Black Polar Bear

Tail: Black polar bear or calf hair.

Butt: Pink fluorescent chenille.
Body: Black chenille.
Throat: Black polar bear or calf hair.
Underwing: White polar bear or calf hair.
Upperwing: Black polar bear or calf hair.

Green Polar Bear

Tail: Green polar bear hair.
Body: Silver tinsel.
Throat: Green polar bear hair.
Wings: Green polar bear hair.

Spring's Wiggler and the Clark Lynn Special are two similar Michigan patterns that double as attractor and exact imitation flies.

Spring's Wiggler

Tie a yellow chenille body.
Palmer the body with a brown feather.
Use fox squirrel hair to make an overlay.

Clark Lynn Special

Tie a light yellow body.
Palmer the body with furnace hackle.
Use fox squirrel hair to make an overlay.

Both of these flies remind fishermen of *Hexagenia limbata* nymphs popularly called wigglers. These nymphs burrow in the bottom of many Michigan streams, and emerge, as they grow, to shed their skins. Fly tyers began to add feelers and a tail to the Spring's Wiggler. As far as I know the Clark Lynn Special has always had feelers and a tail. At any rate, the feelers and the tail on both patterns are usually made by simply extending the squirrel hair fore and aft.

When fish are taking emerging *Hexagenia limbata* nymphs both flies get a great many takes. However, the flies are often used for chinook and coho that are not feeding, and for steelhead that may or may not be feeding. Some fishermen feel that these two flies can double as attractor or exact imitation patterns. Other fishermen apparently think that Pacifics and steelhead feed on burrowing mayfly nymphs. Neither of these flies fits the hot, contrasting color criterion that I use for my exciter flies; but both of them can be tied with fluorescent chenilles and hot palmering. In those colors they look like wooly worms with roofs or Goofus Bugs without wings.

The Twenty Mile Fly is a fish-getter on streams tributary to Lake Erie within Pennsylvania. Named after Twenty Mile Creek, it was originated by Rich Young. It's sold in Young Hardware, which is fisherman's headquarters in Union City, Pennsylvania. It's a duller pattern than Brads Brat, a West Coast fly that works well in Pennsylvania tributary streams.

The Twenty Mile Fly

Tail: None.
Body: Hot orange chenille.
Wings: Barred mallard flank tied well rolled.
Hackle: Brown.

Parr Patterns

Juvenile salmonids are important to migratory salmonid fishermen because they provide a fly-tying challenge during off-season fishing. It's possible to catch stream-resident fish in migratory salmonid streams and estuaries by imitating salmon, trout, and char parr. This is good for the migratory salmonid fisherman because he already knows the stream as a result of fishing to spawning runs. He can learn about the stream during times there are no runs by fishing to indigenous fish with parr imitations. It's by-product fishing!

Haig-Brown was a pioneer in this kind of fishing and some of his parr imitation patterns are in this chapter. Sam Slaymaker created three patterns that may help, called the Little Brown Trout, the Little Brook Trout, and the Little Rainbow Trout. Tie these sparsely.

This coho parr was among the historic fish stocked in Bear Creek during the first successful Great Lakes Pacific salmon stocking in 1966. Note parr marks above and on the lateral line. (Photo courtesy Michigan D.N.R.)

In Michigan, natural reproduction of coho and chinook in some streams makes this kind of fishing into a new field. In other Great Lakes tributary streams there is some natural reproduction of Pacifics, but more of steelhead. Fishermen are discovering new models for streamer fly patterns, and the stream fish are discovering the new forage.

It's always helpful to know how to identify salmon, trout, and char parr. Parr marks appear on the sides of juvenile trout, salmon, and some related fishes. A few adult browns retain their parr marks. Adult golden trout (not anadromous) retain their parr marks. In most other adult salmonids the marks fade.

Pink and chum salmon parr head for the sea immediately upon emergence from gravel. They may not have the silvery

TROUT, CHAR, AND SALMON PARR
(2-5 INCHES LONG)

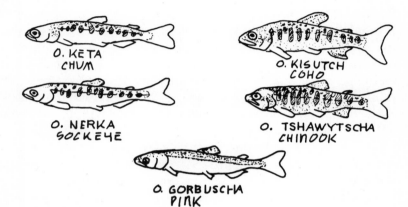

O. KETA
CHUM

O. KISUTCH
COHO

O. NERKA
SOCKEYE

O. TSHAWYTSCHA
CHINOOK

O. GORBUSCHA
PINK

SALMO CLARKI
CUTTHROAT

SALMO GAIRDNERI
STEELHEAD

SALMO SALAR
ATLANTIC

SALMO TRUTTA
BROWN

S. FONTINALIS
BROOK

S. ALPINUS   ARCTIC CHAR
S. MALMA   DOLLY VARDEN

color of the usual seaward-migrating salmonid smolt. Some may not have entirely absorbed their egg sac. Therefore, a *bright* tinsel-bodied fly may not be a satisfactory imitation. Some coho go immediately to sea, but most spend a full year in their stream of birth or in a lake on that stream. Some remain two years in their birth stream. Sockeye parr may move into lakes where they grow for one or two years before going to sea. Chinook may spend up to a year in fresh water, but most of them migrate to sea within three months of emergence. Chinook, coho, and sockeye juveniles are forage fish for adult rainbows, cutthroat, Dolly Varden, and for coho salmon smolts.

Cutthroat fry may move directly from their tributary streams of birth into the larger river or a lake. Some of these fish remain for a lifetime in this habitat, others may go to sea during their second or third year, when they are about 5 inches in length. Some may spend four years in a creek before migrating to a lake. Spring migrations of cutthroat may occur during migrations of juvenile Pacifics resulting in heavy predation by the cutthroat on the Pacifics. Steelhead parr usually migrate to sea after two years. However, they may out-migrate as early as year one or as late as year four. Atlantic salmon parr in most streams grow fast enough to go to sea in two to three years, but in some Scandinavian streams they may not go to sea until they are seven or eight. In the southern rivers of Great Britain, Ireland, Norway, and Sweden, brown trout smolt and run to sea at two to three years of age. They descend in April and May and may return to their river as whitling in early July or somewhat later. They run to sea weighing an ounce or two and return as whitling often weighing no more than 4 or 5 ounces, so I *imagine* that parr imitations would work well at both times. I don't know.

Arctic char parr grow very slowly. Some may migrate to sea when they are from 6 to 8 inches long. Grainger reports that Frobisher Bay char go to sea in the summer at ages five to seven. Anadromous brook trout remain in their birth stream for two to three years. It may be difficult to tell them from nonanadromous species because they spawn in the same places and grow in the same stream habitats. Anadromous Dolly Varden parr from Eva Creek in southeast Alaska go down to sea after three to four years in the stream. Nonanadromous members of the species usually spend a few months in a stream, then move into a lake in the stream system.

Some salmonid parr can be distinguished from others at streamside by the shape of their parr marks and by the position of the marks in relationship to the lateral line. Pink (hump-back) salmon parr do not have parr marks. Most of the parr markings on sockeye and chum are above the lateral line. In chinook and coho the parr marks extend below the lateral line. In all trout and char the parr marks extend below the lateral line.

J. W. Jones says that Atlantic parr can be distinguished from trout parr by examining the adipose fin. The trout parr's adipose fin is edged with red.

The fins of chinook parr are usually not colored. On coho, the forward margin of the anal fin is usually white. The lower and caudal fins are tinged with orange and tipped with white. The backs of sockeye parr are bluish or greenish. This is not enough information about coloration to make it possible to tie flies, and the colors of species probably vary from stream to stream. This and other pattern problems, such as hook sizes, have to be worked out with regard to local stream conditions.

Haig-Brown created a number of migratory salmonid parr patterns for use in both streams and estuaries. He published various versions of some of his flies suggesting alternate patterns from book to book. I like that because it gives a more clear-cut understanding of the ideal to which he strived. No pattern ever fully satisfies the tyer's vision. It may take a lot of fish, but there's always some imperfection of color or form. The more versions published the easier it is to see where one ought to go with revisions.

Haig-Brown Pink (Humpback) Fry Patterns

I. Tail: Green swan.
    Body: Flat silver tinsel.
    Hackle: Scarlet tied small.
    Wings: Blue hackle back to back enclosing one white strand and two blue heron strands.
    Cheeks: Pale blue chatterer.

II. Tail: Yellow.
    Body: Silver.
    Hackle: Yellow.
    Wings: Mixed blue and green bear hair and a few strands of peacock over that.

Haig-Brown Sockeye Fry Patterns

Haig-Brown also suggests two sockeye fry patterns. He used tandem hooks. These were devised in cooperation with Tommy Brayshaw.

I. Body: Flat silver tinsel.
    Wings: Moose hair. Use white or white tipped with dark brown.
    Hackle: Badger.

II. Body: Wrap flat silver to the shoulder. Shoulder scarlet floss silk, ribbed with oval silver.
    Wings: A few peacock herl strands, covered with two furnace hackles, jungle cock cheek, and a few blue macaw strands. (Macaw is optional.)
    Hackle: Under hackle scarlet, over hackle blue macaw.

Haig-Brown Steelhead Fry Pattern

Tail: Pink swan.
Body: Silver.
Wings: Barred summer duck (or grizzly) enclosing yellow swan.

For coho fry in July Haig-Brown recommended:

Tail: Orange feather.
Belly: Silver.
Wings: Golden pheasant tail string with orange bear hair inside the strips.

10

The Rig

There are three riggings for lead-weighted drifting. In two of them the fisherman leaves a blood knot length dangling from the joining of the terminal length of leader and attaches lead— either round or pencil—to it. In the third rig the fisherman dangles surgical tubing for a weight carrier.

In thin water running over stones or pebbles a small, round lead weight will roll along the bottom ahead of the current pressure. The water is like that in many Great Lakes tributary streams where I use Split Shot Sinkers with spreading ears. Because these lead weights are round, they roll well. They have spreading ears and can be easily opened and removed from the line with plier pressure on the ears. Split Shot Sinkers are made by the Water Gremlin Company in White Bear Lake, Minnesota. I use TSS-5 weight, and add one or two more if needed. One can be cast with ease on a number nine Scientific Anglers rod. Two can be cast with annoyance, and three can be cast with disgust. I hate using so much lead in a fly rod, but I'd add an anvil if needed because I know that my lead must roll bottom while my leader bobs the lure about 6 to 9 inches above bottom through the fish's exciter zone.

In deeper water, which often runs over larger stones, pencil lead or hollow core lengths cut off a coil are the best weights.

The pencil lead can be slipped over the blood knot dangle and crimped with the cutting pliers. A two-way swivel can be used between the main line and the terminal leader to prevent monofilament line from twisting. A tag end for the pencil lead dangles from the improved clinch knot used to tie the leader to the bottom two-way swivel eye.

When using pencil lead, guess at the length (or weight) needed. When depth dictates weights that overtax a fly rod, spinning or casting rods must be used.

In deep, fast water running over large rocks or flat rocks that are tipped on edge or rolled into jumbles, surgical tubing acts as an elastic tripping mechanism for the dangling, catching weight. The tubing is attached to a three-way swivel. Solid lead cut from a coil is inserted into the tubing. When the lead catches on the bottom the surgical tubing acts as a shock cord while the fisherman goes through the antisnagging dance. If the hang-up can't be cured the lead will pull out of the tubing or the tubing will fray off. The fisherman gets his rig back minus the lead. In fast, deep water running over jumbled stones, that's a bargain.

The surgical tubing rig is more complex than a blood knot end dangling from the joining with the final leader length. A three-way swivel goes into the same spot. The three-way swivel to be used has one eye at a right angle to the plane of the other two eyes. On the right angle eye, attach surgical tubing perhaps 2½ inches long. Tie it firmly with light wire or strong monofilament. I buy these already made up. When I'm ready to fish I tie my main line to one eye, and my terminal piece of leader to the other eye—it's in a continuous plane with the main line eye.

It can be a job to insert solid core lead into surgical tubing in cold weather. I carry a wooden lead pencil in my pocket to aid that chore. I insert the point far enough to stretch the tubing, then roll a collar back onto the wood. The pencil comes out easily, the lead goes where the pencil was, and my fingers roll the rubber collar over the lead. It hangs there securely. I protect myself from stab wounds by sheathing the pencil point in a discarded felt pen cover.

Carrying lead and pliers on the stream is a nuisance. The lead is heavy and I know of no way to make it lighter. Remember that the pound of feathers you're carrying tied to 3 pounds of hooks are just as heavy as 4 pounds of lead. Add the weight of your pliers and it may be clear to you why fishermen who slip sometimes drown.

Belting your waders may turn them into bags buoyant enough to offset the gear weight if you fall in. And the wader belt can be used to dangle a plier sheath outside your fly jacket where it can be easily reached. The HMF Manufacturing Company in Grand Rapids, Michigan, makes a pair of fisherman's pliers light enough to be carried on a vest from a Pin-On Reel (Yo Yo). These are the easiest to carry.

In streams crisscrossed with logs and sticks, a three-way swivel and droppers to both lure and sinker are needed. The dropper to the sinker should be lighter than the dropper to the lure. Both are of lighter test than the leader. In such bottoms it's possible to get either the sinker and the lure caught—or both. Some sections of the Misery are paved with my lead weights— a hazard to feeding mergansers.

It's impossible to know how the fish feel about the vibrations that travel to the lure from the bump, bump, bumping of the lead weight over bottom rocks. It transmits to my rod handle, so it must transmit to the lure. Of course, there's tension between my hand and the lead weight. There's less tension between the weight and the lure because the slack there dampens the vibrations, but there still must be vibration that the fish can feel by lateral line sensing.

I've observed fish lying in the path of a bumping weight coming down the drift bottom. They swim to one side and move without much fear, as though making way for another waterlogged piece of debris, so apparently our weights don't spook the fish. Still there's the possibility that the fish we don't catch are the fish that do avoid that kind of sensation. We're crashing our leads across the stream bottom. It may be that the fish that avoid them are the fish that will breed survivors. I don't know. Perhaps a generation of fish will rise up and laugh at our rigs. Ruffed grouse have been transformed from tree limb sitting dodos to birds of avoidance behavior patterns including running instead of flushing. If the generations of fish can summate a kind of genetic learning, we may need to think up rigs that creep the bottom quietly.

In drift fishing the weight is to bump bottom, not the lure. It is true that some resting fish are near or on the bottom. Furthermore they may find security within a bottom basin, but many in-migrating salmonids hold 1 to 3 feet above the bottom. In general, fishing the lure right on the bottom is not productive.

The lure is on a leader about 2 feet or less in length. The lure may be buoyed by a drift bobber that is an exciter lure in its own right. The fisherman thinks in terms of bouncing bottom with his weight and drifting his lure through the exciter zone of a fish somewhat off the bottom—how far off bottom varies by season and current pressure within the stream.

Extending from the weight in one direction is the line that goes to the fisherman's rod. Extending from the weight in the other direction is the terminal leader that goes to the lure. Those three parts make up the rig.

No matter how weights are rigged they're awkward to cast with a fly rod. An alternate method is to use a weighted line, many of which cast fairly well. I sometimes use a length of Shakespeare Thin Troll wire (.012 diameter; I think 20 pound) between my monofilament butt and the terminal leader. A 3-foot piece will take lures into the exciter zone in many water situations. I make loops in each end of my Thin Troll Wire with size 5 Berkley Connector Sleeves. Stan Lievense carries Thin Troll Wire of various lengths, and switches them as he moves through drifts of various depths. They cast easily.

These are the rigs for weighted drifting. Happiness is casting thin spoons or weighted flies in thin water where lead weights aren't needed. But fish swim where they will, and fishermen must rig to reach them. The purpose of the rig is to present lures to the fish's exciter zone.

11

Drift Fishing

Drift fishing has a history and a vocabulary. The method developed on the Pacific Slope where drifts have been used by migrating salmonids for generations. (An excellent book on drift fishing is *Steelhead Drift Fishing* by Bill Luch. Order it from the magazine *Salmon Trout Steelheader*.)

A drift is a section of water where fish lie. For migratory salmonid fishermen "drift" does not mean "float." One floats to drifts in one's drift boat. The boat is not a "drift," and drift fishing is not done from a floating boat. A drift boat is floating transportation to sections where fish lie, called drifts. One may beach or anchor the boat opposite the drift and fish from it, or one may get out and wade.

Some fly fishermen often fish from a moving boat and may jump to the conclusion that a "drift boat" is that kind of boat. It is possible to achieve a drag-free float with a dry fly or a sub-surface wet fly from a moving boat with a floating line. The drag-free float, in many instances, will be short. But it isn't possible for a rig to drift bottom at current speed while the boat from which it is cast is drifting the top at current pressure speed. If a lure is fished from a floating drift boat it must be held back by gentle rowing, and an unweighted lure is used. So drift fishing is not fishing from a free-floating boat.

Frank Amato, editor of *Salmon Trout Steelheader* magazine, anchored and casting into a drift from his drift boat. A drift boat is transportation through white water to drifts—places where the fish lie. (Photo courtesy *Salmon Trout Steelheader* magazine)

The best drifts are long sections of water that permit the rig to drift the lure across a bottom that doesn't have too many hang-ups. Fish like these drifts because they are resting places (sometimes called holding water) that have adequate aeration and cover. Such drifts have a head, a body, and a tailout. Usually the head is deep water, the body has the most cover, and the tailout is shallower water draining into a rapids. Fish lie in various kinds of cover in resting places or holding water in all three parts of the drift.

Typical lies in the body, or middle, of a drift are in front and behind underwater obstructions, behind a log that extends from the bank into the stream, under slicks, near eddies, and under overhanging branches. An in-migrating fish thinks of a drift in terms of comfortable resting lies, aeration, and cover. The in-migrator is not as concerned about cover as is the stream fish.

Many migrating salmonids are sometimes careless about picking their lie. A steelhead may swim near the bank and lie under a low-hanging branch that gives enough security for a short time. Don't ignore such places, and don't look at the lies from the point of view of a selective trout fisherman. Most of the lies are resting places between swimming sessions. All of them must have good aeration if the fish is to remain in them for a long period of time. But unless these fish are settled into an over-summering or over-wintering lie, they are transients. They may be in the ideal selective trout lies, but they may also be less particular about cover and will be in other spots. So drift your lure through the marginal spots, and watch them through your polarized glasses.

We can't always fish the drifts that provide a long glide through many possible lies. Sometimes fish can be found in pockets between rocks or in other foreshortened drifts. Remember that a drift can be long or short—3 feet is a drift, 200 feet is also a drift. A long drift is better because your rig passes through several lies, but search the short drifts as well.

The streamlined shape of migratory salmonids allows them to lie in swift-moving water with comfort. Steelhead are happy in smooth, flowing water running from 3 to 18 feet deep. The same kind of water may be inhabited by in-migrating chinook, coho, Atlantics, browns, and cutthroat. Chinook and coho may be found in deeper, quieter pools.

When reading the water of a drift look for those small sections of quiet water that are comforting to the body of a fish. The turbulence just over a roily, sandy bottom may be a sand blasting place for a fish. Just above that there may be a quiet place. The turbulent water just behind a boulder is a place of agitation and rippled barriers to vision for a fish. Just below that turbulence, the water may smooth. A good rule is: Drop the rig into turbulence and drift the quiet area.

The head of the drift and the tailout may vary greatly from drift to drift, but the head is usually deeper water, the tailout relatively shallow. The head of a drift is more productive for summer fish than for winter fish. I've been disappointed often at the head of drifts, but I always cover that water quietly and carefully.

The tailout is the first section in a drift a fish enters, and that entrance is often through the rapid turbulence that drains the drift. In a gigantic river the in-migrating fish is tired. Even in a small stream, where there are many slicks, the fish has exercised. These are inviting, but they are often shallow. It's easy to spook the fish out of a tailout slick.

In general, eddies do not hold fish, but the area near an eddy may hold fish. Moreover, the pocket waters close to shore, maybe within a few inches of shore, are not eddies. Those pockets are prime spots for fish to rest, particularly if they are buttressed with boulders that seem to create a fenced pond. There may be very little overhead cover in such places, so they should be approached with caution. A light lure with no weight can be used in these pockets, and they should be covered before one fishes the rest of the drift. The George River has many such places, and fishermen can drop small Exotic Bombers into them from the shore. The Atlantics, surprised by the landing of a small missile, often rise with fury, and, catching their fisherman on a short line, quickly break off. So avoid eddies, but fish near them, and do not confuse shore pockets with eddies.

Searching for the Bottom from the Top

If you've learned to read the waters in a good drift and memorized every stick and stone on the bottom and in every lie, if you've returned to that drift year after year and seen the changes the waters make, if you've taken many Pacifics and trout from that drift, and if you value it more highly than your most treasured possession, then you know how to fish nearly any kind of migratory salmonid water. Every migratory salmonid fisherman should have his own special home drift. One of the dangers of overcrowding is that, in the future, some people may be deprived of that heritage.

Coho, chinook, cutthroat, browns, and steelhead can be taken by drift fishing. It isn't done for Atlantics because they're supposed to move to the fly, although not all Atlantics will rise to the fly. If you've sighted an Atlantic lying on the bottom and it won't rise to your fly, put on a rig and hit it in the teeth with a drifted fly. If you suspect that your catch could be improved in waters where Atlantics lie unseen, give the rig a chance to carry an invitation to the fish's exciter zone.

It's not so hard to cast a rig into a drift. It can be done with a spinning, casting, or fly rod. Water conditions, the amount of weight on the rig, and personal preferences dictate the equipment. The casting varies somewhat for each kind of rod, but there's little difference in the goal, which is to bump bottom through every possible lie to present a lure to a fish's exciter zone. In shallow water the target may be seen, but in most instances it's an imagined process. One has faith there'll be a fish in a few of the lies. Knowing something about the progress of the run and when and where different species have been caught in the stream results in the conclusion that there are fish in the lies. The objective is to pass one's lure through the drift often enough to stimulate a take.

There are two main tasks to be performed on the drift—sensing the take and learning the bottom. Touch your left wrist with your right hand index finger. If you can feel it, you've touched harder than the impact of a steelhead taking a lure onto its sensitive tongue between its jaws. Of course steelhead sometimes take hard, and may take with any level of impact, but the sensation that's hard to learn and comes most often is the light take.

These light takes teach fishermen a lot about the hang-ups in drifts. Each hesitation in the line, each peculiar bump of the weight, each stop requires a setting. It could be a steelhead. Spring chinook and fall browns will take equally lightly. Over and over the question arises: "Did a fish take my lure?" You must set to find out, but you don't have to tear the bottom out of the stream. Take up slack and tighten your line. Usually a steelhead feels different from an obstruction, and careful striking prevents setting the hook hard into a log or rock crevice. You have to set often in the beginning, although eventually you'll learn how to interpret light takes.

Fish behavior causes light takes. The fish are lethargic without interest in food, often lying in cold water. Winter steelhead take the most lightly; summers a little harder. Spring chinook take lightly; fall chinook take seldom. When they take on drifts, coho will take with good intensity. These fish take the lure, mouth it, then spit it out.

Another thing that can happen is that the fish may take the lure into its mouth and travel downstream with it. This causes the action of the rig to change slightly. Learning to feel the change in that action, more than feeling a complete stop, is what gives the veteran drift fisherman the signal to set.

By rigging properly for pickup the fisherman can improve his ability to feel the take. It's important to maintain line tension so that feelings are telegraphed to the fingers that hold the line. I always hold a section of line in the fingers of my left hand. I watch the line carefully. Sometimes I can see it stop before I feel anything. Use a rod with an action that properly telegraphs takes to your hand. The setting and playing action of the rod is not the only action built into a drift rod. It has to have a sensing action also. Finally, rig your terminal leader length properly.

Terminal leader slack delays the transmission of a take to the fisherman. Imagine your lure floating ahead and above the weight and the terminal leader floating straight out ahead of the lead at maximum distance. Let's say that you've decided on 30 inches of leader. The leader enters a fish's exciter zone and is taken at 30 inches from the lead. The fish is stopped. The lead must now travel 30 inches to get to the fish. At that point the leader has made a u. The lead must now travel another 30 inches before the slack is out, and a take is telegraphed to the fisherman's hand. This means that the weight traveled 60 inches before the take was felt.

Many things can happen while the lead makes that 60-inch travel—the fish can spit the lure out, the weight can snag or spook the fish, the fish can drop downstream ahead of the weight with the lure still in its mouth. Thirty inches of leader is too much; 2 feet is about right.

Of course the leader doesn't travel straight out, it travels above and to one side. It may even u back toward the fisherman because of differences in current. If the lure is assisted in its float by a drift bobber, it'll be riding somewhat above the lead. So leader lengths can be difficult to figure. Sometimes I shorten mine to 1 foot.

A drift fisherman is feeling from the top for the bottom. It's a distance type of Braille. The fisherman may look like he is trying to get a fish to take, but he's really gathering stream-contour data. When the data is gathered the drift fisherman knows when the boulder bump is coming, and that the sunken log bump will follow. He knows when to throw slack in order to get a little more sink for a drop-off, and when to do the line weave to shorten line for a shallow area. This knowledge cures the set-and-yank jerks and reduces the expenditure for lost terminal tackle. Still, there are many hang-ups even on a known drift.

While searching for the bottom, don't forget current pressure, which varies at different stream levels. Your job is to keep your lure traveling at current speed. Fish don't accept lures that travel too fast or too slowly, so watch your line. Is it and the whole rig moving at current speed? If too slowly, you may have rigged with too much weight. If too fast, there could be bellies in the line or you could be using too little weight. I like to pay out line at demand from current. I let out enough line to keep the lead bumping. I don't want a belly that gives the current assistance in moving the lead, I want the line tight enough so I can feel what's going on just above the stream bottom.

I use the lightest amount of lead possible to secure a natural drift. An upstream cast will allow a light lure to sink to the bottom and make a natural travel from the sector beginning opposite the fisherman's boots to the limit of the line. A cast somewhat farther upstream will allow the lure time to sink somewhat above the fisherman's boots. The length of the drift can be improved by throwing slack line as the leader progresses downstream. I usually start with light lures and upstream casts; in fact, nearly all of my casts are upstream casts. Upstream cast, drift through, and two steps downstream; upstream cast, drift through, and two steps downstream. That's my drift pattern.

Having started with a light lure I switch to heavier lures for lower bottom contours. Many fish are missed because they lie in basins and the lure passes above their exciter zone. I'm always changing weights. I add lead for drop-offs and basins; take lead off for shallow areas; add and remove lead to regulate drift speed. Use the lightest possible weight, and keep switching.

Drift bobbers keep the lure up above the weight and near the fish's exciter zone. They also help to avoid hook hang-ups, but they won't lift the weight over obstructions.

I do not use treble hooks on spinners that I drift. They are bottom grapplers anchoring themselves onto rocks, tree limbs, boots, tires, beer cans, canoe bottoms, and dead muskrats. (I've successfully fought and landed every one of these trophies.) I dress my spinners with Blue Tail flies; either double-salmon or single hooks. In most instances I've been satisfied with their holding quality.

A spinner blade need not flail the waters to excite takes on the drift. A slow-moving or limp blade will take fish. Furthermore, it will usually do no good to crank or pull the spinner back to your stand. Fish on drifts won't follow that kind of lead but they will sometimes follow a hook pulled at the end of a drift, providing the pull starts gently and moves the weight continuously along the bottom. On a drift a spinner should be drifted, not cranked.

As winter progresses and water gets colder, the fish will move less distance and need more drifts through their exciter zones to stimulate taking. Cover cold water more closely and with more casts than warm water.

I may start on a drift with a clown (chartreuse with spots) spoon dressed with a Blue Tail Fly. The next lure I'll use will be the Two-Egg Sperm Fly—usually weighted. After that I'll rig with a drift bobber dressed with a third fly—perhaps a hairwing fly. The last exciter lure I try is a spinner. If all of these lures have failed to stimulate a take and I have sighted fish on the drift, I dress a Glo-Go with a fly and some spawn.

So far in this section I've been describing drift fishing with a weighted rig. In many shallow water streams the weight isn't needed. In such water the following fly-fishing maneuvers usually take fish.

1. A downstream cast to create a dead drift right to the fish's mouth.

2. A quartering upstream cast to drift the fly in a slow swing in front of the fish. In this cast, the fly does not travel the length of the exciter zone, and the intention of the cast is to provoke a follow if the fish does not take at the moment the fly is near its mouth.

3. A pulsed retrieve after either of the above presentations. This is done by weaving line into the right hand with the intention of stimulating the "cat-following-a-string" take.

4. The teasing cast. Make a downstream cast and pay out line to present in a downstream dead drift. When the lure reaches the point where you expect the fish to be lying, take two actions designed to tease the fish into taking—make wide rod tip sweeps, or twitch and pull the lure back and forth in a zone in front of the fish. This may stimulate a hard strike.

Thin Drift Fishing

Two Doe Riffle (ficticious name) is a thin drift on the Pere Marquette near Baldwin, Michigan. My field notes show that on March 20, 1976, I hooked six steelhead there and landed two of them. I'd luckily found a pod of fresh-run fish there.

The stream was still running high with snow melt-off. The February thaw came late, then a heavy snow put more moisture on the banks, which melted slowly as each afternoon sun pushed the mercury a few degrees above the freezing mark for an hour or so.

I poked along the banks searching the waters for signs of fresh-run fish that might take readily and fight hard. I wanted fish too green to spawn still moving on their in-migration or holding beside spawning gravel for the water temperature to drop. These are the spring fish that I like to fish to—not the spawners on their redds. The spawners fight all right when fresh to the redd, but their takes are not quickly solid. Teasing them is a chore of a thousand casts.

At the head of the long run that divides the two drifts I found three fish over a newly started redd. Two were darkly colored with reddish brown and had well-defined stripes— definitely over-wintering fish. They had probably run in during late October or November. The third was bright silver—fresh-run. Through the Polaroids it seemed to have a thin, pink stripe along its side. When I first saw the fish they were chasing each other without much discrimination. None seemed to be dominant. I couldn't be sure which was female and which male, but after ten minutes of watching I saw the fresh-run fish turn on her side to pump the gravel. She was in water so thin that her side was out of water as she worked. Her belly was pearly white, her fully spread tail fin gleamed translucent in the sun between snow squalls. The two males continued to chase each other and the female. It would be a day or so before they'd spawn in that cold water.

One male was about 25 inches; the other maybe 27. The female was largest—probably 29 inches, and might have gone 12 pounds.

It was a temptation to fish for the spawners. They'd fight frisky enough, but it wasn't what I wanted. And beyond them in the lower middle of the first drift I saw a dark fish roll on the surface. I wasn't sure whether it was a large stream brown or an over-wintering steelie. The snow came in again falling to melt into the running waters. When the snow shower stopped I cupped my hands beside my Polaroids and stared intently. There were two fish shapes in the water upstream from the stump—were they fish or logs? I changed vantage points getting my vision into a cross shadow where I could see nothing. I went far upstream, crossed and got directly opposite the spawners. The fish shapes in the water still lay more like logs now, but one moved, then the other. And a third fish letting itself downstream from the raft picked up speed, seemed to charge the two moving shapes, then took to the air to show me silver sides. That fish went on through the drift into the shallow water beside the long run and "kicking" its way in fright over the shallow, open place disappeared into the deeper downstream waters. Then I saw two more fish run through past the spawners into the long run.

The fish were on the move. I'd hit the time right. The spawners could be ignored. It would be fun to have them behind me while I two-stepped the drift. I realized they'd probably hold for tomorrow. I had two days to fish.

I started at the head pool opposite the raft. I was rigged with one TS-Five "cannon ball," and each cast was a long upstream one so the cannon ball would be bottom ticking as it swung opposite my boots. The Two-Egg Sperm Fly was presenting the length of the drift about 15 feet from me. As I got to the stump pool I added one weight. The spawners behind me were an added complication. I didn't want to spook them, but I didn't want to belly up to the spot where I'd seen the fish shapes and spook that supposed target. The morning sun was still too slanted to give me a look into the waters while wading. I could see well only from the added bank height.

Finishing the drift out I waded midstream below the spawners (one had made a hightail kick sending a spray of water into the air) and got onto the bank to search the waters. This time there were four shapes in the water above the stump. Two swam away, but two held. Marking the spot—about two rod lengths upstream from the stump—I went to the head of the riffle, slid down the bank on the ice, and worked my way downstream. I started my casts well above the marked spot, and felt each line drift with an increasingly nervous apprehension. Now the tails lashing in the nest behind me made me increasingly jumpy, and it was a hard fight not to turn and put a cast through the redd.

I put three casts to the shape. "Maybe under," I thought. The fourth cast went over farther to the bank than I had thought right, but I felt the fish, and I instantly went hysterical. Instead of raising the rod tip calmly I jerked. Instead of letting the line pass through my fingers, I dropped it and the slack came up too suddenly and too tight, but the fish keeping underwater seemed to be taking out the line well. Then everything went slack. I reeled in feeling foolish.

Staying put I sent a cast to explore the base of the stump, and was instantly on. The fish came up slightly above the surface in a tired effort to leap. It was a dark fish, spawned out and thin, and came off as it took line across stream and toward the cover of the long run.

About noon I saw six fish move out of the long run. Swimming against the current, they went toward the raft at the head of the upstream drift. Then a female did some sunfishing in the shallow gravel just below the stump pool. She was considering making a redd. She had no males with her, and she wandered back and forth over the gravel turning on her side occasionally to move a little gravel, then righting herself to swim erratically to another testing spot. Finally she went behind the stump. Then I saw two fish letting themselves down from the head pool. They circled above the stump and dropped into still positions holding off the bottom, maybe a foot. I couldn't see how far off the bottom, actually.

Getting into the water and moving slowly into position I shaded my eyes hoping to see them. I thought I could see one shape. I cast for it, and it moved slightly—maybe disturbed by the weight. I tried to remember whether the second fish would be upstream or down. I couldn't remember. But the next cast was right. The fish was on solid, then the leader broke. I hadn't put on too much pressure. The monofilament came limply to me. It looked as slack as I felt. It had been rubbed on rocks. I saw scratch marks.

I tied in a new leader and put on a new Two-Egg Sperm Fly. By this time I was blaming myself and feeling terribly rattled.

Fish number four was out of the water before I knew I had her. Bright silver and huge, she splashed water when she landed and instantly rose into the air again. I lowered my rod tip, and saw the hook fly out of the fish's mouth. There'd been no time to set it. Then the fish came down on the fly and was foul hooked somewhere in the rear end. I had a fighting fish by the tail end! She was instantly into the long run and under the tag alders. Running alongside her in the shallow water I kept my rod tip pointed low and took up slack. Midway in the long run she came toward me into shallower water and I could feel the wiggles of her muscles as she fought frantically. I tried to hoist her so she couldn't get a purchase in the water with her tail, but she would have none of that and went back into the run stripping line from the free spooling Pflueger as she swam. We went under all the tag alders all right. The fish shot into the eddy at current's end and leaped there twice. How she could do it with my line anchored to her tail I don't know. In the long glide the fish kept my rod tip bowed and I tired her, but it was not until I'd gotten through the deep water and around the bend that I could beach her, and dragging her up the beach tail first was a hard job. She was foul hooked in the anal fin.

Twenty-nine inches long! A beautiful fish. I couldn't decide whether to keep her. It wasn't fair to keep a foul-hooked fish, but she'd been fair hooked until her second leap. And no one had seen me. I got the stringer off my fly jacket hanging loop and looked around for witnesses. There was no one there. I was on my knees in the sand beside the fish. She flared her gills. I held her upright in the water until she swam out of my fingers. She headed upstream. I regretted not having marked her fin. I might catch her again and not know.

When I returned to the stump pool the spawners were gone. Probably I spooked them during the struggle with the fish foul hooked in the tail. I cast for an hour, and heard them again splashing behind me.

Fish number five took the fly after it sank just as I felt the lead really ticking well along bottom. The fish ran between the stump and the low bank and I waded out into the pool to get my rod tip over the stump to prevent having the fish belay the line around it. The water there was above my waist and I moved awkwardly as the fish reversed direction and headed upstream. It wanted to go under the raft. Knowing I'd lose the fish, I put the pressure on, and it came to me, then turned downstream and ran back to the stump, where it leaped twice on a long, slack line. The water droplets flew off the line on each leap and I saw the lead weights wrapping round and round the monofilament leader. The angle of the fish's body in the water seemed odd. I couldn't be sure it was fair hooked, but the connection was in the head area.

The fish took me through the run under the tag alders, but I kept control and wore it out in the head of the long glide. Tired, it let me lead it to a beaching on the opposite bank. It was a good fish, hooked solidly in the mouth corner. Bright with green on the dorsal surface, and a trace of pink over the lateral line. A female, I judged, too green to milk, but the belly was bulged pregnantly. Measured 28 inches on my pocket tape. I tied the fish to a bush that overhung the water.

I went back upstream to the stump and watched the waters for a while. The clouds had settled in and it was too dark to see into the waters. As far as I could tell there were no more fish. The snow had settled down now to a steady fall. I could see that the cloud bank overhead would probably break, but I began to worry about turning the Chevy around and getting it out.

Thick Drift Fishing

When I decided to go out to the Pacific Slope and get my head together on some of the streams there, I gave Frank Amato a ring. He'd published a feature of mine in *Salmon Trout Steelheader* and helped edit a couple of selective trout features published by Steve Raymond in *Flyfisher*. So we knew each other through working correspondence, and he volunteered to fish with me for two days on one of the streams near Tillamook. I was hungry for fishing when I crossed the Columbia and headed down the coast to rendezvous with Frank.

Frank rattled in to the motel yard with his green, wooden drift boat on the trailer behind him. Seeing that boat I knew that we'd be fishing deep water. We put into the Wilson at Mill Bridge, and floated the coastal plain in deep water, through green pastures, with long oak oars creaking.

There are two types of drift boats—Mackenzie River and Rogue River boats. Authorities disagree over the difference between these two boats. They are both for white water and they're both copies of East Coast dories. Many Pacific Slope drifts are in canyons or other places that cannot be reached easily on foot or by vehicle. The easiest way to reach a number of drifts in one day is to float to them. Because the same terrain features that prevent access on foot create whitewater, the boats must be whitewater boats.

On the lower section of the Wilson we floated calmly over gentle waters. The following day in the upper canyon we floated one short whitewater section. Frank, an experienced whitewater drifter, made easy passage with strong-muscled oar strokes.

The waters of the Wilson look green where they run deep and a bit milky in the shallows. The stream is edged with large, dirty white boulders, and the bottom has the same stones. They are larger than I'd expect a fish to move, but the fisheries biologists tell me that there is some spawning in this lower section. The stream's edge is low and gentle in most stretches of this section.

Frank and I floated until we reached a drift. Some of the drifts were classic with well-defined heads, beautiful middles, and excellent tailouts. Other drifts were long glides having just a middle. All the tailouts on the Wilson are good. Many of them have a slick spot or so, and nearly all of them have shallow water lies among rocks or in little pools encircled by rocks. In general, the Pacific Slope tailouts are classic, and provide adequate aeration and cover for steelhead. Great Lakes tailouts can be unsatisfactory, however. Many of them end in a miniature waterfall with a shallow riffle beneath that.

At the drifts we could either cast from the boat or get out and wade the edges. The drifts were too deep to wade through in "middle-of-the-stream" fashion.

Frank pronounced my Shakespeare Quick Taper rod and Zebco Cardinal 4 reel okay for casting the drifts. He left a tag on my leader blood knot for a dropper, and put a coil of hollow core lead on the seat beside me. I broke off a longer chunk than I thought I needed and pinched it onto the dropper. The lure was a Glo-Go, the tiny red bead it spun on, and a bare chromed hook. Nothing more. A real, live exciter lure!

Glo-Gos are plastic football shapes with molded integral wings that bite into the water causing the lure to spin. They are winged drifters that spin and float. Mine was a barber pole fluorescent red and white. Several other fluorescent colors are available.

Naturally, since it was my first time on the Wilson, and my first time to fish a Glo-Go, I caught a steelhead, then a cutthroat. Frank put them both back into the water—they were kelts. "We're looking for bright fish," he told me. We soon came to a yellow, aluminum drift boat occupied by a lone drifter who had boated a bright fish. He held it up for us to see. Bright fish were running up; kelts were working down. It looked like a good day.

Since I didn't know the water, I discovered the depth of the drifts by trial and error. On my home stream I can nearly always set up my rig weight from memory. On the Wilson I usually began with too much lead, and, after hang-ups, adjusted the length with the pliers.

Between drifts we used the transportation fly, a Tadpolly. Frank made the Tadpolly vibrate the rod tip of the 8-foot Eagle Claw drift rod he loaned me. Without weight the Tadpolly dug deep, searching the water between drifts. I had already caught a steelhead, so I stretched out my legs, sipped some coffee, and bingo!

The strike was hard and the fish showed its silver sides in two exciting leaps. Frank rowed hard to beach the boat, and the fish running toward the boat leaped twice more only a couple of feet from the boat. I thought it might jump in. I had stood to get out of the boat and I had to bow my rod for each jump—just as I did for Atlantics on the George. When the fish tired and went on its side, I led it up a beach that was so studded with willow whips that I couldn't find an opening wide enough to pull the fish through.

Frank got a piece of toweling and tailed the steelhead. Both steelhead and browns can be tailed. Their thicker shorter wrists are harder to grip than a Pacific species or an Atlantic salmon, so hand position and finger grip are important. For all species the power squeeze should be with thumb and first finger, and should be at the head side of the fish's wrist. The remaining fingers should rest slackly over the tail fin. If the whole hand is gripped with power the tail is compressed, the greased-pig effect is increased, and the fish slips away. I squeeze my thumb and forefinger together with as much power as I can muster. I want to make the fish's steel-hard muscles yield, and I want to cut through the mucous coating.

I stay ready for slips by keeping a high rod and a slack line. I don't want my dropped fish to bounce at the end of a tight line. Usually the fright of getting untailed will energize a fish and another short fight may ensue. It's often possible to try tailing again. However, many fish gain premature releases from tailing efforts frustrated by poor grips made in slippery conditions to a moving fish. A good way to obtain an adequate grip is to lead the fish by moving the rod hand as you grasp with the tailing hand. A fish moving through the water has a greater sense of security, and won't make those counteracting flops that a fish lying dead in the water makes as it sees that approaching hand and arm.

Mucous is a problem. A tailer, a loop of stringer, or a piece of dry cloth or leather can be an aid. During this landing Frank grabbed the towel that lay between us on the boat seat to dry our hands against cooling evaporation. His grip didn't slip, and he delivered the flopping fish to the boat bottom where it got its picture taken.

When you have a choice between beaching and tailing, choose beaching. The gravity weight of the fish is always against you when you tail. There are more chances for slips and stumblings. An exhausted fish can be led up a surprisingly steep bank, and can be skidded over small logs and sticks. Back up the bank and into the brush while facing the fish. Point your rod tip at the fish. If it resists or flops at the edging of the beach, stop operations. Be ready to raise your rod tip and return to the water to play the fish. Do not back under brush that arches over the rod tip and prevents you from raising it. The fish is now on its side at the edge of the beach. The rod tip is pointed at the fish. You are coming with the fish's weight first floated in water, then dragging a bit in water washing under the body and down the beach, next skidded over sand and log on the fish's slime. (The mucous is now working for you.) You are backing, backing. The fish may lash its tail. That will only drive it farther up the beaching. You've landed the fish!

A 15-pound leader will start a 28-pound fish out of water and pull it, if the strain is even, up a beach and over a log. But if the fish interrupts the even strain, or catches on an obstruction, yield to that. Sometimes a half-beached fish body catches on an obstruction, but the fish doesn't flop and fight. In such a case move gently (don't frighten the fish; keep the rod tip raised slightly) into a kicking or beaching position and place kick or throw the fish up the bank. A companion following behind the dragging fish can act as safety man.

If the fish's body catches on an obstruction and it begins to flop about, raise the rod tip, move between the fish and the water, and if the fish regains the water before you can block it with your foot or a tailing grab, play it further while giving line to it. You can see how well hooked your fish is after it's exhausted. A well-hooked fish will stay hooked provided you keep an even strain that always yields to the fish. A flopping fish wants to return to the water. Don't panic when beaching flopping occurs. Give slack so that there's no fulcrum purchase from the flopping.

Despite all this sage advice, fish are lost while beaching. "Quick releases," we call them. They are disappointing, but practicing your beaching can be fun.

12

The Pacific Slope Region: Southeast Alaska, British Columbia, Washington, Oregon, and California

Representative Pacific Slope streams include streams of the island-estuary habitat of southeast Alaska (Evah, Saook, Hood Bay, and Petersburg creeks), short streams running off the face of the Coastal Range (the Capilano and the Wilson), long interior streams (the Skagit, Rogue, and Klamath), streams of the Olympic Peninsula (the Hoh), and short, coastal streams (the Gualala).

The Pacific Slope region, native home of Pacific salmon, cutthroat, and steelhead, extends from the Mexican border through Anchorage and down the Alaskan Peninsula. It has three major climate zones: Mediterranean, marine, and subarctic. The Mediterranean zone is a dry, summer subtropical area with cold, wet winters; it extends from Mexico to 40 degrees latitude —somewhat south of the Eel River. Although steelhead at one time ranged into the Mediterranean zone to the Mexican border, man's ecological usage of these rivers now restricts that range. The marine zone, which has mild winters, cool summers, and more precipitation in winter than in summer, extends from 40 to 60 degrees latitude.

Most of the Pacific Slope precipitation includes both rain and snow falls from October 15 to May 15. For the steelhead fisherman this means freshets that encourage successive runs. In the summer there may be periods of drought similar to those in Mediterranean California. The autumn rain that often falls in late August encouraging Pacific salmon runs may be followed by frost and a dry, warm spell when rivers return to fishable levels. Winter snows occur everywhere in the marine realm, but rain is more common in the lowlands and heavy snow in the higher mountains. This is why Roderick Haig-Brown had 2 to 3 feet of snow on the banks of his beloved Campbell River on Vancouver Island while it was raining on the banks of an Oregon steelhead stream. Despite snow in some parts of the marine climate, the winters are mild—the average winter temperature is 35° F.

The January normal daily minimum temperature map for the whole Pacific Slope is a study in mildness when compared to the Great Lakes or the arctic. The coldest temperatures are 20° F and 10° F for two mountain tops north of Seattle. These variables create some interesting contrasts for fishermen. In one day it is possible to leave one's home in the rain and go higher into the mountains and fish in the snow. Or one might leave those mountains and head for an estuary emptying into the Pacific and fish in sunshine.

Because of the many climates and subgeographical regions along the Pacific Slope, it's hard to give specific information that makes it possible for a migratory salmonid fisherman to plan ahead. It can rain quickly and hard and put the rivers up. People in the East can hop a plane, it can start raining as the plane takes off, and streams can be up too high to fish when they land. It takes an average of two days for many of these streams to clear and drop to fishable levels.

In August, Pacific Slope streams are waiting for fall to happen. California streams run low and clear after the hot, dry days of summer. The fish have not yet run; the fisherman hopes that they are approaching the river mouths. In Oregon the streams that head in the Coast Range also run low and clear. Steelhead and salmon fingerlings swim in the streams at Idleyld in North Umpqua Canyon where the waters are swift and the wading is hard. Fishermen look for frost and the autumn rains. Every fisherman tries to get his work finished, for the fall rains will begin a calendar of migratory salmonid fishing that will interfere with work through March. Fall is often ushered in by a rainstorm in late August or near Labor Day; then it frosts and hot weather may return. In Oregon there may be a dry spell before the fall freshets make a full beginning.

The fall freshets bring the jacks upstream, and with them run the other fish that were waiting in the sea. It also sends river water farther out to sea where schooling fish are drawn to the mouths of their streams of birth.

In many Oregon streams October is a time of roily water and heavy rains. Fishermen may have difficulty using flies. On the Klamath the early fall steelhead run may be followed by low, warm water. As the season advances fishermen in each region adjust to their memories of the cycle of winter rains. In California, December may bring schools of steelhead into certain streams where an extended dry season after the fall rains puts the waters into condition for winter steelhead fishing. In January, on the Eel, fishermen may be wearing wool shirts, but no coats. Canvas duck hunter hats may be comfortable headgear. At the Santa Ynez, January mornings may be frosty and the rivers turbid. The day will be warmer. On the Stillaguamish there may be a tawny flood in January, and the Campbell may rise in full freshet. The Campbell might be running just at freezing temperature and be dressed with 2 feet of snow. Under the gravel the salmon eggs will be cool and eyed. Where it rains in winter the Slope steelheader stays out and gets chilled. If it's in a canyon, the damp cold may become as unpleasant as the dry snow cold of a 20° above zero day on a Great Lakes stream. In winter there can be low-water periods also. In many streams the high water roiled with glacial silt makes bottom bouncing with a weighted rig more productive than by fishing.

In July the last snows have melted out of most Pacific Slope mountains and the rivers come down to summer level. As the fishermen mark off the August days, the streams may come down even lower exposing the dry shoulders of glacial rocks on either side of a channel trickle. Then the autumnal rains come again.

From these examples it is clear that it's hard to judge the freshets, the conditions of streams, and the in-migration of the species. Fishing success in these streams depends on runs and water conditions. When the water level is correct and a new run has arrived, fishing will be superb. A sudden rain may color the stream and reduce the catch.

Although steelhead use most of the Pacific Ocean tributary streams, the best runs usually occur in rivers that have the following characteristics: the upper branches reach into the mountain foothills; they are fast-flowing streams that run over rocky bottom (many, like the Hoh, are glacial); they often have tributaries that flow through box canyons that have pools between whitewater rapids; the upper sections have good gravel for spawning steelhead, Pacifics, and cutthroat. Near the gravel there are resting pools where salmonids can wait until they are ripe enough to lay eggs.

In southeast Alaska and British Columbia the migratory salmonid habitat is in island streams, saltwater estuaries and sounds, and mountain streams. Many of the stream systems include lakes—both inlet-outlet lakes and outlet lakes. This habitat extends south of Vancouver Island into Puget Sound to Olympia.

Because netting by militant Indians or changes in planting programs can reduce the usual runs, check with local authorities before traveling long distances to fish Pacific Slope streams.

ALASKA

There are typical southeast Alaskan streams on Baranof, Admiralty, and Kupreanof islands located between Juneau and Ketchikan, and near Sitka, where the Alaskan Department of Fish and Game conducted the southeast Alaskan studies. The streams in these studies were Evah, Saook, Hood Bay, and Petersburg creeks. The life histories of Dolly Varden and cutthroat are highly dependent on research done on these streams.

The Petersburg Creek system includes a lake, Petersburg Lake. The main stream and two short-length inlets run into the lake; the west fork enters the stream below the lake. Lower down, Shakey Frank's Creek enters the main stream. Near the tide flats Split Creek and Cold Creek enter the stream mouth. The system is on Kupreanof island. Dolly Varden, cutthroat,

Ward Creek tributary to salt water in Ward Cove north of Ketchikan is typical of southeast Alaska streams. A lake-stream system river draining from Ward Lake, it has steelhead, coho, sockeye, and cutthroat runs. (Photo courtesy Alaska Historical Library)

steelhead, and Pacific salmon, including pinks, use Petersburg Creek.

Eva Creek and Saook are on Baranof Island. Their mouths are 10 miles apart by water on the Peril Strait, but their head-waters are closer because the Saook Creek drainage points toward the source of Eva Creek. Eva Creek has a lake, and Saook does not. Saook Creek Dolly Varden come home from salt water to spawn, then run into Evah Lake to over-winter with spawned-out Evah Creek natives and nonanadromous Dolly Varden.

There's an inlet with two branches into Eva Lake and the outlet called Eva Creek that runs into Hanus Bay. The lake is a 260-acre oligotrophic lake near the northeastern corner of Baranof Island about 30 air miles from Sitka. The creek is only seven-tenths of a mile long. Saook Creek is 4 miles long, and has a branch that enters the main stream from the west.

Evah Creek Dolly Varden may begin their spawning run as early as May and the run may last through December. That's a six- to seven-month in-migration. The peak is usually from July through September. Out-migration may begin in March and last through July. The peak of out-migration is May. Pacific salmon use Evah and Saook creeks. The Dolly Varden in-migration usually begins before the salmon run. I do not know what Pacific species use these two systems, nor do I know the extent of steelhead and cutthroat migrations.

Hood Bay Creek, located on the southwest section of Admiralty Island, empties into the South Arm of Hood Bay in Chatham Strait. The system does not have a lake. The creek, which is 2.7 miles long, has only one major tributary. The stream gradient is steep with one waterfall about 4 feet high that is leaped easily by salmonids during normal flow. The stream is used by Dolly Varden and three Pacific species: pinks, chum, and coho.

BRITISH COLUMBIA

All migratory salmonid streams in British Columbia drain into the Pacific either directly or through the Columbia River.

Because the mountains come right down to the beach leaving very little coastal plain, many of the streams are short run; some are blocked in a few miles by waterfalls. On some rivers in British Columbia ice forms on streams restricting the fishing near the end of the season.

Three places fished by migratory salmonid fishermen in lower British Columbia are the Capilano, which runs through greater Vancouver; the Cheakamus Squamish System; and the Vedder in the Fraser Valley. The Cheakamus, a tributary of the Squamish, will still have steelhead in May. The Vedder has good steelhead runs in November, and produces many fish for British Columbians.

In winter there may be a foot of snow on the Squamish River banks, but just a trace at the Capilano. On the same day fishermen may be chilled at the Vedder by the wind that blows down the Fraser Valley. On a dark, damp day Capilano Canyon can be a chilly spot for winter steelheaders.

THE CAPILANO RIVER

There are 3 miles open to fishing on the Capilano—all below Cleveland Dam. Most of the stretch is in Capilano Canyon. The stream has urbanized banks. Below the dam there's a park and fish hatchery. Dog Leg Pool is reached on a park path with wooden steps to ease the climb down the canyon walls. There are two suspension bridges. Downstream from the park there are houses and farther downstream bridges and department stores. Fishing near the outlet into Burrad Inlet is done behind a shopping center. Although the banks are urban, the water is pure and the fish are wild.

When Captain George Vancouver sailed into Burrad Inlet in 1792, Capilano River and the lake 14 miles upstream had heavy runs of coho and steelhead. About 200 years later the species were threatened with extinction because they were cut off from their spawning grounds by Cleveland Dam, the major source of Vancouver's water supply. By 1971, Capilano River Hatchery was in full operation and chinook salmon were added to the river's species.

In October 1975 all of the hatchery brood stock, eggs, and fry—with the exception of some steelhead fry—were killed in a chlorine spill. The spill possibly occurred from back pressure in a line called the Seymour Creek water line. Death occurred in a few minutes, and wiped out the year-classes affected. The well-managed hatchery has adequately recovered the loss.

This urbanization of stream and hatchery illustrates several significant points regarding current fishing conditions. Fishery personnel, not only in British Columbia but also across the salmonid range, are adjusted to obtaining clean waters and good fishing despite a human population that grows into every ecological niche. Also, not all of the Pacific Slope fishing occurs in unsettled wilderness, and fishermen in a highly urbanized slot that extends from Vancouver down Highway Five to Olympia continue to have good migratory salmonid fishing.

The Capilano Spawning-Run Calendar

The Capilano has a scanty run of summer steelhead. They run from June through October and lay in the stream until April and May when they spawn. Winter steelhead in-migrating in December, January, and February lay in the lower reaches of the river and spawn in April and May—the same time as the summers. Some steelhead in-migrate in the fall.

Fall chinook run in from August through October and spawn October through November. This run started in 1969, so it isn't completely clear what the peak run time is—probably October.

The coho run starts in early June and continues through January. Hatchery records show that Capilano coho have always run over a long period. The coho begin spawning in November and continue spawning through December with occasional late spawning in January and February. The peak of spawning occurs November through December.

There are some runs of native chums and pinks below Canyon Pool. An increasing population of cutthroat use the stream and can be fished in some part of the stream throughout the year. They spawn in April and May with the steelhead.

WASHINGTON

The eastern edge of the Puget Sound country is a sunken intermountain basin. In a sense Washington residents have two coasts—the Puget Sound area and the west coast of the Olympic Peninsula. Salmonid streams empty into both of those coasts. The Olympic Peninsula and Puget Sound geography and climate differ from southeast Alaska and British Columbia. Puget Sound represents the ending of a dominant saltwater and stream estuary kind of habitat.

THE SKAGIT RIVER

The Skagit and its tributaries is the largest river stream in the Puget Sound region. It lies within the Skagit Basin that also includes the Samish River and five smaller, independent drainages. Because the Skagit includes a great variety of habitats, most of the anadromous species of the Puget Sound region use the river.

The Skagit's lower mainstream is nearly as wide as Montana's Yellowstone near Livingston, and from the mouth up to Rockport the water reminds me of the Yellowstone. Wading fishermen get small nibbles at the edges; in other places they fish from the bank, but most fishing is from drift boats. The steelhead lies at the junction with the Baker River are marked by spots stomped free of grass by fishermen's boots. "Stomping lies," the fishermen call them.

The dam site on the Baker is popular with bank fishermen because fish bunch up below the Baker River Fish Collection Facility waiting for their truck ride upstream. Fish of the post-dam era really get around. Seeing a salmon being trucked to spawning gravel is a very strange sight!

There are boat landing sites all along the stream, some dedicated to local sportsmen, others to local clubs. All of the towns along the stream profit from the steelheader's trade and want to provide services. At Rockport there's an excellent streamside camping park with pleasant sites and tables.

The Skagit, a long, interior stream, has headwaters in the Cascade range. A canoeist traveling upstream on the Skagit from Marblemount would travel deeply northeast into the Cascades, then turn and travel north across the British Columbian border to the foot of Silvertip Mountain. Unfortunately, he'd have to portage three dams.

The Skagit has heavy snow runoff during most springs. Two beautiful, large streams—the Sauk and the Cascade—empty into the Skagit. Both streams are hosts to some steelhead, salmon, Dolly Varden, and cutthroat. It's a long way for the salmon and steelhead to run to spawn, but a few manage the trip. Dollys and cutthroats also have a mileage problem, but since some of them make a seasonable feeding home in the Sauk and Cascade tributaries, they have a higher residential density throughout the year. Neither stream is very fertile. Both streams have a few nutrients and are too cold for high production of bio-organisms. The pH level of the streams isn't high enough to support many insects. So both streams run down through beautiful country but neither supports large resident trout populations.

The Skagit has 162 miles of mainstream length. Flowing to the sea it crosses the Canadian border about 70 miles east of Baline and runs south for about 33 miles nearly to Newhalem. There are three dams in this section, and it is a steep-walled narrow valley that has been cut through the rugged high Cascade Mountain range. The river turns southwest below Newhalem running in that direction to Marblemount. The Cascade enters from the east at Marblemount.

Below Marblemount the Skagit runs through a broader valley floor with excellent pool-riffle sections. It flows west by southwest for about 10 miles to Rockport. The Sauk enters below Rockport.

The Sauk has two major tributaries—the Whitechuck and Suiattle—that have headwaters in the high Cascades. The last 4 miles of the Sauk runs through a delightful valley, but the rest of the stream flows through more rugged country.

The Skagit flows by Rockport and runs about 12 miles to Concrete where it receives the waters of the Baker from the north. Below that confluence the river runs west about 33 miles to Sedro Wooley and turns south. From Sedro Wooley it's about 23 river miles to the confluence with Skagit Bay near Conway.

The Cascade, the Sauk, and the Baker are all large rivers that deliver the volume of water that makes the lower mainstream a mighty river.

Below Marblemount the Skagit Valley floor broadens into open farm land. There are some sections of deciduous cover to Concrete; below that it's mostly farmland with some industrial sites. Anadromous fish like the pool-riffles from Marblemount to Sedro Wooley, and that usage is important to the economy of the area.

Below Sedro Wooley the mountain stream is tamed. It becomes a flatland drainage that meanders quietly with long deep glides and pools. The farmland is giving way to increased industrial usage, and river lovers are concerned about that usage.

The Skagit Spawning-Run Calendar

The Skagit is host to all five Pacific salmon species, two trout species (steelhead and cutthroat), and one char (Dolly Varden).

Winter steelhead begin to enter the Skagit in November. The run continues through May and peaks in December-January. Spawning occurs from late February to June, and kelts may be in the stream as late as July. Winter steelhead spawning areas are found throughout the watershed from tidewater to headwaters.

Summer steelhead begin to enter the Skagit in April. The run continues through October, and peaks in June-July. Spawning occurs from late February to May, and kelts may be in the stream as late as June. Summer steelhead spawning areas are the same as for fall/winter fish with the exception of natural runs that occur in Finney Creek, Dog Creek, and the Suiattle River.

Sexually mature cutthroat enter the Skagit on their spawning run beginning in September, and run through February. The run peaks in October, and spawning occurs from February through May. Cutthroat prefer to spawn in tributary headwaters. Some cutts will still be coming downstream in May.

There are three stocks of Skagit River chinook—spring, summer, and fall. The spring stock is considered to be a distinct group mostly because its migration pattern and spawning area choice is different from the summer-fall stock. Spring in-migrating chinook spawn in the riffles and patch gravel areas of the upper Skagit tributaries. These include Goodell, Bacon, Diobsud, and Illabot creeks, the Cascade River, and the upper Sauk River drainages. The Sauk drainages used by spring chinook are the upper mainstream, the lower Whitechuck, the Suiattle, and the following Suiattle tributaries: Sulphur, Downey, Lime, Buck, Straight, Tenas, and Big creeks.

Some spring chinook are trapped below Baker Dam and given a 14-mile truck ride. After that "hitch" they swim to spawning grounds in the Baker mainstream and sections of its tributaries.

Skagit spring chinook enter the river in early April and continue to run into July. On some grounds spawning begins as early as late July. Spring chinook spawning is usually completed in the system by early October. Juveniles live in the system for more than a year and go to sea early in their second year during spring runoff, usually between mid-March and mid-July.

Summer-fall chinook usually spawn on the riffle areas of the mainstream and the larger tributaries. The mainstream grounds are between Newhalem and Sedro Wooley. Spawning also occurs in 16 miles of the Cascade and 32 miles of the mainstream Sauk. The major fall chinook spawning areas in the Sauk are below Darrington. Tributaries of the Sauk, Cascade, and the mainstream Skagit are hosts to summer-fall spawners.

Summer-fall chinook begin entering the Skagit about mid-July. The run continues through September. Spawning begins in the first part of September and is usually finished by the middle or end of October.

Juvenile summer-fall chinook live in the stream about three months. Their out-migration begins about the same time as the spring juvenile out-migration mid-March, but it lasts longer. Some juvenile chinook have been recorded out-migrating in nearly every month of the year.

Most of the streams and tributaries in the Skagit Basin that are big enough are used by migrating coho. Heavily used Skagit River tributaries include Bacon, Diobsud, Goodell, Newhalem, Martin, Cascade, Illabot, Finney, Grandy, Davis Slough, Barnaby, Wiseman, Savage, Red Cabin, Muddy, Alder, Jones, Day, Nookachamps, and Carpenter creeks. In the Baker system coho spawn in every accessible tributary to the mainstream, and to Baker Lake. Sauk River tributaries that are host to coho are Beaver, Dan, Dillinger Slough, Hilt, and Rinker creeks.

The Skagit Basin coho spawning migration begins in mid-July and continues into December. In some upper Skagit tributaries there is an earlier run. Spawning in some areas begins as early as mid-October, and in many areas continues until mid-January.

Juveniles live in the system for a little more than a year before going down to sea. They migrate early in their second year. Their peak out-migration occurs between mid-March and mid-July during spring run-off time. Some juvenile coho have been recorded out-migrating in nearly every month of the year.

The major spawning ground for Skagit chum is the mainstream in areas of channel splitting where sloughlike conditions occur. There must be suitable flow, depth, and bottom type. A middle-western muddy slough bottom isn't the exact type desired. They use the mainstream up to Newhalem. Chum salmon also use Alder, Barnaby Slough, Bacon, Day, Goodell, Grandy, Illabot, Jones, Mundt, Savage, and Thornton creeks; the Sauk and three of its tributaries, Dan, Hilt, and Rinker creeks; plus the lower Cascade.

Chums begin to enter the Skagit in early to mid-September. Spawning begins in early November and continues in some areas into mid-or late January.

Juvenile out-migration begins in early February and continues through early June. They run as soon as their egg sac absorption scar heals.

Skagit Basin pink salmon spawning occurs almost entirely in the Skagit. They spawn mainly in the mainstream. They like the broad riffles that combine with areas of moderate channel splitting beginning above Marblemount and extending downstream for 50 miles to below Lyman. Many Skagit tributaries also are hosts to pink salmon spawning. These include Alder, Bacon, Boulder, Day, Diobsud, Finney, Goodell, Grandy, Illabot, Jackman, Pressentin, and Thornton. The Cascade and two tributaries—Clark and Jordan creeks—entertain spawning pinks. They also run into the Sauk and two of its tributaries—Dan and Hilt creeks.

Pink juveniles begin out-migration soon after emergence from gravel, and spend much of their early life in the Skagit, Sauk, and Cascade mainstreams. These sections and the estuarine waters are important to the early rearing of pinks. For that reason industry and farming sources of pollution are carefully watched by river lovers and fishermen. Out-migration is usually completed by the end of May.

Adult pinks return to the river on odd-numbered years during early to mid-July. Spawning begins as early as late August. It's usually completed by late October.

Skagit Basin sockeyes are indigenous only to the Skagit River system, and are mostly found in the Baker River drainage. For that reason the Baker River elevators at the fish trap are significant. Without them the species might become extinct in the basin. The spawning areas are artificial because the original grounds are under Baker Dam water. They're called "artificial beaches."

Sockeye enter the Skagit on their spawning run from early to mid-June. The run ends in August. Spawning begins in late September and continues until mid-December.

Juvenile sockeye usually remain in the system for one year. Their out-migration occurs during spring runoff from mid-March to mid-July.

Dolly Varden Char in the Skagit

Dolly Varden enter the Skagit on their spawning run in the fall. They continue to in-migrate through December and begin spawning in November. Peak spawning is from December through January and spawning usually ends in February.

Dolly Varden spawn in the upper tributaries. There is estuary fishing for Dollys the year round, and flies imitating salmonid fry work well in fall and late spring.

THE HOH RIVER

The Hoh, the gem of the Olympic Peninsula, springs from a glacier in Olympic National Park. The waters falling over a gradient more gentle than many Pacific Slope streams do not scour the bottom as badly as, for example, the lower Wilson. Therefore, the spawning gravel extends for long distances and occurs in lower sections of the stream. Seventy-five percent of the lower stream area has spawning gravel. The females dig eagerly in the beautiful white gravel that yields easily to their flanks. The stream banks are forested with gigantic Douglas fir and other luxuriant rain-forest fauna. The Hoh valley is too narrow for ranching in most places, but it is not a narrow canyon and is easily traversed. The Olympic mountains are scenically positioned along the stream. In winter, fishermen lift eyes from the Hoh to the snow-sprinkled green boughs of spruce, hemlock, and Douglas fir growing on the mountains. Despite the fact that the Olympic Peninsula gets about 100 inches of rain during the season, the snowfall in the valley is not excessive. There's very little snowfall on the streets of Forks, the nearby town.

Hoh waters are more like the classic Great Lakes migratory streams than any I've seen on the Pacific Slope. Like Michigan ground-water streams, the Hoh is shallow, clear running, wadable for long stretches, and gives long reaches of spawning gravel to migratory salmonids. The stream often floods in December and January and occasionally in the spring.

The Hoh is in the Soleduck-Hoh basin, a rich fishing resource that includes 569 rivers and streams tributary to the Pacific from Cape Flatery south to but excluding Kalaloch Creek. The major watersheds are the Ozette, Quillayute, Suex, and Hoh.

The Olympic mountains are the source of the two largest systems in the Soleduck–Hoh Basin—the Hoh and the Quillayute. The smaller drainages begin in the low foothills at the base of this range. While the mountain drainages are steep in their headwaters, the rivers have many miles of moderate gradient and lowland channels in the lower sections. Adequate stream flow comes from snow-pack runoff, a few glaciers, and the heavy Olympic Peninsula rainfall.

All Pacific salmon species (chinook, chum, coho, sockeye, and pink run in the Soleduck–Hoh Basin streams. There are over 600 miles of suitable spawning-migration water in the basin.

The Hoh Spawning-Run Calendar

Winter steelhead enter the Hoh in November; there is good fishing to them until around April. The fishing peaks November through April, but fish are still available through May. They spawn from February through May.

Summer steelhead enter the Hoh in June; there is good fishing for them until around October. The fishing peaks June through September; they spawn from February through May. In general, there's steelhead fishing year round in the Hoh. Cutthroat run in the Hoh from August through December.

The Hoh has the most significant spring and summer-fall chinook run in the Soleduck–Hoh Basin. Most of these fish spawn upstream from the South Fork, and in the lower 10 miles of the South Fork. Some spring and summer-fall chinook spawning occurs in Winfield Creek upstream nearly to the mouth of Glacier Creek. In the basin the spring chinook upstream migration begins in March and ends in the middle of August. Spawning occurs from the middle of August through the middle of October. The summer-fall upstream migration begins in mid-August and continues through November. Summer-fall fish spawn from the middle of September through the middle of December. In the fall chinook spawners concentrate between the mouth of Nolan Creek and the South Fork; they also like Winfield Creek and the South Fork; and they will do some spawning in Nolan, Owl, and Mt. Tom creeks.

Coho like to spawn in the Hoh. They can get up to the cascade areas near Glacier Creek about mile 49. The south Fork has 10 miles of stream coho can swim, but most of the tributaries above the South Fork are too steep in their upper reaches. Coho can swim into Hoh River south bank tributaries except Maple and Owl creeks which have falls close to their junctions. Braden, Nolan, and Winfield creeks are good coho spawning reaches. On the north bank of the Hoh the tributary gradients are too steep for coho until the stream reaches the

Hoh Valley where Anderson and Alder creeks are hosts to them.

In the basin there's coho upstream migration in early January and spawning throughout that month. Migration occurs from mid-September through December, and spawning for those fish is from mid-October through December.

The Indians catch pink salmon in the set-nets on the Hoh, but the average annual escapement for the whole basin is only 500 fish. So don't go pink salmon fishing, although you might see a few swimming upstream in the Hoh from mid-July through mid-September, or spawning from mid-August through October. The fish stinking on the banks in the fall that looks like a pink may really be a pink.

Sockeye have never officially been seen swimming in the Hoh or caught in Hoh nets. Chum salmon may someday make an official call, but it won't happen often.

OREGON

The boundary between Washington and Oregon is the Columbia River, which has headwaters in British Columbia and Idaho. The majority of the Oregon streams of the Pacific Slope south of the Columbia flow west to the Pacific from headwaters in the Coastal Mountain range. Two rivers, the Rogue and the Umpqua, flow west to the Pacific through the Coastal Mountains from headwaters in the Cascades.

The Oregon coastal strip is long, narrow, and rugged. The mountains protect some of the fertile forested valleys along the lower portions of the major streams. Bays and tidewater areas jut inland where rivers enter the ocean. Forest roads, some paved, run along most of the streams providing fishing access.

The Rogue and Umpqua are important because they provide sufficient flow and volume to support summer runs of migratory salmonid including cutthroat, salmon, and steelhead. They both have spring salmon runs as early as March with good runs in April, May, and June. The steelhead that enter these streams in spring may not reach the upper waters until August. In August, coho and chinook enter the Rouge and Umpqua; their spawning peak is usually October.

THE WILSON AND TRASK RIVERS

The coastal plain scallop is wide at Tillamook, Oregon, and the fisherman who wants to explore short coastal stream systems has five to choose from: the Miami River system, the Kilchis River system, the Wilson River system, the Trask River system, and the Tillamook. If a fisherman has a family that doesn't want to chase salmonids, he can leave them on the beach to gather firewood, clams, and crabs while he catches and releases fish. In the evening the family can reunite for seafood around a beach fire.

The Wilson is of medium width, and runs deep across the coastal plain. In the lower canyon beneath Siskeyville there are sections that can be waded and other sections that can be fished effectively from the bank. The drift boat is the best approach to these waters because one can cover the drifts and the deep runs and holes. Rains sweep in from the ocean and the stream can become too high and too cloudy for fishing in a short time. When these rains melt snow on the upper canyon slopes, the stream rages between its banks with an awesome power. Tillamook Bay absorbs a terrific discharge of water when all its systems are affected by a general rain.

Highway Six to Portland follows the Wilson River Valley into the upper canyon to its headwaters at the top of the Coastal Range. On the east slope of the Coastal Range the waters flow east and find their way to the Pacific via the northward-flowing Willamette and the westward-flowing Columbia. The upper canyon waters become progressively thinner flowing into drifts that shrink to pools. The thin water is rough, and probably not easy spawning territory as it might be in the Great Lakes region.

Although the Tillamook area streams run through the region of greatest oceanic moderation, the January Tillamook fisherman should expect to be as cold as the fisherman in the early November snows of Michigan.

The Trask Spawning-Run Calendar

In a letter dated February 3, 1977, Ernest Jeffries, Oregon

Fish Culture Supervisor, described the Trask salmonid smorgasbord as follows:

> Winter steelhead enter the Trask in early November, there is good fishing around Thanksgiving, the fishing peaks near Christmas but fish are still available through March. These fish spawn from mid-February through April.
>
> Summer Steelhead runs are smaller in number and some of the fish may be strays from hatchery plants in other Tillamook Bay streams. They enter the stream in late April, peak in June, and remain in the stream till spawning in April and May. We do not plant either the summer or winter steelhead in the Trask River.
>
> Spring chinook are available in Tillamook Bay starting mid- or late April. The fishing in the stream takes place mostly in May and June and they spawn early September through October.
>
> Fall chinook enter the bay in October and start to spawn from mid-October through December.
>
> Coho enter the bay in September, the spawning peaks in late October and November and extends through December.
>
> Sea-run cutthroat enter the bay and tidewater areas in mid-August, spawn in late winter, and some are still in the streams when trout fishing begins in spring.

THE ROGUE RIVER

The Rogue rises at the summit of the Cascade Mountain range and cuts through the Coastal Mountain range. The Rogue River Basin covers nearly all the southwestern corner of Oregon and a chunk of northern California. The watershed, which is 110 miles long and about 60 miles wide, covers 5,161 square miles. The terrain is rough and mountainous except for the narrow, central inland valley located east of the Coast Range between river mile marks 85 and 145.

The river runs from an elevation of 5,600 feet southwest for about 215 miles, to the Pacific north of Gold Beach. Above river mile mark 145 the river drops sharply at 60 feet per mile through a narrow canyon. In the agricultural land of the central valley the gradient decreases to 10 feet per mile, but becomes more steep in the Coastal Range where it flows through a wonderful gorge that drops 33 feet per mile.

The tributaries that have some great fishing include the Illinois, Coquille, Grave, Evans, Applegate, and Bear creeks, and Little Butte and Big Butte. The Applegate and the Illinois are the two major tributaries. They head in the Siskiyou mountains of California and flow north to enter the mainstream at river mile marks 95 and 27 respectively. Big Butte, Little Butte, and Bear Creek enter from the south between mile marks 152 and 126. Evans and Grave creeks enter from the north at miles 111 and 68 respectively.

The stream runs at peak in January because of winter rainfall. A second peak, not so high as this, runs off in May from melting snow in the Cascades. Some of the inland valley tributaries run dry in summer.

In general, Rogue River fishing weather is mild. In the higher elevations of the Cascades it can get bad, but fishermen don't climb up there. Wear a raincoat in winter, and expect hot, dry weather in summer. It'll be cool in the canyons.

The estuary is short, shallow, and narrow. The tidal influence extends for about 4 miles upstream. In summer the saline water that intrudes inland is cool.

The river has gained protection through legal declarations. Some sections of the stream have been designated National Wild River and State Scenic Waterways.

Fish can now get over Illinois Falls where a fishway was constructed. The Illinois Canyon from Kerby to the mouth of Briggs Creek is a popular fishery for winter steelhead. Drift boats seldom take the stretch because of difficult access and white water. Fishermen have to hike from the road into the canyon.

In fall, chinook pile up at the mouth of the Applegate waiting for a rise in water level. They can't get over the riffles there until fall rains bring the river flow up.

The Rogue Canyon from Agness at mile 32 to the mouth of Grave Creek at mile 68 is a good section for summer steelheading. It has white water, rapids, and beautiful scenery, and has been given National Wild River and State Scenic Waterway status. Guides for running the river are necessay for strangers.

The road doesn't go to the river, but a trail runs the length of the stretch.

The Oregon Department of Fish and Wildlife keeps track of run populations passing over Gold Ray Dam. Personnel seated in a counting chamber can see the fish passing over the dam.

Above Gold Ray Dam where there had been a lag in fall steelhead runs, the fishery is now excellent. This is a result of hatchery-reared summer steelhead smolt releases in the upper Rogue Basin. The run population spawning in the Grants Pass stretch below the dam is also good.

The Rogue Spawning-Run Calendar

The Rogue is Oregon's most productive anadromous salmonid stream. Adult salmon, steelhead, and cutthroat runs provide fishing throughout the year. The steelhead half-pounders provide a quality fishery.

There are three steelhead runs in the Rogue system—spring, fall, and winter. They are often smaller than in many other Pacific Northwest streams because they become sexually mature and make their first spawning run at an earlier age. Usually steelhead make their first spawning run when they're four, but a large percentage of the Rogue fish spawn in their second and third year after spending only three to five months at sea. There'll be some larger fish, and most of them will be making their second or third spawning run.

When water temperatures rise spring steelhead enter the stream; fall steelhead start up river in August after the hot summer water cools, and winter steelhead run in the months shortly prior to spawning time.

With the exception of the Applegate and Illinois branches and the lower 50 to 60 miles of the mainstream Rouge, fishermen can present lures to a potpourri of steelhead during most of the year. As winter-run stragglers leave the headwaters, the spring-run leaders arrive. They remain available to fishermen while over-summering to spawn the next winter. In the middle section of the mainstream spring kelts backing downriver meet fresh winter-run fish still coming upstream.

Steelhead fishing time gaps occur on the Applegate and Illinois calendars because they entertain only winter-run fish. There are time gaps in the lower Rogue because the lowest section of the mainstream, spring kelts backing downriver meet not a tarrying section. Above the canyon races intermingle, and the upstream and downstream migrations overlap.

The majority of the fall-run steelhead are half-pounders that entered the ocean in May of their second year and return to spawning grounds three to five months later. They run with fish of other ages.

Spring Steelhead

The warmer spring water temperatures occur when water rises, and spring steelhead in-migration may not be noticed because of the covering waters. The first springs cross the Gold Ray counting station in April. The run peaks in July and tapers off in September. They begin to take lures in August, and most anglers start fishing to them then. Most of the fish are 15 to 20 inches long with a few 23- to 25-inch-long fish in the run. Because they spend a long time in fresh water the fish do not have as much sea growth as fish from other runs.

Fall-Run Steelhead

Fall-run steelhead enter the Rogue after it cools from maximum summer temperatures. Some fish arrive to visit in pools of the lower 6 miles during July, but the upstream migration usually doesn't start until the last week in August.

Most fishermen take fall steelhead in the lower canyon; most fish are caught near the Illahe-Agness area. Fishing is all right through the canyon as far as Robertson Bridge.

The fish are small, averaging between 10 and 15 inches; weighing about $1\frac{1}{4}$ pounds. There are a few larger fish that have been at sea for a year and a half or are returning to spawn the second or third time, but most of the fish have only been to sea a few months.

Winter Steelhead

Winter steelhead run in after fall rains raise the water level. When temperatures are warmer than 40° F., they run upstream. Warm water accelerates their upstream rate of swimming speed. When water temperature drops below 40° they hole up. November is usually the calendar date for the in-migration; December can be a good migration month that may start with a warm southwest storm. The run reaches the middle Rogue in early or mid-January and peaks at Gold Ray in March. The fish fan out to nearly all Rogue system tributaries. The heaviest spawning occurs in the mid- and lower sections of the system; the lightest in the upper river waters.

The fish from this run that swim into the Illinois and Applegate are called the Illinois and Applegate races. These fish average 7 pounds and some grow to 16 pounds or more. Fishermen like the Illinois Canyon from Kerby to the mouth of Briggs Creek. The Applegate race will still be running until March or April.

Winter fish are the largest because they follow the four-year life cycle common to most Pacific Slope steelhead. Some precocious fish may return in their third year, but they are larger than the spring-and fall-run fish because they've spent from four to seven months longer in the ocean. Some late winter fry migrate to the ocean during their first year, and grow even longer in salt water.

Winter-run fish are the largest population in the Rogue. They run during high water, and many escape anglers. Most of the catch is taken in the Agness-Illahe area because cold-water conditions have delayed them there. Many are harvested in the middle section of the mainstream.

Chinook

Spring-run chinook enter the Rogue when water temperatures rise in February or early March. They'll still be running through the mouth in early June. The peak of the river-mouth fishing is April and May. The fish prefer to spawn in the main channel of the upper Rogue; early arrivals go high in the basin and late arrivals settle progressively lower. Spawning occurs in September and October.

Chinook column-heads form where the water first reaches 50° F. At first the river mouth is the 50° line. As the river warms the head of the run follows the 50° mark upriver. March 5 through 20 are the arrival dates in Grants Pass. Fish arrive at Gold Ray in mid-April and peak there in June. Some of them are still being counted in September, and most of them pass over Gold Ray.

The fish like the Rogue Elk to Shady Cove holdover section best, and give second preference to the area from McLeod downstream to and somewhat below Bybee Bridge. Some fish move into Big Butte Creek, the only tributary used by spring-run chinook.

Rogue River fishermen are used to tidings from the Gold Ray counting station and they frequently ask, "How long does it take a chinook to swim fifty miles of river at fifteen miles per hour?" Questions like that cause biologists to get out their slide rules. The answer is not easy because there are variables in addition to water temperature. Water height, turbidity, and increase in altitude also influence the chinook's progress. The fish are overcoming gravity by swimming uphill, prefer certain temperatures, and like to see where they're going.

Because the sex organs of fall-run chinook and coho start an earlier maturation, while they are at sea, they overcome gravity at a faster rate of speed. Fall-run chinook and coho enter the Rogue together in August and September. Fall chinook spawning peaks in November and December, chinook continue to enter the river as late as January.

The chinook spawn on the gravel where they happen to be at their delivery time. Water conditions may permit them to migrate a certain distance, but egg maturity stops them where they will. The bulk of the fall chinook spawn in the main channel from points overlapping those used by spring-run stragglers to bars located near to tidewater.

However, there's an Applegate tributary race that waits in the Rogue for fall rains to bring the water level high enough so they can enter the Applegate, and some of them may still be spawning in January and early February. Another group of chinook wait at Illinois Falls for suitable water to run up in.

There are not many coho using the Rogue Basin. Most of them are caught in the lower 30 miles of the river, but some are caught in the Illinois near Illinois Falls. Rogue River coho swim 165 miles into Big Butte and Elk creeks. Others reach Butte and Applegate creeks.

Some jacks enter with the Pacific runs. In the Rogue a chinook jack is usually three years old and a coho jack is two years old. Some of the female fish are also sexually precocious.

Sockeye and chum have been planted in the Rogue, but few have returned. Atlantic salmon have also been planted without success.

Spring-run chinook salmon fry emerge from gravel from late December to early May. They spend their first year migrating slowly downstream, hold through their first winter in the lower 30 miles, and enter the Pacific Ocean in the spring of their second year. Coho leave their redds about the same time as chinook, spend their first year in the main Rogue channel, and start their migration to sea in the spring of their second year.

The Rogue River has suffered many ecological accidents and repairs. It is the only stream I know of that was improved through direct, violent, radical activity. In 1927, the Ament Dam between Grants Pass and Savage Rapids, which had partially blocked in-migration for eighteen years, was removed when a "conservation-minded person" exploded a boatload of dynamite on the dam.

CALIFORNIA

The Smith and Klamath River country in northwestern California is the region of heaviest precipitation in the state. The coast seldom gets snow, but it falls on interior mountains above 1,000 feet. At Crescent City, about half-way between the Klamath and the Smith, January temperatures will be only 13° below the August norm. Forty-five miles up the Klamath the difference between summer and winter temperatures is about

34°. Happy Camp temperatures may range into the hundreds in summer, but the lowest temperature recorded for winter is 6°. In this country the Douglas fir and hemlock rain forests change to California redwoods.

South of the Smith-Klamath area there's a region of small coastal plains and mountains that I call the Trinity-Eel country. That name is all right providing one remembers that the Trinity runs out of the area at Weitchpec where it joins the Klamath. Fishermen are aware that the Van Duzen parallels the Eel and runs into it near the juncture of mile marks 36 and 101. This is rugged country and the streams cut through some high elevations. There's little difference between summer and winter temperatures in this region. The coast gets 121 days of rainfall. The lowest recorded temperature in Eureka (elevation 43 feet) was 20° F. The lowest recorded temperature at Forest Glen (elevation 2,340 feet) was —2° F. Fishing clothing should include a raincoat and one pair of light wool trousers. The Mad River, its fishable length foreshortened by Sweasy Dam, runs north of Eureka and south of 299.

I call an area centering around coastal Fort Bragg with the outer perimeter enclosing the Russian River at Ukiah the Little River country. There are ten short-run rivers in this area. The headwaters of the Russian are included because they run through this climate area, but it is not a short-run river. The northern short-run river is the Ten Mile; the southern is the Garcia at Point Arena.

The lowest temperature recorded for Fort Bragg was 24° F., the highest 90° F.

Some of these short-run streams have lagoons at the mouths; some do not. Some are open year round, while others are closed by tidal bars. Some require a drift boat for productive, comfortable fishing. All of these streams have steelhead runs, most (except Greenwood, Alder, and Brush) have coho, and two (the Garcia and the Elk) have a few chinook. All are fishable in November or later depending upon rains.

The fisherman will notice increased population density as he shifts from the Gualala to the Russian River. Rising in the northern mountains it flows south through them into lower banks lined with summer homes. South of the Russian there are coastal plains of various widths with attractive beach resorts. The streams are within an easy drive of San Francisco, and they are short-run streams fishable after November, depending upon rains. The streams include Salmon, Walker, and Papermill creeks. They lie between the Russian and the San Francisco Bay area north of the Golden Gate Bridge.

There are two salmonid streams emptying into the east side of San Francisco Bay—the Napa River at the north and Alameda Creek at the south. They're both fall and winter steelhead streams. Alameda Creek isn't recommended for fishermen who live so far away that they can't keep in touch with daily developments.

South of the Golden Gate there are several short-run streams between Half-Moon Bay and Santa Cruz that are also within easy drive of the San Francisco complex. This is the Pacific Coast side of the San Francisco Peninsula. The marine climate is warm in summer and winter. The lowest temperature for Half-Moon Bay is 49°. The lowest temperature for the bay region north of Golden Gate is 19°. It's the shirt-sleeve salmonid fishing area!

The Saquel, Pajaro, Carmel, and Big Sur rivers empty into the marine climate, Monterey Bay region. Big Sur does not empty into Monterey Bay. They are also short-run, November or later streams. Although it's a marine climate, the temperatures here will be a little nippier than in the San Francisco Bay area. The temperature has dropped to a staggering 21° F. at Monterey. Better bring two shirts!

From the Garcia south, fishermen do not expect to catch chinook though they technically range to Monterey Bay. Coho aren't usually caught south of Papermill Creek; however, a few do run into Pescadaro Creek, Scott Creek, San Lorenzo River, and Soquel Creek.

There are some streams south of the Big Sur that once had steelhead fishing. Malibu Creek, Santa Clara, Ventura, and the Santa Yeenez used to have runs, but ecological changes brought about by increased population and water usage have altered the streams.

The Sacramento–San Joaquin Valley

San Joaquin River salmonid fishing extends to the Dos Reis angling access point. Sacramento River salmonid fishing extends to Keswick Dam north of Redding. There are eight salmonid streams tributary to the Sacramento—Battle, Mill, Deer, and Butte creeks; Feather, Yuba, American, and Mokelumne rivers. The Mokelumne was marginal in 1977; the Fisheries Division expects to rebuild the runs.

Coho (silver salmon) are rare in these streams. They all have steelhead and fall-run chinook except Butte Creek, which has no steelhead and a spring run of chinook. The Sacramento, Mill Creek, and Deer Creek also have spring chinook runs. Mill Creek, Deer Creek, and the American River have some summer steelhead.

Some tributaries to the Sacramento run off the western slope of the Sierra Nevada Mountain range, and they cool the river that runs through a relatively warm agricultural valley. Moderating winds warm the valley. The nights are cool, but freezing weather is extremely unusual. In the lower Sacramento Valley the Sierra Nevada foothills seldom get snow. Even at high altitude, snow doesn't last for more than a few hours on the western side.

THE KLAMATH RIVER

The Klamath, the second largest stream in California, flows through a narrow, forested canyon in mountainous terrain. The wide estuary extends upstream for about 4 miles. Above that, the stream width varies from 100 to 300 feet. It's a series of riffles, rapids, and pools with both fast-dropping water and relatively calm, deep holes.

Most of the river flowing through the Klamath and Six Rivers National Forests is paralleled by State Highway 96. The lower 40 miles flows through private property including Indian lands. The lower 10 miles is not within range of the highway, but boats make noisy trips into this area.

The Klamath-Trinity River system achieved long interior stream status by cutting through the Coastal Mountain Range, called the Klamath mountains, from the slopes of the Cascade Range north of the Sacramento Valley. The Trinity and the Klamath, two branches extending from a short main stem, embrace a Coastal Range uplift called the Salmon mountains. The Trinity has its headwaters east of the Salmon Uplift and makes a half circle around its southern side to join the Klamath at Weitchpec about 40 river miles upstream from the Klamath River mouth. The Klamath branch of this system is much longer. It has headwaters in the Oregon Cascades above Klamath Falls, and many miles below that encircles the northern side of the Salmon mountains.

The river is fishable most of the time; however, turbid water often slows action. Fall rains can occur early in September, but most of the precipitation is from November through March. Snowfall is unusual below Happy Camp.

Fishermen following runs upstream on the Klamath progress through different geography, climates, and flora. The climate gets colder in the increased, upstream elevation with some snowfall above Happy Camp, about 100 miles above the mouth. The vegetation growing in different amounts of rainfall changes from redwood rain-forest growth at the mouth to juniper-hardwood clumps in the upper river. The wide estuary changes to a narrow canyon that breaks into rolling hills and basalt cliffs near Iron Gate Dam.

Although the snow isn't deep on the Klamath, the canyon can be cold. Small warming fires are a Klamath Canyon custom.

The fish cannot swim into the headwaters of the Klamath because of two reservoirs. Fish and fishermen alike come to a grim halt before Iron Gate Dam. Knowing where to fish is difficult because the fish have miles of stream to swim and freshets interrupt their rest periods in holding pools sending them farther upstream at random. Fishermen can roar up and down the roads or talk with a series of guides and tackle-store dealers by phone without achieving a satisfactory lie pattern. The problem is complicated further by the fact that a climb down the canyon rim or a float down a certain stream section may be a day-long reconnoiter. A saving grace is that when one is well into a season, successive runs may distribute fish over a wide length of the stream.

The California Fish and Game Department has published a helpful guide for locating winter steelhead (I've added rough river mileage estimates). Weitchpec (north of Trinity), August 8—roughly 44 miles upstream; Orleans, August 20—54 miles upstream; Somes Bar (mouth of Salmon River), August 24—64 miles upstream; Happy Camp, September 7—100 miles upstream; Scott River, September 20—140 miles upstream; Shasta River, October 3—175 miles upstream; and Klamathon (below Iron Gate) October 8. The schedule varies and the tributary pattern is dependent upon it. I don't know a good rule of thumb for locating salmon, but fishermen check at the mouths of streams, a favorite resting area for them.

The Klamath Spawning-Run Calendar

A few fall-run steelhead enter the Klamath with chinook about the last of July. This run peaks in the lower river near Labor Day and, depending on rain, continues into October and November. Most of these early fall steelhead are "half-pounders" ranging from 10 to 14 inches. A succession of steelhead runs continues through the fall and winter. Larger fish move in as the season progresses. Fall steelhead fishing at the junction with the Trinity continues through October or later. Good fishing may continue through the winter. Most of the winter fish are taken in the upper river below Iron Gate Dam; January and February are the best times. It is difficult to set calendars for fishing the tributaries, but many fishermen have established times and seasons that suit their home waters.

Summer steelhead enter the stream in March. When the run coincides with the spring runoff, fishermen may not be able to fish for them at the start. The fish over-summer in the main stream and cooler tributaries, including the Trinity and Salmon rivers.

There are steelhead available in the Klamath every month of the year. Steelhead will hold in a stream for many months, so a statement of availability to fishermen includes both entering and holding fish (over-wintering or over-summering). Spawning has been observed from December through May.

Fall chinook enter the stream about the first week of July. In the lower river the run peaks between the middle of August and Labor Day, and is usually completed by the month's end. Chinook reaching the Shasta River mouth by the first of September continues to run through October. Spawning in the river and tributaries starts at the last of September, peaks in October, and may last through December.

A small run of young chinook enter the stream during March, April, and May. Spring runoff frequently prevents fishing to this run in the lower river, but the fish that lie in the Trinity, the Salmon, and Woolsy Creek can be located and cast to.

Coho enter the Klamath about mid-September.

Sea-run cutthroat run in the lower Klamath in fall, winter, and spring. While the known fishing seems to be restricted to the estuary and tidewater tributaries, exploration would locate cutthroat farther upstream.

THE GUALALA RIVER

The Gualala is a beautiful coastal stream. It has redwoods, mountains, the Pacific Ocean, and a Russian past. It has known Spanish, Russian, and American cultures. A few fishermen know it well and love it. It is not a major migratory salmonid stream from which fishermen land state trophies. It has only two species, and their runs to spawn are not prolonged or spectacular. There are no summer steelhead, half-pounders, or king salmon runs. The nature of the stream dictates terminal tackle and fishing methods that do not include the full range of steelheading techniques. It is an example of a quality fishery on a small coastal stream with classic winter steelheading. There are many of these streams in California including the Garcia and a cluster of streams near Fort Bragg.

The Gualala River, shaded by redwoods, washes out its tidal bar to let coho and steelhead swim to riffles fished off the South

Fork Gualala Road. The river empties into the Pacific through a curving beach that houses a few people in the town of Gualala. The coastal plain is about a mile wide.

Highway 1, the migratory salmonid fisherman's throughway, rolls through Gualala and spans the river. The formerly Spanish area was an important logging center, and there are ruins of a logging mill in Gualala. South on the coast and upstream on the river, there's the Kruse Rhododendron State Park where 20- to 30-foot rhododendrons bloom in May. Near the head-waters of the South Fork is a restored Russian fort that stands on the site of a Russian American Fur Company enterprise that failed after the sea otters were all skinned.

The estuary has an average depth of 10 feet, is 200 feet wide, and about 1.5 miles long. Fish soon swim to the major river fork, the confluence of the Little North Fork and the South Fork. The short main stem of the river runs northeast; the two forks, branching at right angles, point in opposite directions to support widely spaced tributaries.

There are coastal orchards nearby. The Little North Fork, running parallel to the coast, has headwaters northwest of the town of Gualala; the South Fork, running parallel to the coast in the opposite direction, has headwaters southeast of the town. The headwaters of the Little North Fork extend nearly to the headwaters of the South Fork of the Garcia, and an easy country road joins the two. On the Garcia, Californians practice winter steelhead fishing in relatively mild weather among beautiful redwood trees. The headwaters of the South Fork extend southeast of Fort Ross and point toward the Russian River. Fishermen that roam the Russian and the Garcia use the Gualala for a season reference point that provides alternate fly fishing and steelhead lies.

The stream flows through a temperate rain forest of coastal redwoods. There are several groves of virgin or old-growth trees on the lower reaches, and many of the productive pools are beautifully set in them. Lies where fish are battled before huge redwoods are Miner Pool, Thompson Pool, Donkey Pool, and Switchville.

The trees grow in marine terrace soil and the stream flows from snow melt, some groundwater springs, and precipitation. There are several winter floods and a spring runoff that make the stream unfishable. The stream bottom does scour, but pools and riffles do not lose their traditional shape. The stream is about 40 miles long with about 10 miles open during the winter season. There are no natural or man-made obstacles to fish passage, and water diversions are minor. In some places the stream gradient causes a swimming problem for the fish.

Fish swimming upstream on the Little North Fork soon come to the confluence of the North Fork and the Little North Fork. The North Fork has four short tributaries: Billings, Robinson, Bear, and Stewart creeks.

The first major intersection upstream on the South Fork is at the confluence with Wheatfield near Valley Bridge. Between the main stem and Wheatfield Fork there are two tributaries emptying into the South Fork, Rockpile and Buckeye creeks. Rockpile, Buckeye, Wheatfield, and the South Fork above Valley Bridge and their tributaries are flies only from Memorial Day through October 31. (Check current regulations.)

East of Kruse Rhododendron State Park another tributary—Sproule Creek—empties into the South Fork. Sproule Creek has two tributaries, Carson and McKenzie creeks. East of Fort Ross the South Fork embraces Brain Ridge and draws water from Turner Canyon. The Russians used to trap on the headwaters of the Gualala.

The Gualala Spawning-Run Calendar

The Gualala spawning gravel begins about 2 to 3 miles inland and extends, with skips, into the headwaters.

Dennis Lee, a California fisheries biologist, says that steelhead enter the stream in November and run through March. The peak of the run occurs from December through January. The fish spawn from March through May. The peak fishing time is December, but fishermen continue to fish until the February 28th closing. The steelhead return to the ocean from

March through May, and they're nearly all out of the stream by June 1. About .05 of 1 percent of the fish may hold over.

Coho enter the stream from October through November, and a few late swimmers straggle in through December. They spawn from November through early December. The fishing peaks in late October, but it is not a major fishery. The fish responding to storm flows normally move quickly through the estuary, so they are not exposed to estuary fishing for long. They mature rapidly, and fishing in the upper areas is productive for only a short time.

There are no cutthroat or chinook runs in the Gualala.

13

The Great Lakes Region: Michigan, Minnesota, Wisconsin, Illinois, Indiana, Ohio, Pennsylvania, New York, and Ontario

The Great Lakes are the adopted home of most of the migratory salmonids. The only natives are the char called the brook trout, and the trout called the Atlantic salmon. Atlantics were native in Lake Ontario but disappeared at the turn of the century. Brown trout were imported from Europe; Pacific salmon and steelhead from the Pacific Slope; experimental Atlantic plantings have been made with stock from Sweden and Canada.

Four of the five Great Lakes dangle from the subarctic head of lakes (Superior) into the interior lowlands. Some steelhead streams on the Lake Superior Keewenaw Peninsula get 180 inches average annual snowfall with blizzards and temperatures that occasionally plunge to 20° below zero. Winter temperatures in Ontario streams tributary to Lake Superior may fall to 40° below. Other steelhead streams in the snow belt of Lake Erie have relatively mild winters.

The streams tributary to the southern shores of the southern Great Lakes (Erie and Ontario) run through a snow belt in winter and a foggy belt in summer just like Lakes Superior and Huron and the northern half of Lake Michigan. The only major exception to the cold, misty effect in the Great Lakes streams is the southern part of Lake Michigan that extends into a plain of muddy slow-moving streams polluted by a large assemblage of steel mills, factories, and river traffic. Southern Lake Michigan streams are in a continental effect from the plains; Lake Erie and Lake Ontario climate is affected by the other Great Lakes. So, with one exception, Great Lakes tributary streams can be treated as a single climate unit. However, as one moves south of 45° north latitude, the waters become increasingly warm for salmon trout. Because steelhead and salmon can live in cool Great Lakes waters in summer and run into southern streams when they are cool in fall, winter, and early spring, successful runs can be planted in marginal streams—the streams of southern Wisconsin, northern Illinois, northwest Indiana, southern Michigan, and northern Ohio. In this respect these streams are somewhat like the steelhead streams of Mediterranean southern California, but the Pacific Slope streams have headwaters in the cooling mountain canyons, a habitat that can incubate eggs for natural reproduction. Most of the southern Great Lakes streams cannot support natural reproduction.

In general, continental winters are cold with average temperatures ranging from 15° to 30° F. and the summers are warm with the average temperatures ranging from 60° to 70° F. The subarctic generally has light precipitation with cold winters averaging 15° to 20° F. and cool summers averaging 45° to 60° F. But in the Great Lakes the moderating lake effect makes temperatures near the lake warmer in winter and cooler in summer. The lake effect causes more snow to fall on the southeastern shore snow belts of Lakes Erie and Ontario. In certain other areas there may be less snow as one moves from inland toward the lake.

The Great Lakes are a flowage; they are not five ponds. They are all inlet and outlet lakes. The flowage begins at the point of highest elevation, the St. Louis River, at the head of the lakes in northern Lake Superior. All the tributary waters flow over Niagara Falls into Lake Ontario and out of Lake Ontario through the St. Lawrence River into the Atlantic. From every tributary stream, in every lake, pressure builds to form a current that flushes each lake in its relative time period. It takes two-and-a-half years to flush Lake Erie, and fifty years to flush Lake Michigan.

The Great Lakes are the largest body of fresh water in the world. Lakes Michigan, Huron, and Superior rank among the world's six largest lakes. But the system drains a relatively small area and the tributary streams are all small.

Freshets motivate Great Lakes fish to enter and swim the streams during their spawning run just as they motivate Pacific Slope fish and salmonids the world over. But the Great Lakes have less precipitation in winter than in summer—the opposite of the marine climate zone of the Pacific Slope. In fact, the Great Lakes area is relatively dry during the fall months when Pacifics and steelhead begin to in-migrate.

On the Pacific Slope a general wet-weather pattern brings rains in fall. In the Great Lakes there is no general wet front. Instead, Great Lakes fishermen watch for rather localized weather conditions that bring freshets the length of a stream system.

During the winter successive freshets may be caused in the snow belts of the lee side of Lake Erie by melting snow sometimes followed by rain. In the northern parts of the Great Lakes snow lies on the ground all winter and streams may run low and clear. A February thaw in the northern lower peninsula of Michigan creates freshets in some streams. Spring runoff brings in more steelhead into nearly all of the Great Lakes streams. That freshet is succeeded by early spring rains.

On large streams like Michigan's Big Manistee there's sufficient volume and flow to bring fish in without rains. But other Michigan streams, such as the Betsie and Platte, need precipitation.

October in Michigan is often a season of warm days and cool nights. Early frost kills the mosquitoes, and a local rain or two occurring just before frost often brings fish into the streams. It's usually a comfortable season to fish. By winter snow freezes the lines in our rod's line guides. In November we fish for coho in snow squalls with our waders bulged with underwear and down jackets. By January we can no longer swish the ice out of our line guides by holding the rod underwater. Then we grind ice with spinning reels, and suck line guides with chapped bleeding lips. To warm up we exercise our wader legs in knee-deep snow on the banks. Even the southern streams of northern Ohio are chilled with ice channels, and we beach our steelhead on ice floes. The October warmth is precious to us. We hang our chinook from tree limbs among colored leaves, and turn our faces up to the afternoon sun.

Because changes in planting programs can reduce the usual runs, check with local authorities before traveling long distances to fish Great Lakes tributary streams.

MICHIGAN

Michigan Adopts Pacific Salmon

The first white men to fish the Great Lakes tributary streams were searching for the Northwest Passage. They didn't find it, but if they returned today they could fish for Pacific Ocean fish in the world's largest body of fresh water. Two Pacific Ocean species now live and naturally reproduce in the Great Lakes drainage. They are steelhead trout and Pacific salmon. How were these fish transplanted from the Pacific drainage? Why do they survive? What ecological niche have they filled?

The changes that men made in the Great Lakes created an ecological gap that Pacific species have been planted to fill. Before the Welland Canal was dug, and before the Great Lakes commercial fishery, there were plenty of native fish in the lakes. It is true that tributary streams were not being used by fish for fall- and spring-spawning runs, but neither fish nor men noticed. The Welland Canal opened passage to sea lampreys and alewives. Overfishing reduced the indigenous species. Lampreys continued the reduction. Alewives flourished and became a nuisance fish because there were no big fish to eat them. In those days there were alewives everywhere. They clogged municipal water inlets. They died on beaches and made the beaches uninhabitable because of the stench. This continued until Howard Tanner and Wayne Tody, two biologists with the Michigan Department of Natural Resources, noticed something interesting about steelhead trout.

The biologists responsible for starting the planting of Pacific salmon in the Great Lakes returning from trolling for chinook in Lake Michigan. (Photo courtesy Michigan D.N.R.)

After the anadromous sea lampreys were brought under control by using a specific pesticide that worked better than the original electric weir control program, the steelhead began to reestablish their runs. They were not negatively affected by alewife predation like some other surviving Great Lakes species. Steelhead had an ecological jump on the alewife. They ascended cold streams to spawn out of range of alewives. Their young remained in upper river areas for an average of two years before descending into the alewife habitat. By this time they were large enough in size to be safe from predation; indeed, they were large enough to feed on smaller alewives.

The steelhead program was accelerated, but there were more alewives than the steelhead could possibly control. Furthermore, the Great Lakes that had once supported a profitable commercial fishery were now sterile and no longer making a contribution to Michigan's economy. Tanner and Tody thought that introduction of other salmonid species, which would use tributary stream spawning grounds at times when steelhead were not using them, might result in more alewives being eaten. Commissioners and politicians gave support to Tanner and Tody's objectives.

The following factors gave hope that coho could be successfully planted in Michigan streams tributary to Lakes Superior, Michigan, and Huron:

1. Because of their close morphological similarity to trout (*Salmo*), Pacifics (*Oncorhynchus*) are thought to be of freshwater origin. *O. masu*, an Asian Pacific, is the most closely related to *Salmo*.

2. *O. masu*, anadromous in many Japanese streams, had resident populations in both streams and lakes. The species was transplanted to Lake Biwa on Hondo Island, Japan, where it migrated for spawning into tributary streams. This simple transplant produced an anadromous, freshwater population.

3. *O. masu*, chinook (*O. tshawytscha*), and coho (*O. kisutch*) follow the troutlike characteristic of smolting before going to salt water. The other three North American species have forms that can out-migrate to sea without smolting.

4. Pinks (*O. gorbuscha*) had already survied an accidental dumping into a Lake Superior tributary and were continuing the species by natural reproduction without aid from the fisheries.

5. New Zealand chinook transplants had established a resident freshwater population.

6. Cultus Lake, British Columbia, supports a resident population of coho. (It also is host to anadromous populations running in from the Pacific.)

7. The California Department of Fish and Game had maintained coho in fresh, hatchery waters for three generations.

8. Coho planted in 1933 in Lake Erie by Ohio yielded some survivors.

9. Atlantic salmon were native in Lake Ontario, and reproduced there prior to the 1900s.

10. Steelhead, formerly a saltwater-freshwater species, enjoy natural reproduction in many Great Lakes tributary streams.

This evidence supported the theory that coho and chinook could be established in an entirely freshwater lake-stream system with sufficient spawning grounds in the streams and sufficent food in the lake. Michigan tributary streams and the Michigan Great Lakes had the right habitat.

In 1966, smolt hatched from eggs stripped by Oregon Fisheries personnel from coho at Bonneville Dam were released in the Big Huron, the Platte and Bear Creek. The plants were successful and all U.S. Great Lakes tributary states took cognizance.

Coho have a three-year cycle. To ensure runs each year, plantings were made on three successive years—1966, 1967, and 1968. The 1967 releases were made from smolts hatched from eggs supplied by Oregon, Washington, and Alaska. The eggs were from adults that spawn in stream and weather conditions similar to Michigan.

Michigan planted chinook in 1967 from eggs donated by Washington from females that ran into the Toutle River. They were planted in the Big Huron, the Little Manistee, and the Muskegon. Survival of chinook in Lake Michigan was good. It was not as good in Lakes Huron and Superior, perhaps due to lamprey predation in Lake Huron and food scarcity in Lake Superior.

While launching the Pacific planting program, Michigan increased its steelhead program, and gave policy affirmation to the continuation of the rare coaster brooks fishery, and the lake-run brown trout.

First successful planting of coho salmon in a Great Lakes tributary, Bear Creek. Michigan D.N.R. personnel release smolts during a March snowstorm. Commissioner Carl Johnson was on the stream bank. (Photo courtesy Michigan D.N.R.)

Stan Lievense battling coho in Michigan's Bear Creek. Bear Creek, one of the first streams selected for coho plantings, sustained natural reproduction so well that runs continued in the stream without stocking. Pacifics are now screened from entering the stream by a weir. (Photo courtesy Michigan Travel Bureau)

Because access to the Big Huron is poor and Bear Creek is too small for a sports fishery, Pacific plantings were soon discontinued in these pioneering streams. A significant migration of stray chinook and coho into the Bear continued to provide fishing for many years. Furthermore, significant chinook natural reproduction in the Bear continued that run in viable numbers. But in the fall of 1977, because of a change in stream-management policy, a weir was built at the mouth of the Bear to screen out Pacifics. In the Huron there's been significant migrations of coho strays and significant natural reproduction, so coho runs there continue to support a fishery. The establishment and continuation (until screened out in Bear Creek) of natural reproduction in two streams of adoption show that properly established Pacifics can adapt to an entirely freshwater habitat.

When Michigan chinook and coho returned to their streams of imprintation and established their first spawning runs, the success of the Pacific program was demonstrated to the American Great Lakes public and to other state fisheries departments. Tanner and Tody's research sparked planting methods that worked in the other Great Lakes States. Michigan provided eggs from which Indiana, Wisconsin, and Illinois made their initial Pacific plantings. Pennsylvana's first release was from U.S. Fish and Wildlife Service eggs. Subsequent plantings were made from Michigan eggs. (Although Pennsylvania now milks eggs from home streams, the state still depends on Michigan for some coho and chinook eggs.)

The public of the Great Lakes States got its first taste of migratory salmonid fishing, and programs for planting other species were expanded or implemented in most states. All of the Great Lakes became the adopted homes of Pacific Ocean fish. In addition brown trout, brook trout, steelhead, and Atlantic salmon programs were given further thought, implementation, and funding. The success of the Pacific program publicized the utility of filling all parts of the Great Lakes ecological niche, and reinforced intentions to continue and implement an anadromous trout and char fishery.

Michigan Streams and Geography

Michigan's tributary streams have three Pacifics (chinook, coho, and pinks), three trout (steelhead, browns, and Atlantics —experimental), and a char (brooks—habitat reduced). Michigan is the meeting place of fishing techniques from many places in the world—Atlantic salmon fishing techniques from Great Britain, and steelhead fishing techniques from the Pacific Slope, for example. Hundreds of men and women on the streams and in the flyshops of Michigan considered cross-referential data. Old-timers remembered coaster brook fishing methods. Steelheaders across the state developed new local methods specific to their home streams. Stream techniques for

Stan Lievense tailing a dark chinook in Michigan's Bear Creek. Stan tossed
the 28-pounder onto the log in the background, it slid down the bank, lashed
its tail twice, broke off and got away. (Photo courtesy Michigan Travel
Bureau)

Pacifics were pioneered. Snow-fishing techniques for over-wintering steelhead and browns were developed. This creative ferment is now being oriented into a new salmonid fishing consciousness.

Michigan has two land masses jaggedly out-thrust into four of the five Great Lakes. The state is literally surrounded by water. It has the longest shoreline (3,177 miles) of any inland state. No point within the state lies more than 85 miles from one of its four great lakes. It has tributary streams nearly the length of the north to south range—from the Lake Superior subarctic to the southern Michigan tip. Michigan has large salmonid rivers (the Big Manistee), and small (the Little Elm). The state has the best ground water streams and spawning gravel on the American side of the waters.

The gradient of most Michigan streams is gentle because there are few high uplifts at stream mouths. Glacial tills provide an abundance of spawning gravel between stretches of sand laid down in older, larger lake periods. For spawning salmonids there may be long areas of sand through which the migrations may pass rather rapidly. Most holding pools are near the areas of spawning gravel.

There are two mountainous uplifts in the Upper Peninsula, the Porcupine and Huron mountains. These lie in the Superior Upland that covers the western part of the Upper Peninsula. Many of the short-run streams within this area descend precipitously from a rugged plateau lying 1,000 to 2,000 feet above sea level. They do have waterfalls and some barriers to fish passage, but most streams are passable to fish. Despite the easy falling of the waters, the flow is rapid enough to sustain good aeration and, in many streams, the volume and the rate of flow is sufficient the year round to bring fish in with relatively small freshets. It doesn't take a cloudburst to increase the fall stream flows to swimmable passages.

The Great Lakes Plains cover the eastern part of the Upper Peninsula and the entire Lower Peninsula. Within this region in the Upper Peninsula there are many bogs and swamps. Throughout this plain, the fishing is easy because the wading is easy.

Many of the streams flow through small lakes near their sources. These are lakes created by glacial action along the present Great Lakes shores. Streams having this characteristic include the Jordan, Pere Marquette, Boyne, Platte, Muskegon, White, Pentwater, and Betsie. The Little and Big Manistee enter Manistee Lake. These lakes can be staging areas for fish on their spawning runs. They enter the lakes and wait for freshets before ascending further. The water warms in these lakes and may act as a barrier to upstream migration. Steelhead may over-winter in these lakes before spawning.

Because it has good volume and rate of flow throughout the year, the Big Manistee presents little barrier to the upstream passage of fish even during the generally low-water periods of late summer. Steelhead enter the stream early in the year and continue to in-migrate in successive waves until spring spawning time. This is the reason the stream is favored by guides. Few of the other streams have such good stream contour and rate of flow, but streams that do not require high-water freshets include the Muskegon, the Pere Marquette, the Grand, and the Betsie. (These have all been drag-lined at the mouths for shipping.) In comparison with the Skagit and other large migratory salmonid streams, Michigan's are short. The Grand River (tributary to the lower peninsula Lake Michigan) is the longest —260 miles. Fish passage in that stream has been opened as far as Lyons. On an upper Grand River tributary, Fish Creek, which empties into the Maple, fish can ascend to a dam in Hubbardston.

Major rivers in the Upper Peninsula include the Ontonagon, Two Hearted, and Manistique. In the Lower Peninsula (tributary to Lake Michigan) the principal rivers on the western side are the St. Joseph, Kalamazoo, Grand, Muskegon, Pere Marquette, and Manistee. They are all migratory salmonid streams. On the eastern side (tributary to Lake Huron) the Au Sable is a major river having runs of migratory salmonids, but they are blocked at Foot Dam. Most Lake Huron migratory salmonid streams are relatively small.

Outdoorsmen in Michigan dress for misty, moist, cool weather. The state has cloudy days six out of every ten summer

David MacLeon, Michigan D.N.R. Fisheries Habitat Biologist, with coho he landed in the Little Manistee. The lure in the fish's mouth is a Stanley Streamer. (Photo courtesy Michigan Travel Bureau)

days; seven out of every ten winter days. It ranks with western New York and Washington as one of America's three cloudiest regions. Rain squalls in summer and snow squalls in winter are the hallmark of Michigan weather. In summer and winter, loose-fitting, water-repellent duck hunter's caps with brims and turn-down ear loppers are the best headgear. Some wealthy sportsmen wear more expensive Tyrolean hats that achieve the same effect with more style. In winter several layers of underwear should be carried at all times, and in summer one down jacket should be available for use during the frequent chilly periods.

There is good natural reproduction in many Michigan streams for all species (Atlantics still experimental). Many streams have runs of two Pacific species (chinook and coho), and one anadromous trout (steelhead). Several streams have runs of three Pacific species (chinook, coho, and pinks) and steelhead. Two streams (the Falls in the Upper Peninsula; the Betsie in the Lower Peninsula) have runs of two Pacifics (chinook and coho) and two anadromous trout (steelhead and browns).

The Upper Peninsula three-species (chinook, coho, and steelhead) streams are: Huron, Chocolay, Anna, Black in Gogebic County, Black in Mackinac County, Presque Isle, Big Iron, Cedar, Dead, Two-Hearted, Carp, Manistique, and Whitefish. Small or short-run Upper Peninsula streams include the Falls and Anna.

The Lower Peninsula three-species streams are: Boyne, Big Manistee, Betsie, Muskegon, Kalamazoo, Paw Paw, Au Sable, Witney Drain, St. Joseph, and Riffle. Small or short-run Lower Peninsula streams are Boardman, Otter, Sable, Pentwater, Ocqueoc, Tawas, Thunder Bay, Huron, and Cheboygan.

Other Upper Peninsula steelhead streams include the Sturgeon, Otter, Ontonagon, Garlic, and Little Garlic. The Garlic and Little Garlic have marginal chinook and coho runs. The listing does not include brooks.

Lower Peninsula streams that have been three-species streams, but may have Pacifics screened out beginning in the fall of 1978, are the Jordan, Little Manistee, the Bear, Platte, Pere Marquette, and Van Etten Creek.

Pinks run on odd-numbered years in the following Upper Peninsula three-species streams: Anna, Huron, Two-Hearted, Chocolay, Presque Isle, Black in Gogebic County, and Black in Mackinac County.

Pinks run in the Ocqueoc, a Lower Peninsula three-species stream.

The most fishable three-species migratory salmonid streams in the Upper Peninsula are the Two-Hearted, Huron, Chocolay, Carp, and the Black in Mackinac County. They are easily waded, have cold water, a full run length from the Big Water, and spawning gravel that allows the fish to go through the entire reproductive cycle. None of them is blocked by dams. In all of these streams the full range of migratory salmonid fishing techniques may be practiced. Anyone having access to these streams has fishing as good as royalty in Europe can buy. They have everything the Pacific Slope fisherman has except char, and there are a few places in the Upper Peninsula where brook trout still run.

There are many three-species migratory salmonid streams in the Lower Peninsula that meet these fishing criteria. Among them I'd name the Big and Little Manistee, Betsie (browns) Au Sable, Muskegon, St. Joe, and Grand.

With spawning-migration calendars for the Chocolay, Two-Hearted, Silver, Muskegon and Jordan rivers, fishermen should be able to time the runs in both Upper Peninsula and Lower Peninsula streams.

The Chocolay Spawning-Run Calendar

Coho begin to enter the Chocolay in the Upper Peninsula in September and continue to in-migrate through October. The peak of the run occurs from the beginning of October to mid-month. Spawning begins in October and continues through early November. The spawning peak is in mid-October. There is fair natural reproduction.

Juveniles remain in the Chocolay for one year. The smolt out-migrate in April during warming, rising water conditions.

Chinook begin to enter the Chocolay in September and continue to in-migrate through October. The run peak occurs from about mid-September through early October. Spawning that begins in October peaks in that month and is usually completed within the month. There is fair natural reproduction.

Juveniles remain in the Chocolay for two months. They out-migrate in May during warming, rising water conditions.

Steelhead begin to enter the Two-Hearted in the Upper Peninsula in September and continue to in-migrate through May. The peak of the run is late April and early May. Spawning that begins in April and continues through May peaks in early May. There is good natural reproduction in the Two-Hearted.

Fry emerge from the gravel in June and remain in the stream for two years. They smolt and out-migrate during May when waters are rising and warming.

Michigan steelhead may begin to enter streams as early as late August. They continue to in-migrate on successive freshets until the river waters cool (become no warmer than the lake water in January and February). About the last of February as the waters warm, in-migration continues again and hits a spring peak about mid-March through mid-April in the Lower Peninsula, and early May in the Upper Peninsula. Surges of fish come in on fall rains, winter thaws, spring warming, and spring rains.

Apparently, in the late fall and early winter, the fish move upstream for varying distances in one swim, then rest for a period that varies from a few hours to several days, then take another swim to another distance, depending upon water conditions that develop during the swim and upon their energy level. Manistee River guides who spot the steelhead in one place but cannot locate them there the following day run upstream until contact is reestablished. Contact for wading fishermen in the flies-only section of the Pere Marquette can be reestablished on the same basis, but the reestablishment in a third or fourth day of fishing may be upstream from the limits of the flies-only section.

During winter, the fall- and early winter-run steelhead overwinter in holes and runs. They're often in heavy cover, but may lie under a slim overhanging branch. Despite the severe winters and ice channels in some Upper Peninsula streams, steelhead over-winter in large, slow holes and in the lower sections of streams where estuaries have formed at the meeting point of their stream and the Big Water. Steelhead are more likely to over-winter in larger Upper Peninsula streams such as the Two-Hearted and the Ontonagon.

Most steelhead that survive spawning out-migrate soon afterwards. Usually they swim actively downstream, but some may let themselves down tail-first. Enough fall spawning during October and November occurs in Lake Michigan and Lake Huron tributaries to suggest the development of a significant spawning-migration behavior pattern. There isn't a lot of spawning now, but a potential exists.

In streams that are open, fishermen should begin to watch for spawning steelhead in January and early February. Michigan does not have any immediate plans to establish runs of over-summering steelhead. In Upper Peninsula streams, runs may continue somewhat later than Lower Peninsula streams. Perhaps into June.

The Muskegon Spawning-Run Calendar

The Muskegon River runs wide and deep without barriers to fish passage from Croton Dam to Lake Michigan. Glacial tills upthrust into the river bed provide good spawning grounds for chinook, coho, and steelhead. They begin below Newaygo and continue intermittently to just below Croton Dam. Between the gravel uplifts there are fine holes that can best be reached from a boat. The spawning areas can be waded with caution. Croton Dam, used for power generation, is opened at various times raising the stream to dangerous wading levels.

Migratory salmonid fishermen in the Lower Peninsula can set their calendars according to the following migration information for the Muskegon. Chinook begin to in-migrate in early September. The in-migration continues through October and peaks from late September to early October. Spawning begins during early October and continues through the month. The peak is between October 5 and 20.

Chinook smolts go down to Lake Michigan during warming, rising water conditions in May.

Coho begin to run into the Muskegon in early September. They continue to run through October, and the run peaks during the early part of the month. Spawning begins in early October and continues through early November. The peak occurs in the last part of October.

Kent Miller tailing a chinook with a loop in the stringer. This 27-pounder was taken in Michigan's Muskegon in late October on the Blue Tail Fly. Landing a chinook with a looped rope requires extreme caution in approaching and a lot of luck.

Coho parr smolt and go down to Big Water about March or April.

Steelhead run into the Muskegon in early October. The in-migration continues through the winter and into early May. The fish come in surges during fall rains, winter thaws, spring rains, and spring warming trends. There are two major peaks— November and April. A line graph of in-migration would begin in late September and show a peak in November; successive smaller peaks would be graphed for December, January, February, and March, and the highest peak of all would be graphed for April.

In the Muskegon and most Michigan streams over-wintering steelhead begin to spawn in late February and early March. Other fish in-migrating in late winter and early spring begin to spawn in late March, and spawning may continue as late as early June. The spawning peak is mid-March to mid-April.

Pinks

Pinks have spread from Michigan's Upper Peninsula Lake Superior tributary streams to Lower Peninsula streams tributary to Lakes Michigan and Huron. They have spread as far west as the Ford River and as far south as the Ocqueoc. Their life history in the Great Lakes is generally the same as for the Pacific Slope. In the Upper Peninsula Silver River pinks begin to enter the stream on odd years in October and continue to in-migrate through November. The peak of in-migration is October, and spawning begins in that month. It continues through November, and peaks in late October. In many rivers pinks spawn in early September.

Although Michigan biologists have not released any anadromous browns in streams, significant runs have established themselves in the Upper Peninsula Ontonagon and Falls rivers, and the Lower Peninsula Jordan and Betsie rivers. Both the Jordan and the Betsie have lakes in their system. Browns released in streams may not grow very large; released in the Great Lakes they forage and attain trophy sizes. There is natural reproduction.

Browns

Anadromous Jordan River browns enter the stream about mid-June, and their in-migration continues through July. The peak of the run seems to occur in late June and early July. The fish use spawning gravel located about 20 miles from the mouth. Apparently they begin to spawn about October 1. The spawning peak is about mid-October and spawning continues through November.

Brooks

The anadromous brook trout population in Michigan has dwindled. Apparently there are runs now in only one remote Upper Peninsula stream. Brad Durling, Upper Peninsula Regional Fisheries Biologist, reports that the department is trying to obtain a brood stock of anadromous brooks to begin a restocking program. He suspects that the life history of the species is similar to that of other fall-spawning anadromous fish in Lake Superior. That is, they ascend streams to spawn in September, complete their spawning by November, probably over-winter in the stream, and return to the Big Lake the following spring. Nothing is known about the migratory patterns of the juvenile fish or the feeding pattern of in-migrating adults. It is suspected that the adults do not feed during their spawning period.

Atlantics

Michigan biologists are working to establish runs of Atlantics. To date, efforts to establish runs of brood stock from which eggs can be milked have been frustrated. The state is still dependent upon imported eggs from stock not adapted to the state's waters. At present, Atlantic smolts are being released in Cherry Creek a tributary to the Chocolay, the Little Manistee, and the Pere Marquette. It is hoped that Michigan Atlantics can be established that will in-migrate from June through August and spawn from October through November. Natural reproduction is desired, and it is expected that parr will go to sea after one or two years in their birth stream.

MINNESOTA

The St. Mary's River, which flows through Minnesota, has the highest tributary elevation in the Laurentian (Great Lakes) Flowage. The point where it flows into Lake Superior is the head of lakes. The Minnesota sector of the Superior watershed is short and precipitous. Most tributary streams are 15 to 25 miles long in their total drainage, and some descend 1,300 feet from their source. The Knife River has 70 miles of stream that fish can swim. In nearly all of them the last 400 feet of fall occurs over a 1- to 3-mile-series of waterfalls and cascades. These falls bar upstream migration of anadromous salmonids, so stream sections available to them are short. There are fifty-nine streams within this watershed.

The stream beds have some gravel and glacial drift. A few of the streams run from small lakes, but most of them are dependent upon surface runoff. There are few swamps or other sources of ground water storage. The streams are not comfortable over-wintering places for steelhead and those that do make fall runs usually return to the lake before freeze-up. This precludes snow fishing in Minnesota.

North Shore streams are usually very low in the fall—often too low to allow Pacifics to swim in. But Minnesota has some Pacific salmon fishing—it has steelhead, kamloops, and brown runs. There are a few anadromous brook runs.

The state had discontinued its coho program. When runs occurred in the Baptism, Cascade, and French rivers, cohos entered the streams in September, peaked in November, and spawned in November. They sometimes continued to run and spawn through December. Michigan and Wisconsin coho migrate along the North Shore in mid-summer and are taken by anglers. Some of them stray into Minnesota streams.

Minnesota plants of chinook in Baptism, Cascade, and French rivers are experimental. Survival of 1974 plants was low. There were no eggs available for the 1975 stocking and 1976 fingerlings were lost by disease and mortality before planting. Chinook are expected to return to the Baptism, Cascade, and

French rivers in 1977. Their spawning migration calendar cannot be predicted.

The news that pinks had survived the accidental planting made by Ontario in 1956 came when Minnesota fishermen caught them in their streams in 1959. Since then spawning runs have occurred in alternate years in most Minnesota tributary streams. It is their major Pacific species fishery.

There's no natural reproduction of chinook and coho in the Baptism, Cascade, and French rivers.

In-migrating, sexually maturing anadromous brooks in Minnesota are limited and occur in scattered streams.

A kamloops fishery begins in late winter off the mouth of the French River, the stream where they were stocked. They generally run in earlier than steelhead to spawn, so it makes a late winter fishery. None of the Minnesota kamloops run in early fall or over-winter. Apparently the major fishery is at the river mouth.

Minnesota releases browns. There are periodic runs in the French, Sucker, Lester, Knife, and Stewart rivers. The runs are sporadic because of low stream flows in the fall. Minnesota browns do not over-winter in streams where they have spawned, but Minnesota brooks do over-winter in streams where they spawn in the fall.

KIMBALL CREEK

The major migratory salmonid fishery in Minnesota streams is to steelhead where there is good natural reproduction in most of the fifty-nine North Shore streams. Kimball Creek, flowing east of Grand Marais in Cook County, is typical of these streams. This creek, which drains an area of about 15 square miles, runs over Keweenawan lava flows and intrusions. These rocks are covered with stony water-worked soils and glacial drift that support a forest cover of aspen, birch, and spruce. Alder grows thickly along stream banks. The Kimball flows from three small lakes, Kimball, Mink, and Boys. A few tributaries drain areas that do not provide much flow. The creek, about 7 miles long, flows through beaver dams and over falls—the highest is 10 feet. After the falls the creek flows into a steep-walled canyon and descends rapidly to Lake Superior. The water is soft; the medial pH is 7.4. Steelhead can swim 8,395 feet into Kimball where they encounter the first impassable upstream barrier.

Kimball Creek Spawning-Run Calendar

Steelhead in-migrate into Minnesota in the spring. They make exploratory runs in the fall, but the harsh winter and the steep gradient does not create a comfortable over-wintering habitat. Biologists have not observed fall spawning in Kimball Creek. There's very little fall fishery and no over-wintering fishery in most of the short streams. Spring ice break-up and flow from melting snow trigger the in-migration. The in-migration beginning dates vary from April 19 to May 4 in Kimball Creek. The runs last through mid-June with 50 percent of the run completed by May 20 and 80 percent completed by May 30. Ripe females run from the last week of April through the middle of June.

Kimball Creek steelhead that survive spawning descend to the Big Lake by late June. They begin out-migration about the first week of May and the peak occurs during the last part of May and the first part of June.

WISCONSIN

Wisconsin streams running through two different habitats are tributary to Lakes Superior and Michigan. The Lake Michigan streams become increasingly warm as one travels from the northwoods into the Central Plains. The coast of Lake Michigan has little regulating effect from the other Great Lakes and it's warmed by a prevailing westerly wind from the heartland. The same wind cools as it passes over Lake Michigan and gives some cooling effect to the west shore of the state of Michigan.

According to Ronald J. Poff, Wisconsin Great Lakes Supervisor, Lake Michigan tributaries are poorly suited for spawning and survival of trout or salmon. Only one stream has significant natural reproduction and this stream is a small native brook trout stream. Lake Superior tributaries, on the other hand, are extremely suitable for salmon spawning and significant numbers of coho and chinook have been observed in at least twelve streams on Lake Superior. (Poff said that Wisconsin doesn't plant Pacifics in Lake Superior tributaries because they might compete with native trout.)

Wisconsin has minimal runs of anadromous brooks, some runs of anadromous browns in both lakes, good runs of naturally reproducing pinks in odd years, some splake runs (they are not believed to be anadromous), chinook and coho runs in many streams in Lake Michigan, stray chinook and coho in some Lake Superior streams, and good steelhead runs.

Wisconsin began steelhead plantings in 1963 in Door County streams. Between 1964 and 1967 fish were planted in Lake Michigan between Sheboygan and Rawley Bay. Since 1968 there has been an active stocking program in Lake Michigan tributaries. In 1968 eight of Wisconsin's Lake Superior streams were stocked, and in 1969 plantings were made in the Baptism, Beaver, Sucker, and Talmadge rivers. Lake Superior plantings continue. With some minor exceptions, Lake Superior fishing regulations in Wisconsin close steelhead streams to fishing from November 15 to April 2 because winter conditions are not conducive to stream fishing. Jim Moore, a Wisconsin fisheries biologist and practical migratory salmonid fisherman, reports that he does not know of stream fishermen working to catch over-wintering steelhead anywhere in Wisconsin.

Wisconsin chinook return to thirteen streams tributary to Lake Michigan, and the coho return to ten. The following rivers now have both chinook and coho runs: Ahnapee, Pike, Kewaunee, East Twin and West Twin, Little, Pensaukee, Sheboygan, and Little Manitowac. Streams having chinook runs only are: Lower Fox River, Strawberry Creek, the Harbor Mouth at Kenosha, and Sauk Creek.

Wisconsin Spawning-Run Calendar

Fishermen can set their spawning calendar for Lake Michigan tributary streams with this migration information for the Little Manitowoc and the Ahnapee. Fishermen using this information to gauge pink runs in Wisconsin or other runs in the western end of Lake Superior should remember that in the fall Wisconsin Lake Superior runs come earlier.

Chinook in-migrations in the Little Manitowoc begin in late September. The migration peak is in late October. Spawning usually begins in mid-October and may last through late December. Coho begin to enter Ahnapee River about October 20 and peak in late November or early December. Coho may continue to run through January, and spawning usually begins about November first. Spawning peaks in late November.

The best streams for fishing for Pacifics are the Root River, Sheboygan, Wewaunee, and Ahnapee. The Root is presently closed to snagging.

The rivers are not well suited to fly fishing for Pacifics. The fish are hard to see in Wisconsin rivers, and no good methods have been worked out to take them on flies.

ILLINOIS

Illinois streams tributary to Michigan are even warmer than Wisconsin streams. Illinois, Indiana, and Ohio tributary streams are the warm-water streams of the Laurentian Flowage. They are marginal migratory salmonid streams, but they do support fish that visit the streams at cool times and runs to cold sections of Michigan and Erie. None of Illinois' larger rivers empty into Lake Michigan. The few small streams that flow into the lake are Kellogg Ditch, at the south end of Camp Logan, east of Zion; the Dead River, near the south end of Illinois Beach State Park; the Waukegan River, which drains several city parks and runs into the lake east of Waukegan; and Pedibone Creek, which flows into the Great Lakes Naval Harbor. (Pedibone Creek may not flow.) Kellogg Ditch, the Dead River, and the Waukegan do have continuous currents. Some of these streams are blocked by sandbars during strong wind storms from the east.

Illinois has circumvented these problems by a unique stratagem—planting in harbors. Pacifics are imprinted in floating cages anchored in the Great Lakes Naval Harbor, Diversey Harbor, and Waukegan Harbor, and fall runs occur in the harbors. Runs were expected in Diversey and Waukegan harbors in 1977. Chinook run into Waukegan River and Kellogg Ditch when there is sufficient rainfall and a minimum of eastern storms.

There is no natural salmonid reproduction in Illinois streams. The streams are not suitable for steelhead runs, and strays occur only occasionally.

Illinois Spawning-Run Calendar

If nature is kind, chinook can begin entering Waukegan Creek and Kellogg Ditch in September. The height of the run is in October. It is not known whether chinook attempt to spawn in these streams. The greatest number of fish are in the stream in mid-October. Snagging is not allowed in these streams, and there is no natural reproduction in them.

INDIANA

Indiana streams are tributary to the bottom of Lake Michigan. Two streams provide steelhead, Pacific, and brown trout fishing. They are Trail Creek and the Little Calumet River. Trail Creek is a short-run stream; the Little Calumet is a larger system that Ts off a short, draglined mainstream to drain from three different directions. Coffee Creek and other tributaries bring water from the east; Salt Creek brings water out of Lake Louise and Sager's Lake from the south; and the Deep River and a more westerly fork brings water out of Lake George from the south and west. The river is slow-moving and mud-bottomed. It has little oxygenation in summer, but cools and provides a habitat for salmonids in fall, winter, and early spring. The upper sections of the stream are pleasantly wild.

Trail Creek and the Little Calumet have runs of chinook, coho, steelhead, and browns, but there is minimal natural reproduction. Steelhead can over-winter in the Little Calumet.

Indiana Spawning-Run Calendar

Although some of the literature distributed to the public used the term, Indiana steelhead are not summer-run. The fish are spring spawners. The Indiana streamers are too warm for over-summering.

Steelhead usually begin entering Trail Creek in August. The run peaks in September with successive runs coming in on freshets throughout September. Steelhead spawn in the stream and the peak spawning period is March. The Little Calumet is also host to steelhead runs.

Coho usually begin entering Little Calumet and Trail Creek in September. The peak of the run is in October. They spawn in both streams, and the peak occurs in November.

Chinook usually begin entering Trail Creek and the Little Calumet in September. The peak of the run is in October. They spawn, and the height of the run is in November.

Browns often enter streams in late September. All of them have been released from the shoreline.

OHIO

The Ohio country bordering Lake Erie is called the Great Lakes Plains. Most of it is affected by precipitation and regulating warmth and coolness from the lake. Ohio's Lake Erie tributary streams flow from a divide that slopes them north. The divide is a series of low hills extending in an irregular line from the northeast corner to the Indiana border in Mercer County. The streams are relatively short run.

Tanner and Tody's successful plantings of Pacifics in Michigan tributaries caused Ohio fisheries biologists to realize that salmon could live in the deeper waters of Lake Erie. However, no one knew whether the species could adapt to Ohio streams. Could the smolt be released into the relatively warm stream waters at times that would allow them to run out before suffering damage from rising temperatures? Could the returning adults, after finding refuge in cooler lake waters outside Ohio's territorial lines, return to streams cool enough to allow their comfortable entry? Or would warm late summer and early fall waters block or injure the fish? After fish have entered streams marginal because of warm water, a change in weather that warms the stream to or above 70° F. can injure them. Ohio, Illinois, and Indiana all have had similar habitat adaptation problems.

Ohio plantings are timed so that chinook and coho leave tributary streams about the middle of May. They migrate west and northwest into deeper Ontario waters and feed parallel to the Ontario shoreline east; then about one-and-a-half years after leaving Ohio they come westward into their imprint streams. This species usage of cooler lake waters in summer and cooler stream waters in spring and fall made Pacific's adaptation to Ohio habitat possible.

Ohio plants chinook, coho, and steelhead. There's little or no natural reproduction.

In District Three Vince LaConte is manager of five streams that are hosts to anadromous fish runs. They are the Chagrin, Conneaut, and Rocky Rivers, and Arcola and Turkey creeks.

THE CHAGRIN RIVER

The Chagrin flows past houses and factories from a dam at Daniels Park in Willoughby, which stops anadromous fish except in extremely high water flows to the lake. It runs with fair gradient over shale that isn't good spawning material.

Many fish run to the dam where they await Cleveland-area anglers. The other lies are in shallow pools and runs with some floated log and debris-covered eddy-type pools. There is little cover from bank brush and trees, and bottom scouring removes most sunken cover from the stream bottom. There are no boulders in the stream bottom that make cover, but there are some pockets in the shale where steelhead will lie. Sometimes the stream runs murky, and that can help hide fish. Near the mouth the stream is deep—probably drag-lined.

The Chagrin Spawning-Run Calendar

Coho enter the Chagrin at the beginning of September. They come in on the first big rainfall, or if there is no big rain they'll enter in the second week of September as the stream cools. The run usually peaks during the first two weeks of October, and lasts through December. Biologists do not know when spawning occurs.

Plantings will continue chinook runs to 1982 when evaluation will be made. The species now enters the Chagrin at about the same time as coho. The run peak is at or near the coho run peak, and runs last through December. Biologists do not have information on chinook spawning.

Daniel Olson, the author's son, with a 9-pound steelhead beached on the ice at Daniel's Park Dam, the Chagrin River in Ohio. The January snow and ice in Ohio can be tough.

Two races of rainbows called spring-run and fall-run are stocked in the Chagrin. The spring-run fish are obtained through the federal government, usually from White Sulphur Springs Hatchery. They may be stream fish. They do not stay in the Chagrin because rising water temperatures force them out to the Big Lake. The fall-run fish are obtained from Ohio's London Hatchery.

The spring-run fish begin to enter the stream in the fall, but the major run is in March and April. By the end of April rising water temperatures send them back to Lake Erie. Biologists have never directly observed spawning steelhead in the Chagrin.

The fall-run fish reared in the London Hatchery begin to enter the stream in the fall. Biologists feel that they spawn in late October and early November. They may over-winter, and fish that are seen in the spring often have worn dorsal fins that may have been rubbed on the ice that covers many stream sections.

THE CONNEAUT RIVER

A Pacific program in the Conneaut was discontinued, and the stream now has good runs of steelhead. The Western Reserve Chapter of Trout Unlimited provides part of the

Daniel Olson beaching a steelhead on shelf ice in Ohio's Conneaut River under a covered bridge. Notice that Dan stands well back from the treacherous, crumbling ice.

funds for the rearing expense of Conneaut stockings. The fish are spring spawners. They begin to enter the Conneaut in early fall and runs continue during freshets through the fall and winter. The major in-migration is in March. The headwaters of the Conneaut are in Pennsylvania, which does not allow winter fishing for steelhead, so over-wintering fish there are protected.

Larger than the Chagrin, the Conneaut has better lies and less population density. The shale stream bottom has little spawning gravel in Ohio, but spawning has been observed on gravel and sand that covers the shale. The stream may be un-fishable because of high water and winter ice channels. It sometimes freezes over. Fishermen may fish lies in the country or within the Conneaut city limits. U.S. Steel owns the mouth of the river, which has been deepened for the entry of coal ships. Lies from the coalyard upstream to the city include "the Arches," under a high railroad bridge, an old dam, and a hole just below the next upstream railroad bridge.

Fishermen who've "hit the Conneaut holes" may also fish nearby Turkey or Arcola creeks in the same day. Both have plantings of spring-run rainbows from the federal White Sulphur Springs Hatchery.

OTHER OHIO STREAMS

The Rocky River, a Cleveland west-side river (the Chagrin is an east-side river), does not have Pacific plantings, but receives stockings of rainbows from both the federal hatchery and the London Hatchery.

In District Two, Lake Erie tributary streams include the Huron, which has Pacific stockings, and the Vermilion, where steelhead are stocked. Much fishing on the Huron is done between Huber and Webber Settlement Roads. The Monroeville Dam, 15 miles from the mouth, is the upstream limit of the runs. Two streams that do not have good road access that lie between the Huron and the Vermilion (Old Woman's Creek and Chappel Creek) occasionally have salmon and steelhead. Some fishermen obtain access by boating along the Lake Erie shore.

Cold Creek has a half-mile stretch of stream below Mill Dam from which strays and returning escapees from private trout-fishing clubs upstream are caught, among which are sea run (bright and silvery) steelhead, browns, coho, and chinook. The browns and the steelhead are either strays or fish that came over the dam from private clubs, and returned to the estuary after feeding in Lake Erie. The Pacifics are strays.

PENNSYLVANIA

Several short-run streams flow through the small section of Lake Erie shoreline that is within Pennsylvania's borders. Most of them are now used for the spawning runs of anadromous species. Three of these streams—Elk, Walnut, and Twenty Mile creeks—have fair runs and are often open to public fishing. Crooked Creek, Six Mile Creek, Godfrey Run, Trout Run, and Twelve Mile Creek are among other streams also having salmonid runs. Six Mile, Godfrey Run, and Trout Run are nursery waters governed by special regulations. (Before fishing any of these streams double check the complicated Summary of Fishing Regulations and Laws.) These streams do not have suitable spawning-gravel reaches. The gradients are steep and mostly shale bottom. Because of the gradient, the streams scour most of the gravel off the shale. Natural reproduction in the streams is minimal, and it's limited to steelhead. Fish from the Canadian side of Erie stray to these Pennsylvania streams. All of them are relatively short run. Elk Creek, the longest, drains an area about 12 miles deep between 6N and the lakeshore. In these streams the season opens with the regular trout season but may close before the trout season closes.

Pennsylvania has chinook, coho, and steelhead runs in Elk, Walnut, and Twenty Mile creeks. Some streams have runs of brown trout originating from releases of nonanadromous stock. There is no natural reproduction of Pacifics. There is marginal natural reproduction of steelhead.

Pennsylvania Spawning-Run Calendar

Chinook begin in-migration in Pennsylvania tributary streams as early as Labor Day. The peak of their run is mid-September. It usually lasts through the first week of October.

The fish begin spawning as early as mid-September, and the peak of spawning is the first week of October.

Coho begin in-migration as early as mid-September. The run peak is late October, and usually lasts through the end of November. The fish spawn from late October to January. The spawning peak is mid-November.

Steelhead that migrate into Pennsylvania tributary streams are mostly spring spawners. There is no fall spawning, although they do migrate in the fall. The in-migration begins in October, and the fish may over-winter in Elk, Twenty Mile, and Walnut creeks. The peak of the run usually occurs in spring—mid-February to mid-March, but may come in early April. Usually, in-migration is completed by the end of March.

NEW YORK

New York has streams tributary to Lakes Erie and Ontario. Some of them run through the Erie-Ontario Lowland that extends inland from the shores of the two lakes. In this region, the lake plains border the Great Lakes and extend inland between 4 and 35 miles. Over these plains, larger lake waters once rolled. The soil is fertile, and it's tilled by orchard growers, nurserymen, and truck farmers.

There are few tributaries to the Great Lakes in New York that could be classified as good or excellent salmonid spawning-rearing streams. Most have natural or man-made barriers close to the lakes; therefore, the mileage available to anadromous fish is restricted unless fishways are constructed. Many of the streams are too warm in the lower reaches during summer months to carry salmonids. Some of the tributaries to main rivers are fairly good, although they are generally small streams. There is some natural reproduction for steelhead. All streams, regardless of size, had some salmonids present in the fall of 1976.

Apparently Canadian tributaries across the lake from New York are similar, although their upper reaches may be more suitable for salmonids than most New York tributaries.

New York fisheries workers hope to equip some of the longer streams with fish ladders. The Black River tributary to Ontario has hundreds of miles of main stream and many hundreds of miles of tributaries branching into the Adirondacks and the east side of Tug Hill Plateau. A favorable cost-benefit ratio could result in opening this stream to salmonid migrations. However, New York is holding on the Pacific salmon program in Lake Ontario because of contaminants.

The New York State Health Department has determined that eating salmonids and certain other species taken from Lake Ontario is dangerous to human health because of the high levels of toxic chemical (including Mirex) in them. Because of this contaminant situation, New York discontinued stocking chinook in Lake Ontario in 1977 and restricted coho stocking. Moreover, emergency regulations were issued on April 11, 1977, requiring that fish taken in Lake Ontario and its tributaries be returned to the water except for smallmouth bass over 18 inches, coho over 31 inches, chinook over 35 inches, browns over 21 inches, and steelhead over 27 inches. These trophy fish must be immediately tagged with a Department of Environmental Conservation tag.

New York tributaries have runs of chinook, coho, and steelhead. A few browns from nonanadromous lake stockings enter the lower portions of some of the streams. Natural reproduction is limited to steelhead. Few of the New York tributary streams now open to fish passage have food and habitat for large numbers of steelhead fry. Enough steelhead fry hatch in many streams to load the habitat's nurturing potential.

THE SALMON RIVER

The Salmon River, formerly an Atlantic salmon stream, provides a good fishery to the three major species, and some browns do run in. The Salmon had steelhead running to spawn in tributaries prior to the Pacific salmon programs. The Salmon flows through Oswego County to empty into Lake Ontario near Port Ontario. The stream is open to fish passage for 15 miles to a Niagara-Mohawk power generating dam above Altmar. A few miles above Port Ontario the stream flows through Pulaski near an exit on Route 81. Pulaski Pond is a Fisheries Section release and experimental site. Spring Brook flows out of Pulaski Pond to a weir at the confluence with the Salmon. Between Pulaski and Altmar there are two feeder streams, Orwell Brook and Trout Brook, which salmon and steelhead ascend. Orwell Brook provides the best spawning sites for steelhead and there is fair natural reproduction in the stream.

There is a no-snagging area near Pineville that fly fishermen like. Sportsman's Hole is a popular fishing spot between Pineville and Pulaski.

The stream depths and rates of flow vary with fluctuations in power needs in Syracuse. Signs on streamside trees warn fishermen of the danger of being swept off their feet.

The main stream has very little glacial gravel. Most of it is bedrock scoured by spring runoff from heavy snows in the upstream Tug Hill area. Here some of New York's heaviest snowfalls occur. Between Redfield and Altmar reservoirs there is a high natural falls that fish couldn't leap even if downstream power dams laddering allowed them to reach it.

Eastern fishermen like this stream, where many of the steelhead are over 10 pounds with some ranging up to 18 pounds. It is a year-round fishery, and 15- to 20-pound chinook were in the 70° F. water in July and early August of 1975. Few fishermen in the East have that kind of opportunity at their doorstep, so the stream is crowded with those who drive long distances to catch large fish. Most of the fishermen are snaggers, and they may gang up in companionable crowds on the bridge in Pulaski. Weekday fly fishermen can find some scanty solitude if they search the stream length.

The Salmon River Spawning-Run Calendar

Steelhead begin to migrate into the Salmon in September. Their numbers increase during the October to February period, with additional new-run fish coming from the lake in March and April. Their major spawning occurs in late March or early April.

Chinook may enter the Salmon as early as July. Fishermen expect to see some of them in August. Some years, chinook have continued until November.

In general, the chinook spawn in October; the coho somewhat later. The coho may still be spawning in January.

Other New York Run Times

Fall salmonid runs in other tributaries to Lakes Ontario and Erie start later than the Salmon River runs, usually September or afterwards. In the western end of Lake Ontario, the Salmon Creek (Creek, not River) and Irondequoit Creek have coho runs in November. The Niagara River also has November coho runs. There is fishing for Pacifics and steelhead in the lower Niagara River during the fall and into the winter. Probably steelhead fishing there lasts all winter. The upper section of the Niagara has brown trout fishing.

In eastern Lake Ontario, North Creek and Sandy Creek in Jefferson County have good coho and chinook fishing. These runs also start later than the Salmon River runs.

The best Lake Erie tributary stream is Cattaraugus Creek, where there has been steelhead spawning in tributaries for many years prior to the beginning of the Tanner-Tody launched salmonid programs. The spawning grounds there are good. Part of Cattaraugus Creek flows through an Indian reservation where special regulations and licenses apply.

ONTARIO

Ontario, the most northern Great Lakes "state," has streams tributary to four of the five Great Lakes—Superior, Huron, Erie, and Ontario. The Lake Superior shoreline is in the subarctic. A plateau in the Canadian Shield separates the rivers that flow into the Great Lakes from the rivers that flow into the Ottawa River and Hudson Bay. For this reason many of the rivers tributary to Superior and Huron are relatively short run. Many of these tributary streams run through relatively wild forest land, but some streams tributary to Lakes Erie and

Ontario run through the Lower Great Lakes Lowland, an agricultural belt. Early cultural pollution of some of these streams may have contributed to the extinction of Atlantic salmon in Lake Ontario.

The northern side of Lake Huron in Ontario is divided into two habitats—the Georgian Bay in northeast Lake Huron, and the North Channel, which at its west end joins the St. Mary's River. Georgian Bay is protected on the south by the base of the Lower Great Lakes Lowland and on the west by the Bruce Peninsula. The Manitoulan Island closes the northwest end of the bay. The entrance to the bay is between Manitoulan Island and the tip of the Bruce Peninsula. The Canadian side of Lake Huron extends on south from the Bruce Peninsula to the St. Clair River.

North of the Great Lakes, Ontario has a superb brook trout fishery in James and Hudson bays. James Bay is the southern branch of Hudson Bay, which is 900 miles long and 500 miles wide. Four times as large as all the Great Lakes put together, it empties into the Arctic Ocean through Fox Channel and into the Atlantic through Hudson Strait. Ontario shares the west side of Hudson Bay with Manitoba and the Keewatin District of the Northwest Territories. The east side of Hudson and James bays lies within Quebec.

In the Great Lakes, Ontario has runs of kokanee, steelhead, browns, brooks, and splake. The splake runs in the Georgian Bay tributaries (Orchard Creek, Sydenham, and Big Head rivers), and the Lake Huron tributaries (Saugeen and Licknow rivers) are probably not spawning runs. In Hudson and James bays, Ontario tributaries are hosts to brook trout. Arctic char do not range into Ontario streams; there are records of only two members of the species having been caught.

Lake Superior has 117 Ontario tributaries with known steelhead runs. Over thirty streams have runs of more than 200 fish. Twenty-six streams in Ontario's southern great lakes have steelhead runs. Brown trout run into many Ontario streams. Five streams in Georgian Bay are host to browns, two in Lake Superior, three in Lake Huron, four in Lake Erie, and several streams in Ontario apparently have brown trout runs.

The major range of Great Lakes anadromous brooks lies in Ontario waters. Outside Ontario spawning runs are rare. In the James and Hudson bays, forty-five streams are hosts to brook trout runs. Seventeen Lake Superior streams have brook trout runs. There are none in the other Ontario Great Lakes. Lake Nipigon, which is tributary to Superior through the Nipigon River, has four anadromous brook trout rivers. There are no Atlantic salmon running in Ontario streams tributary to the Great Lakes.

Ontario's Pacific salmon program is ironic. On the one hand they have restricted plantings of chinook and coho to Ontario's Credit and Bronte rivers; on the other hand they cannot restrict the growth of the pink salmon range that began with an accidental spillage and has never been sustained by plantings. Pinks now run in twenty-two Ontario streams tributary to Lake Superior. They've established themselves in Lake Huron streams tributary to other states, and may have set up housekeeping on odd years in some of Ontario's Lake Huron streams.

For migratory salmonid fishermen in the Great Lakes the Ontario anadromous brook trout fishery offers a wonderful opportunity. This and the Atlantic Coast are the two important anadromous brook trout habitats of the world. Brook runs peak in James and Hudson bays' streams in mid-August. They peak in Lake Superior streams in mid-October. In Hudson and James bays they travel long distances to collect in the headwaters, and they over-winter in the stream to avoid overwintering in salt water. Superior run brooks do not over-winter in the streams.

K. H. Loftus, Director of the Fisheries Branch of the Ontario Ministry of Natural Resources, says that sexually mature anadromous brooks continue feeding after entering their birth stream until the actual spawning period. "Usually they feed well—depending on the length of the stream and the length of time in the stream," he said.

The southern (Superior) fishery in Division 22 is a put-and-take fishery maintained by hatchery stocking. The northern fishery in Division 25 (James and Hudson bays) apparently is maintained from natural reproduction. It is possible to fish to brooks during their entire spawning run in Division 25 where the season is open all year. (The season should be carefully checked by reading current regulations.)

Ontario anadromous brooks go to sea at age three and the females spawn at the end of their third year. Usually they spawn in the same year they enter the stream. Some in-migrating fish are accompanied by males that do not have mature sex organs and will not spawn in that season.

Ontario and Michigan are the two best places in the Great Lakes region to fish for anadromous browns—the best places for sea-running browns outside their native British and European habitat. The peak of the spawning run in Lake Superior streams is late October. The migration occurs in October and November. The fish reach sexual maturity at three to four years, and spend two to three years in their birth stream before running down to Big Water. Most browns return to the Great Lakes to winter, and do not stay in the streams. Brown trout seem to be plentiful in the open and shoal waters of the corner of Lake Superior adjacent to the Sault Ste. Marie. In this water there is no closed season. Loftus says that the browns do not begin fasting immediately after entering streams, but fast when close to the actual spawning period.

There are no summer-run steelhead in Ontario tributaries, and none in the Great Lakes system. Steelhead run into the Saugeen (tributary to Lake Huron) in April and June, but they are spring spawners that return to Lake Huron (that is, they do not over-summer). Some Saugeen steelhead spawn in late fall or mid-winter.

14

Quebec

There are Atlantic salmon streams in many provinces of Canada including New Brunswick, Nova Scotia, Anticosti Island (not a province), Newfoundland, Labrador, and Quebec. Some of these streams also have arctic char fishing, and some of them have coaster brook trout fishing. Some have all three. The Atlantic Salmon Association says the only stream on Prince-Edward Island that has salmon entering is the Moreli River.

Browns are not known to be permanently established in any Quebec streams—perhaps they're present in the Chaleur Bay area. There is no Pacific salmon program in Quebec, although American-released coho stray into the St. Lawrence to a point near Montreal. Quebec has stream rainbows, but no steelhead.

Neither snagging nor redd fishing is allowed in Quebec.

Streams where productive coaster brook catches could be made include the Little Cascapedia, Nouvelle, and Escuminac rivers. Brooks enter the streams in late May and the middle of July. They spawn from the end of September through mid-October.

The life history of Atlantic salmon in Quebec doesn't differ significantly from that in Britain. In northern Quebec, salmon use three streams tributary to Ungava Bay—the George, Whale, and Koksoak rivers—and one stream tributary to Leaf Bay—

the Leaf River. The southern edge of Quebec contiguous to the Gulf of St. Lawrence and the continuation of that land mass along the shores of the St. Lawrence River has many Atlantic streams. The Gaspé Peninsula, the southern land mass at the mouth of the St. Lawrence, also has many Atlantic salmon streams. Anticosti Island, Gulf of St. Lawrence, has nine Atlantic salmon rivers.

Quebec uses French names for its rivers. The Whale, for example, is Rivière à la Baleine.

THE GEORGE RIVER

The George River in northern Quebec has a productive Atlantic fishery. The stream had plenty of Atlantics and anadromous brooks when I was there in the summer of 1976. Arctic char were migrating into tributaries.

The George flows big from Lac aux Goélands, 100 miles northeast of Schefferville as the crow flies. From the air one sees that the country is rock, lakes, scrub trees, and miles of caribou trails. Rivière de Pas has its headwaters closer to Schefferville. One could canoe down it about 150 river miles to the George. De Pas brings plenty of water to the junction with the George, which already has a good flow; this forms a long flowage or narrow lake called Indian House Lake (Lac de la Hutte Sauvage). From this point the George is big water. In some shallow sections one can wade among gigantic stones to a maximum distance of 30 yards. The Atlantics like the edges and I wrestled plenty of them at my feet, but it's really canoe fishing water.

There are no major tributaries entering the George from the west. A thousand brooks babbling from a thousand lakes on either side bring gallons of water into the system. The major tributaries flowing from the east moving from headwaters to the mouth are the Deaf—a stream that has no written name entering at Wedge Point—Slippery Brook, Rivière Falcoz, Rivière Gasnault and the Ford. The stream enters into Ungava Bay at Porte Nouveau Quebec, which is on the tree line. It's roughly 385 miles long.

The George River Spawning-Run Calendar

Atlantic salmon usually begin entering during the first two weeks of August. The run continues through the end of September. It peaks in late August. The major Atlantic spawning ground is near Indian House Lake, where stream depths vary from ½ to 2 feet. The extent of all spawning grounds isn't known to fisheries biologists. In 1975 some Atlantics spawned in deeper water below Culos Camp. Spawning fish are protected from August to October.

George River Atlantics usually go down to sea after six years in the stream, and return from the sea after two years. The fish average from 4 to 17 pounds.

Arctic char and anadromous brooks run into the stream to spawn at approximately the same time as the Atlantics.

FISH EATING ADVISORY

Certain fish of the Great Lakes and connecting waters have accumulated environmental contaminants. Such fish from the waters listed below may contain levels of PCB (polychlorinated biphenyl), DDT or mercury exceeding U. S. Food and Drug Administration (FDA) guidelines for safe eating.

To minimize the potential adverse health impact, the Michigan Department of Public Health recommends:

(1) YOU EAT NO MORE THAN ONE MEAL (½ LB.) PER WEEK OF FISH LISTED BELOW.

(2) FEMALE PERSONS OF CHILD BEARING AGE SHOULD NOT EAT FISH CONTAINING ELEVATED LEVELS OF PCB.

Smaller fish of the species listed generally do not contain contaminants exceeding FDA guidelines.

Levels of DDT and PCB can be reduced by removing the skin and all fatty portions of the fish along the back, side and belly. Barbecuing, broiling or any other cooking method which removes additional oils and fats should be utilized.

Species	Great Lakes and Connecting Waters	Contaminants
Salmon	Michigan, Huron (and tribs.)	PCB
Salmon	Michigan (and tribs.)	Mercury
Lake Trout	Michigan, Superior	PCB, DDT
Lake Trout	Superior	Mercury
Steelhead	Michigan (and tribs.)	PCB
Carp, Catfish (over 17″)	Saginaw Bay, St. Clair R., Lk. St. Clair, Detroit R. and Lk. Erie	PCB
Sheepshead, White Bass (over 10″), Walleye, Muskellunge	St. Clair R., Lk. St. Clair, Detroit R. and Lk. Erie	Mercury
Large- and Small- mouth Bass	Lk. St. Clair	Mercury

15

Snagging and Poisons

Common to Pacific Slope and Great Lakes governments is the problem of regulating the method of taking salmon and trout. Because salmon die after spawning, some Great Lakes States have allowed snagging as a legal means of taking them. Pacific salmon snagging is allowed in Illinois, New York, Wisconsin, Michigan, and Ohio. Indiana, Pennsylvania, Minnesota, Ontario, and Quebec do not allow snagging. Pacific Slope states do not allow snagging for any species because their salmon have commercial value as they are sold for food. (Fish from the Great Lakes cannot be sold for food because they are so laden with poisons that humans cannot eat large amounts of their flesh.) As natural reproduction results from salmon spawnings in the Pacific Slope, it's important that every egg be laid to provide fish to be caught in the ocean. The reproduction is needed to support the commercial fishery. Therefore, Pacific Slope states are more protective of their salmon.

Snagging is a method often used by those too lazy and too uninformed to learn how to fish for fasting species. Many snaggers honestly believe that these fasting fish cannot be taken in any other way. This belief allows them to rationalize the snagging of species other than Pacifics including browns, brooks, and steelhead.

Snagging is a corruption of sportsfishing. It is an odious practice that blocks people from using their brains to develop ethical, humane, and aesthetic fishing methods. In addition to this, snagging allows other fish species and men to be injured. Snaggers have set their hooks into each other and into underwater swimmers. Some states allow snagging on the grounds that Pacifics die and their meat is wasted. On the other hand, all living creatures die and the meat of many of them is wasted. This doesn't justify unsportsmanlike behavior.

Snaggers pull weighted hooks through the water in a series of rod-tip actions and line-reeling motions referred to in Michigan as the Muskegon Twitch. Many of them prefer to snatch fish they sight in the waters, but regulations often force them to twitch blindly in deep waters by feel. That's how a scuba diver searching for lures on a stream bottom was hooked and landed. As the fish fight and the water resistance sometimes helps the fish, the result is that fish lose parts of their bodies or break the line and swim away with the hook. I often see fish swimming in nonsnagging areas with weighted hooks in their bodies.

All of the states that allow Pacific salmon snagging restrict it to certain places and times. Illinois allows snagging only for salmon, and only from the shore in Diversey Harbor and Waukegan discharge channel. New York closes snagging on the Salmon River on November 15 to protect spawning. Wisconsin allows snagging of trout and salmon in tributaries to Lake Michigan from September 16 through December 31. (Be alert for changes in rulings. This is not a guide to state fishing laws.) In Michigan the commissioners set salmon snagging times and places annually on recommendation of the department. The rulings are intended to protect trout.

All readers should be warned about the hazards of eating fish from the Great Lakes. The 1977 Michigan Fishing Guide warning (shown on page 200) states this very clearly.

The same warning applies to species in Lakes Erie and Ontario. In Lake Ontario, there is an additional contaminant— Mirex.

16

Redd Fishing
on the
Muskegon

Carl Richards taught me redd fishing for chinook one October morning in the mists of the Muskegon. The method is simple. Present a fly at exciter-zone level by adding weights and shortening the leader. Usually I'm close enough to the fish to be able to get a fairly good look at the line of travel of the fly along the fish's body. The lead must roll the contour of the redd. There must be enough weight so the fly will be pulled downward into the redd basin. Often fish lie in the pit in the bottom of the redd, and the current may lift the weight causing it to skip over that pit, and letting the fly pass some distance above the chinook. In such instances, lead must be added until the fly falls into the pit. Fall Michigan chinook from Toutle River stock will sometimes rise a few inches to get the fly. Usually the fly must hit them in the teeth. Carl said: "Your lead must roll right on the bottom; these fish are looking at the gravel!"

The flies are simple. Any fly that has two tinsel colors and four fluorescent colors with an egg shape is a good fly. Sizes four and six are large enough to hook securely and small enough for the fish to tolerate it in its mouth. A small hook is more easily taken, and is best for the taste-spit take.

The method may require ten thousand casts. On the other hand, I often immediately take one or two fish from a redd.

Carl Richards setting on a chinook in Michigan's Muskegon.

Though they run in dark, Michigan's Toutle River stock chinook take to the air when hooked. This fish weighing nearly 30 pounds made four leaps. Stan Lievense is the flyfisher. (Photo courtesy Michigan D.N.R.)

If there are many undisturbed redds on a spawning ground and few fishermen, I'll move from redd to redd seeking the quick takers, the easy fishing. The fish that take quickly are more likely to be males that are fighting actively with each other for pairing with the female. If fish are churning and thrashing the waters over a redd, there's more likely to be a quick taker among the males. After the easy fish are skimmed, I settle down to a redd and make my ten thousand casts.

Chinook waiting to spawn will often school in shallow pools between the gravel bars where redd are cut. Some of them will take a free-floating fly.

On the magic October morning when Carl Richards first escorted me the fish were thrashing the waters, chasing each other, and pressing quivering bodies against green-sided females. We crossed the river moving through the mist to the shallows where we could hear the flailing chinook tails. Carl rejected several redds each with six or seven males accompanying a gravel-moving female, and took a stand within 15 feet of a redd where a large male churned restlessly around in pursuit of four other males. The female was on her side. As her belly undulations reflected light I saw gravel rising into the current that carried it a few inches to the side of the moss-cleaned depression under her. Carl put one TS 5 round weight onto the dropper, and shortened his leader to 9 inches. He tied on a Green Butt hairwing fly tied with fluorescent floss.

"Any fly that has a touch of green is a good fly," he said.

The weight plopped into the water a few feet upstream from the redd and sank into it to roll the length of the basin. The fly was a little above the boss male's dorsal fin. Carl shortened the leader, and cast again. One of the smaller males turned his head and Carl pulled the fly away from him. He cast again. This float was at current speed, and so placed that it presented to the fish's teeth, across his eye, and down the total body length. The monstrous fish suddenly drove forward menacingly toward an intruding male and shot out of the redd in hot pursuit. A few minutes later he circled over the redd fanning his fins to brake to a stop upstream and slightly above the female; then he floated downstream while sinking to a position just behind the female. As the female turned upright to rest from pumping gravel, the male moved forward to press the length of his forward-moving belly the length of her dorsal fin. This brought an excited intruder forward again, and the male turned to drive him away. Again he came into the redd in a curving circle that carried him upstream and over the female. He floated downstream while sinking to take up the boss male position immediately behind the female. This time the subordinate males took up submissive positions, fanned out behind the male, and everyone rested. I could see gills opening and closing, fins fanning water, mouths making cud-chewing motions.

Carl cast. The fly presented to the boss male's mouth. Carl twitched the fly ("fluffing it," he says), and as the fly passed the fish's eye the massive head turned, the gills flared, the mouth opened, and the fly was taken. On the set the fish left the water, came down with a splash that scattered frightened males in every direction and took line downstream in a long 80-yard run. Pointing his rod tip at the fish, Carl let the Fin-Nor free spool and began moving along with the fish to save backing.

Meanwhile the female, reacting as she would to any male fracas, turned calmly on her side and began to pump gravel from the redd basin. Carl cranked about half-way down to the fish, which took to the air twice more. I got a great jump shot for my slide show, and a good shot of Carl running after his fish.

For the next ten minutes Carl and the fish ran up and down the shallow water scaring other fish off redds. Finally the fish settled down to being a heavy swimmer on the end of a bowed rod. Keeping the rod tip against his chest, Carl kept the pressure against the fish and led it downstream and around other redds toward a sand spit at the foot of the spawning riffle.

The fish would turn on its side then right itself. Carl tried to lead it up the sand bar, but the fish got an energy surge and went into the deep hole at the foot of the sand bar and sulked. Carl kept the pressure up. "My arms are breaking off," he said. Finally the fish yielded and came to the beach. In one steady pull Carl slid the heavy body up the sand. The wide tail gave a thrash driving the fish farther onto the bar. Carl sat down to take a rest. I shot a picture or two, unhooked the fish, weighed it (28 pounds), and released it. We had a cup of coffee and a doughnut from the lunch basket cached behind a log at the landing beach.

JUMPING CHINOOK

I redd fish for the thrill of hooking leaping, battling fish that weigh up to 35 pounds. I hook chinook that splash all of the water out of the redd when they land from leaps that may carry them 3 to 6 feet into the air.

On its redd a chinook that has not consummated its spawning usually puts up nearly as good a battle as an Atlantic salmon. Lethargic when hooked, they may have to be driven off the redd. Sometimes I have to wade into the pod of fish and force the hooked fish to leave. But once underway, five high leaps are not uncommon. Long runs up to 80 yards are frequent. The fish usually start downstream, but may turn and charge back so quickly that I can hardly pick up the line. I've had returning fish hit me in the shins so hard that it hurt, or go between my legs and break off.

After leaps and running, if the fish is still on I have to reel to it and hope to coax it into a downstream battle ending in beaching. More runs, leaps, and sulking will be the order of the day. A single-action palming reel will put one into close touch with these powerful bodies that range from 10 to 30 pounds. The intimacy of being able to feel every move the fish makes while palming the reel will result in bloody knuckles, fingernails torn off, and a broken reel. I prefer a free-spooling reel with a smooth drag.

Good free-spooling heavy-duty fly reels that I've used include Taurus, Orvis Saltwater Fly Reel, and Pflueger Supreme 577. I have a beat-up Scientific Anglers number nine rod. With it I've caught a 12-foot boat, Doug Niemi, innumerable chinook, coho, Atlantics, brooks, sea trout, steelhead, and a few cutthroat. I'd say the rod has met the test!

Fishing for fish that are on their spawning redds is legal in all Great Lakes States and Ontario. Illinois fish don't have suitable habitat for making redds, but regulations do not

prohibit redd fishing. Pennsylvania fish seldom see top spawning gravel, and the season isn't likely to be open on a stream
stretch where a spawning fish could be reached if it found
gravel, but it's not illegal. Considerable redd fishing is done in
Michigan, Ohio, Wisconsin, and Minnesota.

In Oregon, Washington, California, and Alaska redd fishing
is technically legal in some areas, but most spawning areas with
thin water are closed. Redd fishing over unseen redds in deep
water occurs on the Pacific Slope, but fishermen often do not
know that fish are spawning. Intentional redd fishing isn't done
often on the Pacific Slope.

17

Snow Fishing

Steelheading and fishing for over-wintering browns is the newest sport in Michigan's winter wonderland. It can be dangerous! Survival depends upon good woodsmanship, warm clothing, and dry waders. The following letter, and a couple of excerpts from my diary will illustrate the field conditions.

> Lansing, Michigan
> December 26, 1975

Dear Fred:

River conditions look a little shaky for our filming trip next Monday, the 29th. I was up on the 21st and the Betsie was about 50 percent ice covered with floating ice in the open water. We went to the Little Manistee where the shelf ice wasn't too bad, but ran into my first case of anchor ice on the bottom of the river. It was the coldest weather that I've ever fished in—15° below to 12° above. Despite ice buildup—even the spinner iced up and wouldn't spin —I was still rewarded with three nice steelies for my efforts.

> Tight Lines,
> Jim Bedford

Item: During that trip a fisherman fell in. He returned to his Volkswagen, which had a poor heater, where he spent an hour getting his waders off. Because feet, socks, underwear, and trousers were frozen to the inside of the waders he held his feet against the exhaust pipe to thaw himself free.

January 28, 1975

About daybreak, Jim Bedford, Clyde Allison, Stan Lievense, and I arrived at Crotan Dam on the Muskegon. We got into the water below the dam, but no one caught anything. Gale-velocity wind in the river valley dropped the chill factor way below the thermometer temperature of 4° above. Ice coated my monofilament, creating a dandy weight for casting into the wind, but it clogged the line guides and they wouldn't thaw with underwater sloshing. I had to melt the ice with my lips, and they chapped and bled.

Had a lot of trouble casting because I had gloves on. The glove cloth between my fingers and the rod acted as a cushion

The fly rod gives way to the spinning rod in Michigan's cold winters. Spincaster Jim Bedford and flycaster Stan Lievense compare equipment.

preventing me from holding the line tightly against the rod on the back cast.

We hauled out of there and drove to Baldwin where 3 feet of snow lay on the ground. We fished the afternoon at the Woodchuck Hole section, and waded the snow through the woods to get to the stream. It's exhausting to wade snow in waders. You slip and slide. The waders resist leg movements. It'd be wise to wear snowshoes, but one can't pack them in the stream, and it would be a hard job to wade back to them after going downstream for several hours.

The snow was like meringue. Every tree, every stump had a decoration.

Getting in the stream is dangerous. You must avoid breaking through shelf ice into deep water or slipping on the snow-covered bank and landing head first. I had to sit on my behind and slipper-slide down the snowbank. In many places the snow is so high on the bank that you can't get out. After getting out you may flounder down in the snow onto and between logs, brush, and muck. Because of the snow we like to get in the water and stay in, but the stream in some sections is too deep to wade through. At such places Bedford crawled along the bank hanging onto brush and climbing upon tree limbs, logs, and trees that stuck out of the stream bank. Stan carried an inner tube with a sling like those used by bass fishermen and tried to float from spot to spot.

My Garcia 300 began to grind up ice that formed inside it. Water spray forming on the line was carried into the mechanism where it became ice. Those freezing droplets jammed the gears. When the reel quit working, I disassembled it. The pivot gear was broken.

Standing in the ice water numbed my legs, my abdomen, and my feet. Despite these hardships we took three steelhead. Jim Bedford took two, weighing 8 and 9½ pounds. Clyde Allison took one weighing 10 pounds.

December 22, 1976

Fished the Little Manistee with Jim Bedford, Fred Eyer, and Dick Updegraff. The banks were topped with about 6 inches to 2 feet of snow depending upon the way the winds deposited the flakes. The air temperature was 23°, and the water temperature hung just at 32°. Those water molecules were barely rolling, just on the verge of freezing tightly. The river was extremely low.

Jim and I fished upstream to the second red cottage, the one with the pond. My left wader foot sprang a leak. The good news was that as long as I kept it in the water it was just at 32° —never below freezing. The bad news was that my foot hurt. I kept getting out on the bank and doing a foot-warming dance. The boot eventually filled so much that my body heat couldn't warm the water volume.

After four hours of fishing we reached the red cottage, where I dried my foot, dumped the water out of the boot, and put on a dry sock. Of course we walked in the water on our way downstream, because wading the snow is so fatiguing, so the foot was sopping wet by the time I reached the car. But I had another dry sock waiting. Had to tromp a circular hard place in the snow to make a sock-changing place.

Fred Eyer took a 5-pound steelhead, and a late-wandering female chinook. Jim Bedford took four coho and a brown. Dick Updegraff took nothing. I took pictures.

Cold monofilament is still the world's greatest fishing curse. Jim works with his monofilament all the time to prevent tangling and coiling. He may hold a length of it in his left hand and release it as the lure is cast. The length may be a stubborn length that wants to coil. He'll sense it if some loops jump off the spool, and he'll take them in his left hand and hold the line out from the bail. He closes his bail as the lure strikes the water to prevent tangles. He keeps his reverse button in proper position, so there's no slack produced from the slight turn the spool might make.

I have a lot of trouble with monofilament coming off the reel in loops that tangle. The coils around the reel spool fly off in big loops that curl together and make knots. Also they catch on the reel handle, the bail device, my thumb, and any other thing.

When the temperature's below freezing one can get a frozen sleeve and a cold hand from tailing steelhead, so nets are used. Here Jim Bedford keeps fingers warm by grasping spinner blade.

Monofilament must be properly stretched before going to the stream. I tie mine to the neighbor's fence, pay off a section and stretch it, and so on. If that doesn't make it behave, I soak the spool and line overnight in cold water.

If I have any doubt about my monofilament I go out into the yard on a cold day, tie on a swivel sinker and cast into a snow bank. If the monofilament isn't behaving I can work on it beside the home fires. Touching the bare reel metal while on the stream is a cold experience that aggravates finger sufferings.

The Zebco Cardinal 4 is a good snow-fishing reel. It grinds ice without breaking because it has properly hardened gears with a worm drive. There are other worm gear drive reels on the market that may work equally well.

I don't like nets. They catch on brush and tangle with my camera strap, but in December and January I carry a net because I don't want to get my sleeve in ice water while tailing a fish, and I don't want to freeze my fingers by touching the cold bodies of beached fish.

Walking and wading become very complicated in snow fishing. The one thing to avoid is falling in. So good footing while wading is mandatory. It would seem that felt wader soles would be the answer. They are not. Snow sticks to felt, more than it sticks to rubber. On felts, snow balls up putting the feet into odd positions. Your heels may be elongated—or your toes. This increases the risk of falling in the snow and into the stream. It also makes walking in the snow even more hellish than it is otherwise. It's best to wade snow in your rubber-soled waders, but then you risk slipping when wading the stream. The answer is Super Stream Cleats made by Dan Bailey. They are small slip-ons with cleats for wading slippery stream bottoms. Because they are overshoes, you can carry them to the stream in your fly jacket pocket and walk in your rubber wader soles. If you want to get out of the stream, simply slip the Super Cleats off and walk in your rubber wader soles.

When you fish in ice water, take good care of yourself because hypothermia (loss of body heat that causes vital organs to stop functioning) can kill you. Always carry a dry, spare set of underwear, matches, and a can of lighter fluid for starting a fire. Slide into streams; kneel your way out.

18

Atlantics on the George

I didn't feel that my exciter patterns were authentic until I'd tested them on Atlantic salmon, which fast more consistently than any other trout. Probably they fast as much as chinook. So I saved my money, and spent a high fee for the privilege of fishing at Culos Camp located in northern Quebec 150 miles up the George River from Ungava Bay. I flew to Schefferville by commercial flight, and took a bush plane from there to the camp.

Noah, an Ungava-land Indian, was my guide. Noah, powerfully built (they say he can carry a field-dressed caribou on his back), gave me a paddle-calloused hand. His wife had stitched arctic fox fur scraps around his parka hood. Noah led me to his canoe that rested half out of the water on hewn tree trunks that he had cut, Indian style, to protect the canoe bottom from sand skinnings.

We ran downstream to the big island at the head of one of the worst rapids in the George. Noah turned the engine off, and held up two life jackets.

"Me, old," he said pointing to himself. "You, old," he said pointing to me. "We wear?" His face begged me to throw off all sissy ideas and be a woodsman. I nodded "Yes," and from that moment I felt Noah's spirit warming mine.

"Maybe we catch fish," Noah said.

I held up a Blue Tail Fly. "We *must* catch fish," I said. (I'd been fishless for two days!) Noah looked the fly over with a doubtful expression. "Dyed caribou hair," I said (it was fluorescent bucktail). Noah laughed. "O.K.," he said.

The engine started and Noah's expression became serious as his black eyes scanned the white water for rocks that might tear the canoe planking beneath our feet. As we worked our way down the rapids it began to snow. The snow pellets blown before the incessant Ungava Land winds stung our faces, but we both watched the waters carefully. It was the second day of September.

We made safe passage, and Noah swung the canoe to shore. The river edge was lined with rocks rolled by the current into a reasonably neat edging. Behind the rock edging there's a narrow strip of rocks and sand, then grass to the scrub trees at the foot of Montana-looking, gray hills. On the steep hillsides a few scattered trees lean in the wind, and on the hilltop, there are one or two trees every mile or so. The hillsides are decorated with a lacework of caribou trails.

Noah led me through the snow squall to a ledge about 5 feet above the water's edge. There were two slicks along the ledge, and at the ending, among gigantic boulders, was an eddy.

"Good place," Noah said. "One man here, in this place, caught five one morning." I was impressed by the slicks. In fact, they made me a little nervous. I decided to have a sandwich to fight the nervousness.

Noah went to make his private fire. All the guides make fires. Fishermen who try to interfere with the guides' fires are fools, but some fishermen feel neglected because the guides lie flat down on the ground beside their fires. There is good reason for this. The guides have very little to do aside from canoe management and waiting around all day to net the sport's fish —if he ever catches one. Atlantic salmon come few and far between. The world average is one a day, and the George River fishermen live up to that average. There are many Atlantics in the George; but not many Atlantics take. They are fasting; they are spawning. They are not interested in keeping guides busy.

Noah had pointed out the two slicks beside the eddy where I was to cast. I began to exercise my rod arm vigorously and the long muscles I agitated by casting warmed me. Noah could not exercise because he had to watch my rod tip for signs of an Atlantic to net. Standing erectly still in wind-driven snow would have exposed him to death by pneumonia. He needed to lie down out of the wind beside a warm fire.

Nearly all the George River lies are marked by guides' wind shelters—rock cairns erected over the years. They all have campfire charcoal in front of them. They may have been started first by Eskimos or Indians fishing the resting lies with harpoons. They were continued by the first French and British sports who came into the country with English flies and long, two-handed rods. As I cast I could hear Noah continuing construction by throwing a few more rocks onto the pile. I smelled wood smoke. Noah was warm; I was warm. I looked over my shoulder at him. He raised a huge mittened hand from a rock to show that he saw. His parka-covered head rested on another rock. He had not bothered to brush the snow pillow away. The snow made the rock softer, I supposed.

On the opposite bank across a half mile of blue water I saw the fire smoke of Norm Hyams' guide blown on the winds toward the distant hills. Under the smoke plume I could see distance-dwindled moving objects—a line of caribou coming down to the water. It was fall migration time, and the George lay in the migration path. One day we counted sixty caribou crossing the river. They swam well, their huge antlers looking like brushpiles floating on the water.

I decided to test the Blue Tail Fly. I cast to let the fly swing through the first slick, then by feeding out line and raising the rod tip I got what I thought was a good swim through the second slick.

Each cast had to be sent with a true, tight loop like a bullet into the Ungava wind that blows upriver from the arctic seas and is equally troublesome to either left- or right-bank casters. The wind coming from the arctic over the waters flowing toward the arctic must be cast into first, the water second. The wind resists line and rod so strongly that it would be less work to stand on the stream bottom and cast through the water and into the air. Since Atlantics don't fly, one would catch no fish; but the casting would be easier.

To overcome the wind, fishermen must lean into it, and there's a saying: "When the Ungava wind stops, the fishermen fall into the George River."

I cast for two hours; it seemed longer. I gave Noah several nervous "Should we get the hell out of here?" glances.

"Keep to putting it, Mr. Olson," he called. "Keep to putting it."

I kept "to putting it," but I began to get terribly nervous over the effectiveness of my Blue Tail Fly. I had several standard Atlantic salmon patterns with me. Two fishless days plus two hours had eroded my self-confidence.

I cut the Blue Tail Fly off, and opened the fly box. There were Cossebooms, Gill's Girl Nymphs, and Silver Doctors. Should I yield to the security of traditional patterns? I closed that box and opened the box of exciter lures. The Exotic Bombers in fluorescent greens, reds, and browns looking like rainbow cigars were hooked into the top lid. I put one on. I cast it into the water. As it floated over the slick I twitched it twice, then a third time. I saw a swirl beneath the fly, a pair of jaws, a porpoising back, and I waited for the fish to stretch the slack into a secure take. When that tension came I set once hard against the jaw, and the waters exploded. Opposite me, 25 feet out, the Atlantic rose from the water like a Bouncing Betty. I bowed my rod to the leap, the fish leaped again; I bowed, it leaped a third time. Then the fish bulldogged while I held my arms over my head to continue line pressure. The fish came to my feet. It was now on a short length of line, about 15 feet, and I knew that I had to be ready to let it run. It did run, but only a few feet, then it leaped again.

"Plenty of time. Plenty of time," Noah said. I hadn't heard him approach, but suddenly he was there. And when the fish and I were both tired, he used the net well.

This was my first George River Atlantic. I had landed two on Michigan's Boyne, but they were grilse. This 14-pounder was my first adult Atlantic. We let the fire go out. We no longer needed it.

Brook trout were running to spawn in the George with the Atlantics. I hadn't known that this would happen. Noah put me in an Atlantic salmon lie beside a small stream, and I caught two silver-sided brooks on the Blue Tail Fly. As his knife slit their bellies I saw white milt and orange roe. It pleased me because I wanted to test my exciter flies on char. During my stay on the George I caught nine of these fish. Five of them came from this lie where we knew they were, so I can say I was fishing for them purposively. I guess they were running up the small brook to spawn. That's what Noah said. The other four were taken at random Atlantic salmon lies.

Arctic char were also running and it's possible to take them in streams tributary to the George. I understand that they can be taken in the George near Helen Falls.

In seven days of fishing I landed nine Atlantics. Two were 5-pound grilse. One Atlantic weighed 9 pounds, the others ranged from 12 to 14 pounds. One was taken while trolling.

I used the Blue Tail Fly, the Two-Egg Sperm Fly, and Exotic Bombers. Two fish were taken on Blue Tails fished with a riffling hitch. I also took fish on hairwing patterns.

I suppose that nearly all Atlantic salmon flies are exciter flies. There are few fishermen who use exact imitations for Atlantics because Jones' teaching—"They are all fasting"—is well known to the Atlantic salmon fraternity. Therefore, I can't say that my flies are terribly different from the many other Atlantic salmon exciter flies.

There is not an Atlantic in every lie at the moment every fisherman presents a lure within it. This is particularly true on the gigantic George where there is more holding water than Atlantics. Furthermore, a fasting fish in a lie may not take even the ten thousandth presentation. For these reasons there is a vast element of luck in Atlantic salmon fishing. Whether one pattern will improve the luck much over another pattern is difficult to say. I'm certain that hairwing flies do improve one's take over the take from many other pattern styles. I think that the exciter flies I used are also an improvement. But any small fly that can be included within the general rule—use two tinsel colors, four fluorescent colors, and an egg shape—should work well.

I can be sure that my exciter patterns have worked well for chinook, coho, pinks, anadromous browns, steelhead, Atlantics, and anadromous brooks on their spawning runs. This means that members of all three subspecies of the salmon-trout subfamily have taken my patterns. I guess this doesn't shake the world, but it gives me a sense of confidence about the exciter fishing theory. The patterns should also work for Dolly Varden and arctic char.

19

Salmon

Chinook Salmon

The Latin name is *Oncorhynchus tshawytscha* (Walbaum). *Oncorhynchus* means hooked snout. *Tshawytscha* is the vernacular name for this species in Kamchatka.

SIZE: Chinook are the largest Pacific salmon. Adults range from 33 to 36 inches, and weigh up to 100 pounds. Thirty-pound fish are often landed in Pacific Slope and Great Lakes streams; the average is 20 pound.

RANGE: From San Diego north to the Bering Sea, and south along the Asiatic coast to Japan. Plentiful from Monterey northward; rare in the Arctic Ocean. Also found in the Great Lakes.

COLOR: At sea, bluish-gray on the back, silver on the sides and belly. Many black spots on the dorsal fin, back, and tail lobes. Spots cover two or more scales in one diagonal line and may cover a scale or two on the other diagonal line. The mouth lining is dark with no lighter area on the gums around the teeth. In fresh water as chinook turn dark they have bronze color phases; in some species males have yellow or red phases.

Chinook may run in spring, late summer, fall, or winter. Not all stocks occur in the same river. When two occur together distinctions can be made between summer-fall and spring stock.

Spring-run, upstream migration patterns, and spawning areas usually differ from summer-fall. Summer- and fall-run fish overlap in migration and spawning areas.

Spring stock run into large rivers that have cool, over-summering pools. They usually do not spawn until August, and may continue to spawn through November. Fall strain enter streams in autumn and spawn in October or November.

In California's Sacramento, chinook arrive in the upper river near Christmas. They over-winter and spawn in May and June.

Chinook ascend the Fraser for 600 miles, the Yukon for 1,200. In the Fraser they spawn from July to November; in the Yukon, August to September.

In California water temperatures, eggs hatch in fifty to sixty days. Alevin emerge from gravel in three to four weeks. Most fry smolt and migrate in their first months, but a small number may stay in the stream until they are yearlings. Yukon River fry stay two years.

One chinook planting could lead to runs in every year for a decade because they spawn at ages two, three, four, and five. Most return from the Great Lakes after two and a half to three and a half years.

POPULAR NAMES: A confusing popular name for chinook is spring salmon. Other names are king, quinnat, sachem, and tyee.

Coho Salmon

The Latin name is *Oncorhynchus kisutch* (Walbaum). *Kisutch* is the vernacular name for the species in Kamchatka.

SIZE: Eighteen to 24 inches long; weight about 8 to 12 pounds.

RANGE: From Monterey Bay, California, to Point Hope, Alaska. In Asia, from the Anadyr, U.S.S.R., south to Hokkaido, Japan. Also in the Great Lakes. They've been planted in the Atlantic by New Hampshire, Massachusetts, Connecticut, and Rhode Island.

COLOR: At sea the back and upper sides are gun-metal blue or blue-green. Sides and belly are silver. Black spots on the back, dorsal fin, and the upper tail lobe. The mouth lining is dark with a white strip on the gum crown through which the teeth grow. Spawning colors are reddish for males and bronze for females. In Michigan males may get a wide red stripe somewhat like a resident rainbow's side stripe, but Ohio males do not.

Over their Pacific Slope range coho enter streams usually during the second or third year, and spawn from September through March. Most of them spawn from November through January. Spring-run coho do not occur.

They'll swim up riffles with stream flows as low as 2 cubic feet, and in water as shallow as 2 inches. In streams used by both steelhead and coho, the coho often select spawning areas lower in the watershed than steelhead.

Coho eggs hatch in thirty-eight days in water temperature averaging 51.3° F.; in forty-eight days in water temperatures averaging 48° F. Fry begin to emerge from gravel two to three weeks after hatching. Emergence is complete after ten weeks.

About one year after emergence coho smolt and begin migration to their sea.

POPULAR NAMES: Silver salmon, sea trout, and blueback.

Pink Salmon

The Latin name is *Oncorhynchus gorbuscha* (Walbaum). *Gorbuscha* is a Russian name that took root in Alaskan usage during the Russian domination.

SIZE: From the Pacific Ocean, adults average 24 inches; from Canadian Great Lakes, 18 inches. Pacific Slope pinks range from 2 to 7 pounds; average 4 pounds.

RANGE: From an accidental spilling in Lake Superior's Current River in June 1956 pinks spread to streams tributary to all shores of the lake. They've migrated through the St. Mary's River; now run to spawn in some streams tributary to northern Lakes Huron and Michigan. No other Great Lakes state has stocked them, and Ontario did not make any further stockings. Adaptation to the Great Lakes habitat has been through natural reproduction. This is the most remarkable successful Pacific salmon planting ever. Whether the fish will become an "English sparrow" nuisance remains to be seen.

Like chinook and coho, pinks were once thought to be a species that can't successfully reproduce without living in salt water. Ontario was holding the pink fry in the Port Arthur Hatchery at Thunder Bay for planting in Hudson and Georgian Bays, which are salt. After a seaplane took the fry for official planting to Hudson and Georgian Bays, several troughs of leftover fry were washed down the drain to fresh water. Tanner and Tody had to work hard and used the best scientific methods to establish chinook and coho in the Great Lakes. The pinks were established without funds, administrative effort, or biological forethought.

Pinks occur in the Pacific and Arctic oceans, the Bering sea, the Sea of Okhotsk, and the Sea of Japan. They run from La Jolla, California, to northwestern Alaska and eastward along the Arctic coast to the Mackenzie River.

COLOR: At spawning time males grow a hump between their head and their dorsal fin; become reddish to yellowish on their sides. The females turn olive green on their sides. They don't have a hump.

Pinks spawn every two years. They may run in odd-numbered or even years. Great Lakes strains run in odd-numbered years. (Pinks may, rarely, live to three years.) The Queen Charlotte Islands have an even-year run; the Fraser River an odd-year run. In streams having runs of both odd and even races, one is dominant. The off-year run is smaller and may use different tributaries for spawning. There may be a noticeable difference in the size and weight of the two races.

Pacific Slope pinks usually spawn a short distance from a stream mouth, but may swim as far as 300 miles. They enter streams from June to September. Spawning occurs from mid-July to late October.

Pacific Slope fry hatch from December to late February; emerge from gravel in April or early May. They head immediately for salt water. They may not smolt. They do not have parr marks. They may out-migrate with chum fry.

There seems to be a higher degree of straying among pinks than among other Pacifics—perhaps a factor in their adaptation to the Great Lakes.

POPULAR NAME: Humpback.

Sockeye Salmon

The Latin name is *Oncorhynchus nerka* (Walbaum). *Nerka* is a Russian word for anadromous forms.

Kokanee

The scientific name for kokanee is *O. nerka kennerlyi* (Suckley).

Kokanee is a dwarfed, landlocked form of *O. nerka*. It is easily adapted to small lakes, and widely planted in them. Ontario planted kokanee during 1964 to 1970 in the Georgian Bay hoping to establish a self-sustaining population. That program has been discontinued. The New York Fisheries Department reports catching occasional kokanee. Minnesota, Wisconsin, Illinois, and Pennsylvania have no reports of kokanee strays.

They spawn in streams inlet to their lakes or on shoals in 1 to 3 feet of water.

At maturity they're 8 to 9 inches.

Sockeye

SIZE: 24 inches at maturity.

RANGE: From central California to the northern section of the Bering Sea and south to the Asiatic Kamchatka Peninsula. Abundant from the Columbia River to the southern part of the Bering Sea.

COLOR: Spawning male and female sockeye have green heads. The males' bodies are bright red; females are a darker blotchy red.

Sockeye usually spawn in river systems that include a lake. Most of the fry spend one to three years in the lake before going to sea. The adults may spawn in the lake, in the inlet above the lake, or in the outlet below the lake.

In some areas sportsmen fish for sockeye; however, their major value is commercial.

POPULAR NAMES: Little redfish, Kennerly's salmon, kickininee, yank, red salmon, and blueback.

Chum Salmon

The Latin name is *Oncorhynchus keta* (Walbaum). Keta is the Russian name for this fish.

SIZE: Averages 25 inches; 10 pounds.

RANGE: Rare off California; abundant off Canada and Alaska. In the arctic, it ranges west to the Lena River, east at least as far as the Peel and Mackenzie rivers, perhaps to the Anderson.

COLOR: Spawning fish get blotchy bars of red or black separated with green.

In northern British Columbia chum may be on their spawning grounds as early as July. Farther south they in-migrate from September to early January. There are both autumn and summer runs. They may spawn near the ocean or in some streams, such as the Babine, run into the interior. Some Yukon strains spawn close to the mouth; others run 1,200 miles to Dawson.

Fish often run in ready to lay eggs, and may be in the stream a very short time before dying.

Eggs hatch from late December to late February. The fry head immediately for the sea. They may not smolt. Most parr marks grow for most of their length above the lateral line. They feed on their way to sea, and are eaten by cutthroat, rainbow, Dolly Varden, and coho smolts.

Although they are not a sports fish there is some fishing for them.

POPULAR NAMES: Dog, and keta.

20

Trout

Steelhead Trout

The scientific name is *Salmo gairdneri* Richardson. *Salmo* is the Latin name for the "salmon" of the Atlantic. Dr. Meredith Gairdner (*gairdneri*) was a naturalist employed by Hudson's Bay Company. Sir John Richardson published an early work on the animals of North America called *Fauna-Boreali-Americana*. His cutthroat specimens were collected near Astoria on the Columbia by Gairdner.

SIZE: They range from small to large. Oregon Rogue River fall steelhead average 15 inches and 1¼ pounds (some fish in that run weigh up to 7 pounds). The average for both the Great Lakes and the Pacific Slope is 3 to 5 pounds.

RANGE: The native Pacific Slope range was from northwest Mexico to the Kiskokwim River, Alaska. The southern limit is now California's Ventura River. In all of the Great Lakes with good natural reproduction in northern streams of the Upper Great Lakes.

COLOR: Sea colors for steelhead are steel blue above with gray to silver sides and belly. The lateral line is sharply etched black. In the stream steelhead move through a variety of browns and reds toward resident red side stripes. The lateral line area often becomes pink, but the pink may be covered with reds or browns as pigment cells change.

The life history of steelhead is complicated by the fact that many streams have fall, winter, and spring in-migrating fish, and because the species has many different spawning times. A river system can have fall-run fish that over-winter five to six months and spawn in the spring, spring-run fish that over-summer and spawn in late fall or spring, and winter runs that spawn in the spring. Some perplexing steelhead in southeast Alaska enter fresh water in spring, spawn, then stay all summer and winter and leave the following spring.

On the Pacific Slope some steelhead enter some streams nearly every month.

Summer steelhead generally enter in April and May on dropping stream levels, summer-over in pools during June and July, and spawn in November and December. They may wait to spawn in March or April. Spring-run fish enter while green, that is, with relatively underdeveloped sex organ contents. A warm-water zone at the mouth of a stream (a logoon; a lake) may block them.

Fall-run fish generally enter Pacific Slope streams that are rising from fall rains. In the Great Lakes fall-run fish are usually quite green and over-winter to spawn in the spring. On the Pacific Slope fall-run fish may enter streams from August through July, and may spawn within one to four months of their entry time. Others may wait until spring.

Winter-run fish may come into streams on successive freshets and hold over for spring spawning. During spring in the Great Lakes steelhead run in ripe to spawn fairly immediately and drop back to Big Water. A warm spell in March can accelerate spawning bringing thousands of fish to the beds.

In-migrating steelhead, like coho, ascend on both rising and falling stream levels, but cease movement at flood peaks. This means that fish may move at the beginning of a storm, hole up during the storm, and move again on a weather change—a light rain bringing another rise, a sudden drop, or a warm snap. Ripeness of the fish, stream temperature, and turbidity are further complicating variables in considering stream movement.

If a fisherman has caught fairly ripe fish that cease upstream movement on a flash flood, and cannot find them in upstream spawning areas during succeeding fair weather he might find that because of sexual ripeness they dropped to a downstream spawning area before the stream fell.

This 46½-pound, world-record Atlantic salmon (a trout) was taken by Everett Kircher, President of Boyne U.S.A., in the Alta River. A male on its second spawning run, it was taken on a 12-foot two-handed rod with a Blue Charm. Norwegian Viking canoe behind the fish. (Photo courtesy Everett Kircher)

Steelhead migrate to their seas at various ages and over a long period within a smolting season. They are capable of spawning more than once and may spawn before their first journey to sea. Some fish in both the Pacific Slope and the Great Lakes may elect to remain in fresh water all their lives, even though there are no barriers to migration.

Steelhead may survive to spawn again, but not many do. In some runs second spawners may constitute 36 percent of the total run, but the percentage is usually much lower. Fish spawning a third time form a minor part of runs, and fish spawning more than three times make a negligible contribution to runs.

Steelhead eggs hatch in about nineteen days at an average water temperature of 60° F., and in eighty days at an average temperature of 40° F.

Fry emerge from gravel two to three weeks after hatching.

Steelhead go down to Big Water at a few months to four years.

POPULAR NAMES: Hammerhead, steelie, ironhead, coast rainbow trout, and silver trout.

Brown Trout

The scientific name is *Salmo trutta* Linnaeus. *Trutta* is the Latin name for trout. Carl Linnaeus was a Swedish naturalist who observed browns in their native Sweden. He originated the binomial taxonomic system.

SIZE: In Europe sea trout of 26 pounds have been recorded. An 18½-pound sea trout was taken from the Tay in 1900. The most realistic figure derives from a day's catch of fifteen sea trout taken at South Uist. The heaviest weighed 3½ pounds. The largest come from Alpine Lakes.

RANGE: The native range is Iceland, Great Britain, and the European coast from the northern tip of Sweden (nearly to the Barant Sea) to the southern part of Spain. Atlantic salmon overlap this entire range. Some anadromous runs have developed in streams of the northern Great Lakes from plantings in the lake and in streams tributary to the lake. In most, if not all, instances the plantings were not knowingly of anadromous stock.

COLOR: As browns lose their sea colors they get an underlying yellow and brown tinge. In three or four months they may look nearly like stream-resident fish. Menzies reports that Scottish sea trout may retain a claret tinge. Some females may have a greenish tinge. Males' bellies may turn black with bright red spots.

In Great Britain in-migration begins in summer—June, July, and August. By the end of September most of the spawning fish will be some distance into their rivers, and their sex organs will be ripening. In Scotland the sea trout spawn about two weeks before the Atlantics, usually beginning in October, sometimes in September. November is the peak spawning month, and some sea trout can be found spawning during the entire winter.

At an average temperature of 45° F., eggs hatch in about ninety days. The alevins hatch between January and April. Parr will move into a freshwater loch if there's one downstream. During the autumn of their first year a movement farther downstream may occur.

Juveniles smolt at an average age of two to three years. The more northerly the river the older the juvenile at smolting. In some rivers it occurs at four to five years.

Smolt run to sea beginning in early April and may continue to out-migrate during the first half of May. They feed on their way and may linger in estuaries.

As early as the first half of July they may be on their way back into the rivers. At this time they are called whitling. Whitling are an extra life-stage step unique to brown trout.

In-migration in the Brule River, Wisconsin, usually begins in early July and may continue through early September. The run peak is August. Spawning, at the earliest, starts in October and continues through early December. The peak occurs between mid-October and mid-November. During these times water temperatures may range from the mid-50s in early October to the mid-30s in early December.

After spawning, Brule River fish school in pools, and over-winter. Most of them do not out-migrate until April. By July and August in-migration is in full swing, so they don't spend a lot of time feeding in Lake Superior. During this short time they recuperate their weight loss and may gain more than a pound.

Parr leave the Brule late in the second or early in the third year of life. They spawn in their fourth year. There is no evidence of whitling runs or returns to the stream before the fourth year. The majority of spawners are four or five.

The fish lose weight during their stay in the stream.

The average size of sea-run Brule browns is 22 inches. They range in weight from 1.4 pounds to 13.1 pounds.

POPULAR NAMES: German brown, Loch Leven trout, and European brown.

Atlantic "Not-a-Salmon" Salmon

The Latin name is *Salmo salar* Linnaeus. *Salar* from "salio" to leap. Atlantics are leapers. Pacifics are salmon; Atlantics are trout. Perhaps, at a time when the Atlantic and Pacific oceans were more perfectly joined in the North Pole area, steelhead and Atlantics were one stock. Today they are "near relatives."

SIZE: Weights up to 100 pounds have been reported in Scotland and Scandinavia. Commercially netted fish average 10 pounds.

RANGE: Both sides of the Atlantic. From Massachusetts through eastern Labrador and Ungava Bay on the west side of the Atlantic through Greenland and Iceland to Scandinavia and the White Sea, in the Baltic and North seas, and British Isles, North Germany, the Netherlands, France, the north of Spain, and Portugal. Plantings to establish the species are being tried in the upper Great Lakes and are being considered for Ontario. Plantings are being conducted in the American Atlantic.

J. W. Jones explains that British Atlantic rivers are known by the in-migration season. There are spring fish rivers, summer fish rivers, and late rivers. In spring fish or "early" rivers, the runs come in March. An example is the Welsh Dee. In summer fish rivers, the runs come in summer and autumn. An example is the Cumberland Derwent. In late rivers, the runs come in late summer. In both Canada and Europe, runs can occur during any month of the year.

In Great Britain, Atlantics are near spawning gravel by October and November. They spawn in November and December. The spring fish make a slow upriver journey and are overtaken by grilse that spawn in the high tributary redds. The late autumn fish distribute themselves over lower river spawning areas. Canadian fish also spawn in October and November.

Alevins hatch from eggs in ninety days in water averaging 45° F., and in 114 days in water averaging 36° F. In Great Britain, hatch time is near the end of March and fry emerge from gravel in early May. In *Fishes of Ontario*, MacKay reports that eggs hatch from March 15 to May 4.

COLOR: When they are two to three months old, Atlantics are gray or brown on the back with seven to eleven dark vertical stripes on the side-rolled parr marks. These stripes may be rounded at each end or they may be nearly round. Parr have red or vermilion spots between the marks, black spots on the back and well-forked tails.

Parr go to sea in one year or more depending on the climate location of the stream. The farther north the stream, the longer the stream stay. The majority of British parr are two years old when they go down to sea. Hampshire Avon River fish are an example. In northern Scandinavian rivers parr do not go to sea until they are seven or eight years old.

The sea migration usually occurs in March, April, or May. An old verse helps us remember: "The first spate of May/Takes the smolts away."

J. W. Jones explains that like all the other trout and like char, Atlantic salmon can develop either anadromous or non-anadromous strains. He says: "Several lakes in parts of Canada and the eastern United States have similar fresh-water colonies of fish generally regarded as sub-species of *Salmo salar* which have been called land-locked Salmon, though their access to the sea is not barred in all cases; this would indicate that these fish have evolved a fully fresh-water mode of existence for some reason other than physical inability to reach the sea." Apparently all British Atlantics are anadromous.

ATLANTIC SALMON IN THE GREAT LAKES

Anadromous Atlantic salmon lived in Lake Ontario prior to 1900. By anadromous I mean fish that ran into Lake Ontario tributary streams to spawn. They were not landlocked; and passage from Ontario to the sea was not blocked. A biologist named Blair examined scales of an Atlantic salmon caught in Lake Ontario and preserved in the Royal Ontario Museum of Zoology and decided that the particular specimen had never been to salt water. So it's possible that these stream-spawning fish did not go out to the Atlantic Ocean, but lived in the Big Lake. Apparently the Lake Ontario fish came in during an inland marine development about 11,000 years ago.

Numerous Atlantics ran into many of the Ontario tributaries during the species' existence, and they were used for food by the early settlers. Records show that a fish weighing 40 pounds was taken in Duffin Creek in 1874. A fish weighing 42 pounds was taken from the Salmon River. There is a record of fly fishing for Atlantics on the Credit River.

Reasons for extinction given by Samuel Wilmot were: removal of forests, land drainage, stream-bed clearance, water pollution, spawning-bed siltation, and dams that blocked salmon ascension.

In 1977 three Great Lakes States had Atlantic salmon in hatcheries and state streams, and biologists introduced the fish into Lakes Superior, Huron, and Michigan. Hatchery stocks and eggs from Canada and Sweden have been released into state streams in an attempt to develop stocks that can survive in the Great Lakes, so hatchery personnel can gather eggs at weirs. The field problem is development of stocks that will adopt to the Great Lakes and annually deliver eggs for hatching. After that problem is solved some natural reproduction in streams may occur. The barrier to solving the field problem in Michigan has been that the fish often die before delivering the eggs. In 1975, 7,000 fry hatched from eggs milked from a Boyne River return. Despite all precautions in Michigan's modern

Wolfe River Laboratory, the fry all died. Michigan biologists feel that poisons in the lake such as PCBs may have caused the deaths. They have released Atlantics into the Chocolay River tributary to Lake Superior, which does not have as high a concentration of PCBs as Lakes Huron and Michigan.

POPULAR NAMES: There are few, if any, folk names for Atlantic salmon. The only nickname is "salmon" for a fish that's a trout.

Cutthroat Trout

The scientific name is *Salmo clarki* Richardson. *Clarki* was Captain William Clark, co-leader of the Lewis and Clark expedition. Captain Meriwether Lewis was also memorialized because interior cutthroat represented by Yellowstone area specimens were called *Salmo lewisi*. The fish were first believed to be distinct, but are now considered to be two forms of the same species.

SIZE: Average weight is about 2 to 6 pounds. Some have weighed as much as 30 pounds.

RANGE: From the Eel River north through Seward, Alaska.

COLOR: The skin pigmentation and color pattern of the species varies from stream to stream and between coastal anadromous and interior stocks. Cross transplantation of British Columbia and other Pacific Coast stocks has accelerated these variations. The quick check for distinguishing cutthroat from other trout, although not always reliable, is the yellow or orange to red lines that "cut the throat." These lines are in the skin folds on either side of the lower jaw. They do not cut across the throat. Varying in size and color intensity, they are dim in young trout, and dim to absent in fresh-from-the-sea migrants.

Stream fish are olive green on the back, lighter on the sides, and silvery on the belly. There may be a pink sheen on the gill covers and there may be many black spots on the back and sides. Newly arrived in-migrants are more silvery on the belly and sides, and more bluish on the back. After one month in the stream, southeastern Alaska anadromous fish cannot be distinguished from stream-resident fish. The following chart explains why fishermen may confuse spawning-run fish with residents.

Trout and Salmon of the Great Lakes

Chinook Salmon

Inside of mouth and gums are black, and, according to the Michigan Department of Natural Resources, there are fifteen to seventeen rays in the anal fin. Sea-run chinook are bright silver; spawning adults are often dark olive in color. Average weight of adults is 22 pounds.

Unlike coho, Michigan chinook spend only six months in the hatchery before being released at a size of about 2 to 3 inches in Great Lakes tributary streams. After fall spawning chinook die.

Coho Salmon

Inside of mouth is black; gums are white or gray. The anal fin has thirteen to fifteen rays. Sea-run fish are bright silver and spawning adults are often dark olive in color. Spawning males develop a hooked jaw. Average weight of adults is 8 pounds.

In Michigan coho are reared in hatcheries to one-and-a-half years, released in tributary streams, and migrate to the Great Lakes where they spend another year and a half. Adults die after fall spawning. Although natural reproduction occurs in many Michigan streams, its extent is limited. Lake populations are maintained by plantings.

Kokanee Salmon

Inside of mouth is light in color; gums are dark. Kokanee, the smallest salmon, differ from other salmon by having twenty-eight to forty long, slender, closely spaced gill rakers. Sea-run fish are usually greenish blue and have fine black speckling on the top of the body. Adults average 1½ pounds.

The kokanee was planted experimentally by Ontario in Lakes Huron and Ontario. Ontario has discounted that program. Kokanee die after spawning.

Atlantic Salmon (A Trout)

Inside of mouth is light and gums are light or gray; tongue is narrow, pointed, and tipped with four to six small teeth; upper jaw barely extends to rear of eye. Atlantics are sometimes confused with anadromous browns. Eddy says that the adults have x-shaped spots on their sides.

Atlantic salmon are experimental in the Great Lakes. They do not run to spawn in any Pacific Ocean tributary.

Steelhead Trout

Sometimes confused with coho or chinook salmon, the steelhead differs from these fish in that both mouth and gums are light in color and there are nine to twelve rays (Fry says rarely thirteen), in the anal fin. Adults usually weigh 9 to 10 pounds.

The rainbow need not die after spawning; however, spawning stress does cause mortality. Few fish spawn more than two or three times.

(Continued next page)

Splake

Splake are planted in the Great Lakes. Fishermen may confuse them with lake-run brooks or trout. The splake has ten rays in the anal fin, and usually the tail is less forked than the lake trout and not as square as the brook trout's. Spawning splake may weigh 2 to 3 pounds.

Splake are a hybrid produced from crossing lake trout and brook trout. They mature in three years and spawn in late fall on rocky shoals. They may enter streams, but, apparently, not to spawn.

Pink Salmon

The mouth and gums are dark colored. The anal fin has thirteen to seventeen rays. There are numerous large, black oval spots all over the tail, on upper sides, and back. Sea-run fish are silver; spawning fish are red. Adults run from 1 to 1½ pounds in weight.

Also known as humpback salmon, the pink salmon was accidentally released in Lake Superior in 1956. They mature in two years and spawning runs in the Great Lakes occur on odd-numbered years. Even-numbered-year runs occur in some Pacific Slope streams. Adults die after spawning.

Brook Trout (A Char)

Brook trout have nine rays in the anal fin and the lower fins are usually edged in white with a black border. The tail fin is square in shape. There may be wormlike markings on the back it not obscured by guanine deposits. Sea-run fish usually weigh 2 to 3 pounds.

Lake Trout

Lake trout are not anadromous. They are char.

In the Great Lakes they may be confused with brook trout or splake. They have eleven rays in the anal fin.

Brown Trout

Browns may be told from Atlantics by the following checks:

The brown tongue is broad, square, and tipped with eleven to twelve large teeth.

The upper jaw extends beyond the rear of the eye socket.

Browns have nine to twelve rays in their anal fin.

Browns are well established in many northern Great Lake tributary streams. They spawn in the fall and need not die after spawning.

Michigan Department of Natural Resources artist, Charles Schafer, created this illustration. First published in the September/October 1973 issue of Michigan Natural Resources Magazine, the costs were partly financed by a U.S. Department of Interior grant. Photo by Michigan D.N.R. photographer Robert Harrington is used by permission of the D.N.R. The editorial copy here differs from that published in 1973, and is entirely the author's.

Three Color Stages in Petersburg Creek System During Fall and Winter

Color

1. Sea run; sexually maturing.	Silver when they run in, but will turn dark and look like residents in one month.	One month after fish types one and two enter the stream, all three types look alike.
2. Sea-run; sexually immature over-wintering.		
3. Resident lake; sexually maturing and also will spawn.	Have stream colors and look different from sea-run that have been in stream *less* than one month.	

Cutthroat enter streams on their spawning run in summer, autumn, and winter. In-migration in Petersburg Creek, Alaska, began in May in 1975 and in July in 1972, 1973, and 1974. In those three years it peaked in late September. In Sand Creek, Oregon, in 1946 the run began in October. In streams near Toledo, Oregon, in 1959 to 1963 in-migration occurred from late October until March with a peak in December.

A resident population of cutthroat remain in Petersburg Creek the year round. This is true for most Pacific Slope cutthroat streams.

Some sea-run cutthroat are alternate year spawners, some skip two years, some spawn each year. The sexually immature nonconsecutive spawners run in with the mature fish.

Spawning on the Pacific Slope occurs in late winter or spring. Some spawn as late as March and April, but most spawn in late December, January, and February. Petersburg Creek cutthroat spawn in April and May. Spawning in British Columbia has been reported from late December to early April.

In Petersburg Creek the fish spawn only after darkness. Daytime spawning has been reported in Oregon. Petersburg Creek cutthroat migrate back to sea from early May to late August. In 1972 and 1974 out-migration peaked in June.

Oregon fish near Toledo migrated downstream from December to April in the 1959 through 1962 seasons. Downstream migration for kelts peaked in January and February. Down-stream migration of immature fish peaked in April.

Like Dolly Varden, cutthroat over-winter in lakes of lake-stream systems. In the Petersburg Creek system they spend most of December, January, and February in Petersburg Lake. The sea-run fish that will spawn in the spring, the sea-run fish that are not sexually mature and will not spawn, and resident lake cutthroat—mature or immature—all tuck in together for over-wintering. In this mixed-age class respect they are also like Dolly Varden.

There is evidence that after over-wintering cutthroat leave a lake system in the spring and spawn in nonlake streams of birth, again like Dolly Varden. This occurs when the birth stream is a nonlake stream system. There's a distinction here, however, between Dolly Varden and cutthroat. Dolly Varden, being fall spawners, lay their eggs and milt in their stream of birth and go to a lake to over-winter. Cutthroat, being spring spawners, leave their over-wintering lake to spawn. Cutthroat have a reverse Armstrong syndrome.

Most of the lakes in the lake-stream systems of southeastern Alaska have a mixture of over-wintering cutts and Dollys. Because each species gathers all of its age classes and all of its sexually mature and immature representatives, it makes a de-lightful mixture for fishermen. There's really no way of know-ing which fish is a fasting fish and which is not. In winter some are spawned out (Dollys), and some have not yet spawned (cutthroat).

POPULAR NAMES: Harvest trout, salmon-trout, blueback, coastal cutthroat, Yellowstone cutthroat, red-throated trout, Clark's trout, sea trout, and short-tailed trout.

I'm ending the trout life history with cutthroat and begin-ning the char life history with Dolly Varden so that the similar-ity between cutts, Dollys, and arctics can be stressed. They all escape the full discipline of the exciter fishing theory by run-ning into streams in a delightfully mixed bunch of sexually mature fish that may be fasting and sexually immature fish that certainly are not fasting. Members of all three of these species leave the ocean to over-winter in streams. Dolly Varden and cutthroat in southeast Alaska over-winter in lakes of lake-stream systems. Brooks in Hudson and Georgian bays leave the Big Water to winter in streams. (Brooks in Lake Superior may winter in the lake.) In all of these species the run is a combination spawning run and trip to over-wintering quarters.

The other species that over-summer or over-winter do not bring a lot of sexually immature fish along with them. The purpose of their stay in the stream is to spawn—not refuge from the elements.

All salmon, most trout, and some brook spawning runs are of a reasonably homogeneous population of fasting fish. (They may interrupt their fast to feed.) The exciter fishing theory adequately accounts for their behavior. Among cutts, Dollys, and arctics there are fasting fish, fish that have broken their fast, and feeding fish. No single fishing theory will account for their behavior. The fact that exciter lures work for these mixed populations does not bring consistency to their behavior or to fishing methods.

21

Char

Dolly Varden Char

The Latin name is *Salvelinus malma* (Walbaum). *Malma* is the common name of the species in Kamchatka. Dolly Varden are a native Pacific Slope char. Some fishermen call them the western brook trout.

SIZE: Some weigh only 5½ pounds. In Alberta a large specimen weighed 14 pounds. Thirty-two pound fish have been recorded.

RANGE: From Oregon to the Bering Sea. Dolly Varden and arctic char ranges overlap in Alaska.

COLOR: Sea-run adults have dark blue backs, upper heads, and upper sides. The belly and sides are silvery feathering to white. Spawning fish may have bright red sides. The males get a red touch on the snout. Their lower jaw and parts of their head are black with olive brown on the back and sides. Male spots become more vividly orange-red, and the anal fins get a white leading edge.

Anadromous Dolly Varden enter river mouths from May to December, normally August to September. In some southeastern Alaskan streams the fish may run in as early as late May. In other southeastern Alaskan streams fish in-migrate in early

July. Although the southeastern Alaskan runs may last into early December, they're usually all run in by early November.

In southeastern Alaskan streams having lakes there may be two peak runs—one from sea-run fish born in the stream; the other from fish born in streams where there are no lakes. The latter run is not a spawning run. It is a run of spawned-out fish on their way to an over-wintering lake.

The spawning peak occurs during October in southeast Alaska. In other areas spawning occurs from September to early November.

In southeast Alaska mature Dolly Varden return to sea about ice-out time—April or May, depending on the weather. Young fish first go to sea in their third or fourth year. They often double their weight in the first sea season.

Some Dolly Varden are nonconsecutive spawners. These sexually immature fish run into the streams with the sexually maturing fish. In some streams the in-migration may include immature fish that run immediately back to sea. Probably they find a stream with a lake and eventually enter it to over-winter.

Some do not migrate each year. They skip their trip to feed in the sea, and remain in the stream.

At spawning time there may be five groups of fish in some streams that are definitely feeding. They are: indigenous, non-anadromous fish; nonconsecutive spawners; mature fish that elected to stay in the stream instead of migrating back to sea; fish that are too young to go down to sea; and sexually immature fish that enter the stream to find protection in their over-wintering lake.

At one time people believed that Dolly Varden seriously injured salmon reproduction by feeding on their eggs, and the State of Alaska paid bounties for dead Dolly Varden. The bounty system was designed to protect the commercial salmon industry. Recent dietary studies have proven that Dolly Varden are not a serious threat to salmon populations.

It takes about four and a half months for eggs to hatch. Most hatching is in March and April. The alevins emerge from gravel about eighteen days after hatching.

Sea-run fry from Eva Creek in southeast Alaska go down to sea after three to four years in the stream. Nonanadromous members of the species usually spend a few months in a stream; then move into a lake in the stream system.

An important finding of the southeast Alaska studies made by Blackett (1968), Armstrong (1965), Heiser (1966), Robert Baade, and others was that Dolly Varden over-winter in lakes that are part of lake-stream systems after spawning. Fish that have spawned in a stream (their birth stream) that does not have a lake go back to salt water and swim to a stream with a lake for over-wintering. This trip to winter quarters by spawned-out fish creates another in-migration peak. It isn't a spawning run, and the trip down the stream of birth to the salt (en route to the over-wintering stream) is not a typical out-migration.

Apparently these spawned-out fish do some feeding (in both salt water and fresh water) on their way to their over-wintering lake.

I shall refer to the Dolly Varden kelt migration from their birth stream spawning grounds to their lake-stream over-wintering quarters as the Armstrong syndrome. (It's easier to say Armstrong syndrome than to say: Spawn-in-stream-of-birth; migrate-to-over-wintering-quarters in lake-stream-system.)

POPULAR NAMES: Bull trout, red-spotted Rocky Mountain trout, Pacific brook char, sea trout, salmon trout, and western brook trout.

Arctic Char

The scientific name is *Salvelinus alpinus* (Linnaeus). *Salvelinus* is an archaic word for char; *alpinus* means alpine. Char occur in both anadromous and nonanadromous forms. While many of the nonanadromous forms are landlocked, there are members of the species that do not elect to go to sea and live in streams with no barriers to sea migration.

SIZE: Char grow very slowly. At one year, the time of scale formation, they're often under 2 inches. When they migrate to sea for the first time at age five to eight, they will be 6 to 8 inches long. Char reach full growth at twenty years. Fish that by their scale readings are forty years old may not be much larger than a twenty-year specimen. Trophy char weighing 27 pounds have been caught in North America and a char weighing 34 pounds was caught in Novaya Zemlya, U.S.S.R. These trophies may not have been old fish, they may just have been fat fish—fish that quickly turned food into body weight.

RANGE: Circumpolar. The southern limits of anadromous fish roughly follow the 50° F. mean summer sea temperature line. They are the most northerly of the freshwater fishes. The areas where they range are northern North America, northern Asia, northern Europe (Scandinavia), Iceland, Greenland, and many arctic islands. Freshwater, landlocked forms occur farther south.

The arctic char and Dolly Varden ranges overlap in Alaska. In the central arctic the range of arctic char overlaps with brook trout, and in the European range it overlaps with browns.

Arctic char live in streams entering the west coast of Hudson Bay as far south as the Churchill River. They've been reported farther south in the Nelson River. Brook trout occupy the streams flowing into Hudson Bay south of about 58 degrees north latitude. Possibly the two species overlap in streams between the Churchill and the Nelson. Fishermen can explore combining brook and arctic fishing methods.

COLOR: The fresh-run fish will be bright silvery; the sexually mature fish have orange to reddish hues that range from bright red to deep vermilion. White trim is "painted" on the skin folds under the maxillary bones of the upper jaw and the edges of the pectoral, pelvic, and anal fins.

Some arctic char enter their birth stream and stay in it for fourteen months before spawning, while others enter their birth stream in the fall and spawn shortly afterwards. Some spawn in spring; some in the fall. In some rivers the population is divided into two groups, each spawning on alternate years.

In the Windermere River, a British stream, there are two distinct breeding populations, one population spawning in shallow water in autumn, and the other in deep water in spring.

In northern Alaska all of the char are fall spawners, according to Terrence Bendock, Fisheries Biologist, Alaska Department of Fish and Game. Unlike salmon, however, char spawn over a greater period of time. Bendock says that in the Wulik River (northwest Alaska) and in the Sagavanirktok drainage, char spawn from late August through November with a peak in September.

Wulik River fish enter their stream in the fall, and, without returning to sea, spawn twelve to fourteen months later. Sagavanirktok system adults migrate to sea every year and spawn shortly after entering their birth stream in the fall. These two radically different spawning calendars occur within a relatively short distance from each other, so specific drainages can have different life history patterns.

The following chart summarizes the life cycle of a char following the twelve- to fourteen-month waiting period:

	June 1976 (ice out)	A char runs to sea for its first time.		
Time in Stream	Sept. 1976	The char returns to its birth stream.	Over-winter	Over-sojourn
	Sept. 1977	The char spawns.	Over-summer spawns	
	June 1978 (ice out)	The char runs to sea.	Over-winter	
	Sept. 1978	The char returns to its birth stream to wait and spawn again		

This behavior pattern is bewildering. In the first place one scarcely knows what to call the waiting period that includes over-wintering, over-summering, and over-wintering. I call it over-sojourning. In the second place, it's difficult to know what the fish is doing during the waiting period. Over-summering and over-wintering steelhead fast. But does the char fast for fourteen months? As dumbfounding as it may seem, char do have that capacity, and can rely *mostly* on stored food energy obtained during their last migration to sea. Probably they break their fast frequently, however. The fact that sexually mature fish that may be fasting and maturing fish that have not yet been to sea are often mixed in the same river makes it difficult to distinguish the fasting fish.

Terry Bendock has reported to me that there's a reduction of feeding by all arctic char entering fresh water. Both the fish that in-migrate to spawn and sexually immature fish that in-migrate to over-winter follow this pattern. It seems to occur because of movement from a food-rich coastal marine environment into relatively barren waters.

In his study of char on the west coast of Hudson's Bay, William M. Sprules reported that "The stomachs of all the char taken in Whiterock Lake were empty, which indicates that char do not feed for some time at least after entering fresh water." Opposing observations are reported by J. G. Hunter, a fisheries biologist at the Arctic Biological Station in Ste.-Anne de Bellevue, Quebec. In a letter to me dated March 7, 1977, Hunter said: "Arctic char moving in from the sea on the upstream migration (nonspawning fish) usually have full stomachs. Since spawning, in most cases, occurs under the ice when conditions for sampling are difficult, no stomach samples from spawning fish, to my knowledge, have been taken. However, in aquarium studies (by Eabricus) of spawning char, eggs that did not become washed into interstices in the gravel were consumed by the adult fish."

Arctic char feed very little in winter because cold-water temperatures in most lakes and streams discourage metabolism. Because char do not over-winter in the sea, both sexually mature and sexually immature fish in-migrate in late summer and early fall.

Anadromous and lake-locked char in the Sylvia Grinnel system (it empties into Frobisher Bay) spawn in September and October in suitable gravel or substrata. On Alaska's North Slope near the oil rigs in the Sagavanirktok River system, spawning occurs at spring areas from late August through mid-November. These springs occur at canyon mouths of the Brooks Range, and are open water during winter. Spawning in and near the Wilson River occurs in river lakes under first ice. Eskimos on the Wilson crawl out on the ice, locate redds, and capture char with long-handled spears thrust through holes. Peak migration for char in Alaska's North Slope streams is September. The migration begins about mid-July. Spawning on North Slope streams occurs in late September.

Eggs hatch in late April. In July the fry become free swimming and live on plankton and insects in river lakes and tributaries.

Sylvia Grinnel system char make their first run to sea when five to eight years old (6 to 8 inches). They leave at ice-out, which is early June to mid-July. They do not over-winter in the sea, but return annually to their birth stream in mid-August to late September. Migration to the sea is annual. Some sexually maturing fish over-sojourn during alternate years, and migrate to sea every other year.

Tagged char have been found over 100 miles from their river mouth. Usually they do not travel far into the sea.

Fertilized char eggs may freeze and die in their redds during severe arctic winters when water temperatures fall below 46° F. The alevins are under thick ice between snowy banks in wind-swept country. April 1 has been established as the probable birth date of alevins.

Because the fish linger near their river mouth it is probable that an estuary fishery similar to the cutthroat and Dolly Varden estuary fishery could be developed, using imitations of estuarian aquatic insects and bait fish with flies.

The time to fish for arctic char is mid-July through late September. Ice-out occurs from early June to mid-July, and sea-run char come into the streams about mid-August to late September. In the fish's northern range, mid-July through mid-August is the early season. At that time ice that has not gone out could deter fishing, and, in many streams, sea-run char will not have arrived.

POPULAR NAMES: Eskimos have many names to describe size, color, and breeding phase of arctic char. Their general name is irkalukpik. Other popular or folk names for arctic char are alpine char, Hudson Bay salmon, European char, Greenland char, Quebec red trout, Hearne's salmon, and blueback trout.

Brook Trout—A Char

The scientific name is *Salvelinus fontinalis* (Mitchill). *Fontinalis* means living in springs.

SIZE: Fish weighing 5 to 10 pounds are sometimes caught. The rate of growth varies.

RANGE: Anadromous brook trout occur in the Atlantic Ocean from Massachusetts north. They are found in the Maritime Provinces including the offshore islands, Newfoundland, and Labrador; they swim in tributary streams of Quebec and in forty-five of the Province of Ontario streams that flow into Hudson and James bays. They are found in seventeen of the Province's Lake Superior tributaries, and in some of Michigan's Lake Superior tributaries.

The major anadromous brook trout fisheries are the Ontario streams tributary to Lake Superior and Hudson and Georgian bays; and the Atlantic Coast of North America from Massachusetts northward. On the southern end of the Atlantic Coast, streams may have become marginal.

On the Moser River in-migration begins about June 17 and continues through the last part of July. The peak occurs in mid-July. In Ontario sea-run brook trout have entered the Sutton River (55th parallel) as early as July and continue to run through August. Great Lakes runs for Ontario tributary streams occur from October to December. Runs in Ontario's Lake Superior tributary streams peak in mid-October. Brooks enter—James and Hudson bays streams in July and August. Runs there peak in mid-August.

Some brook trout spawn in the fall of the year they first go to sea; others spawn in the second fall smolting. Anadromous brook trout spawn during late October or early November in Massachusetts tributary streams. In other areas they spawn in October. In Ontario, females usually spawn in their third year.

Moser River fish over-winter after spawning. Cape Cod anadromous brooks out-migrate to salt water in November directly after spawning. Massachusetts brook trout run to salt water after spawning. Brooks over-winter in streams in Minnesota after fall spawning. Ontario fisheries biologists report that brooks do not over-winter in their spawning stream in Lake Superior tributary streams, but do over-winter in streams tributary to James and Hudson bays in order to avoid over-wintering in salt water.

Fry emerge from gravel in April or May. The young remain in their stream for two to three years, feeding on Chironomids and trichoptera.

During their sea stay brooks do not swim far from the mouth of their stream of birth. Fish from some rivers are practically estuary fish. If they are not found near river mouths, they can often be found in clear water along rocky shores in water about 8 feet deep.

They do not stay long in the sea. White found that the sea stay ranges from 42 to 84 days with the average being 64 days.

COLOR: Some sea-run brooks have a purple cast. H. C. White reports that Moser River, Nova Scotia, fish are a dark greenish-blue on the back. Their sides are silvery or with pearl-like iridescence. The ventral area is pearly white. He also reports that Moser River fish have pink spots on the side. Others report red spots on the side.

D. G. Wilder says that by September sea-run fish that in-migrated during the summer have lost their silver sea colors and cannot be distinguished from indigenous fish by color alone.

POPULAR NAMES: Salter, coaster, sea trout, aurora trout, squaretail, speckled char, mud trout, and breac.

Bibliography

Alexander, R. McN., *Functional Design in Fishes*. Tarrytown, N.Y., Hutchinson & Co., 1967.

Ames, Francis, *Fishing the Oregon Country*. Caldwell, Idaho, Caxton Printers, Ltd., 1972.

Armstrong, Robert H., "Some Feeding Habits of the Anadromous Dolly Varden, *Salvelinus malma* (Walbaum)." Alaska Department of Fish and Game, Informational Leaflet No. 51.

———, "Migration of Anadromous Dolly Varden, *Salvelinus malma* in Southeastern Alaska." *Journal, Fisheries Research Board of Canada*, Vol. 31, No. 4, pp. 435–444.

———, "Investigations of Anadromous Dolly Varden Populations in Lake Eva-Hanus Bay Drainage, S.E. Alaska." Alaska Department of Fish and Game, Federal Aid in Fisheries Restoration, Annual Report of Progress 1962–63, Vol. 4, pp. 79–122.

Baade, R. T., Environmental Studies of the Cutthroat Trout, S.E. Alaska. Game Fish Investigations of Alaska. Quarterly Report of Progress, Federal Aid Restoration Project F-I-R-6, Alaska Game Commission, 1957 (unpublished).

Bates, Joseph D., Jr., *Atlantic Salmon Flies and Fishing*. Harrisburg, Pa., Stackpole, 1970.

———, "Conservation: Iceland's Key to Unspoiled Salmon Fishing." *Trout*, Vol. 17, No. 4 (Fall 1976), pp. 24–26.

Bigelow, H. B., and Welsh, W. W., Bulletin, U.S. Bureau of Fisheries, Vol. 40, No. 1 (1925), pp. 1–567.

Blackett, Roger F., "Spawning Behavior, Fecundity and Early Life History of Anadromous Dolly Varden in S.E. Alaska." Alaska Sports Fishing Project F-5-R-6 (1964–65) and F-5-R-7 (1965–66).

Bradner, Enos, *Northwest Angling*. Cranbury, N.J., A. S. Barnes, 1950.

Briggs, John C., "The Behavior and Reproduction of Salmonid Fishes in a Small Coastal Stream." (Prairie Creek) California Department of Fish and Game, Bulletin No. 94 (1953).

Brown, Margaret E., ed., *The Physiology of Fishes*, Vols. I and II. New York, Academic Press, 1957.

Carl, C. G. and others, *Freshwater Fishes of British Columbia*. Victoria, B.C., Provincial Museum Department of Education, Handbook No. 5, second edition, revised, 1953.

Carlander, Kenneth D., *Handbook of Freshwater Biology*, Vol. I. Ames, Iowa, Iowa State University Press, 1969.

Combs, Trey, "Steelhead and Fly Fishing and Flies." Portland, *Salmon Trout Steelheader*, 1976.

———, "The Steelhead Trout." Portland, *Salmon Trout Steelheader*, 1971.

Cramer, F. K., "Notes on the Natural Spawning of Cutthroat Trout, *Salmo clarki clarki*, in Oregon." Proceedings of the Sixth Pacific Science Conference of the Pacific Science Association, 1940, Vol. 3, pp. 335–339.

———, "Notes on Natural Spawning of Cutthroat, *Salmo clarkii clarkii*, in Oregon." Pacific Science Congress Proceedings, 1939, p. 336.

Cooley, Richard A., *Politics and Conservation. The Decline of the Alaska Salmon*. New York, Harper & Row, 1963.

Corti, U. A., *Schweiz. Zeitschrift Hydrological*, Vol. 12 (1950), pp. 288–299. "Die Matrix der Fische Notizen zur postembryonalen Ontogenes von Salmo irrideus" (W. Gibbs).

D.N.R. Staff, Michigan Fisheries Centennial Report: 1873–1973. Michigan Department of Natural Resources, Fisheries Division, Report No. 6 (1974).

Dodge, D. P., and MacCrimmon, H. R., "Vital Statistics of a Population of Great Lakes Rainbow Trout, *S. gairdneri*, Characterized by Extensive Spawning." *Journal, Fisheries Research Board of Canada*, Vol. 27 (1970), pp. 613–618.

Dymond, J., *Trout and Other Game Fishes of British Columbia*. Ottawa, Biological Board of Canada, Bulletin 32 (1932).

Eddy, Samuel, *How To Know the Freshwater Fishes*. Dubuque, Iowa, Wm. C. Brown, 1969.

————, "The Appearance of Pink Salmon, *O. gorbuscha* (Walbaum), in Lake Superior." Transactions of the American Fisheries Society, Vol. 89, No. 4, pp. 371–373.

Everest, Fred H., "Ecology and Management of Summer Steelhead in the Rogue River." Oregon State Game Commission, Report No. 7 (1973).

Fabricus, Eric., and Gustafson, Karl-Jakob, "Further Aquarium Observations on the Spawning Behavior of the Char, *Salmo alpinus*." Limnological Institute of Freshwater Research, Drottningholm, Report No. 35 (1953), pp. 58–104.

Fennelly, John F., *Steelhead Paradise*. Vancouver, Mitchell Press, 1963.

Frost, W. E., "Some Observations on the Biology of the Char." *Verhandlungen Internationale Vereinigung fuer Theoretische und Angewandte Limnologie*, Vol. 9 (1951), pp. 105–110.

Fry, Donald H., Jr., *Anadromous Fishes of California*. State of California, The Resources Agency Department of Fish and Game, 1973.

Grainger, E. H., "On the Age, Growth, Migration, Reproductive Potential and Feeding Habits of the Arctic Char, *Salvelinus alpinus*, of Frobisher Bay, Baffin Island."

Haig-Brown, Roderick L., *Western Angler*. New York, Morrow, 1947.

————, *Fisherman's Spring*. New York, Morrow, 1951. (Reprinted by Crown in 1975.)

————, *Fisherman's Winter*. New York, Morrow, 1954. (Reprinted by Crown in 1975.)

————, *Fisherman's Fall*. New York, Morrow, 1964. (Reprinted by Crown in 1975.)

Hassinger, R. L., Hale, J. G., and Woods, D. E., *Steelhead of the Minnesota North Shore*. Minnesota Division of Fish and Wildlife Technology, Bulletin No. 11 (1974).

Heacox, Cecil E., *The Compleat Brown Trout*. New York, Winchester Press, 1974.

Heiser, David W., "Age and Growth of Anadromous Dolly Varden Char, *Salvelinus malma* (Walbaum), in Eva Creek, Baranof Island, Southeastern Alaska." Alaska Department of Fish and Game, Federal Aid in Fisheries Restoration, Project F-5-R-4 and F-5-R-5 (1963–1964).

Holland, Dan, *Trout Fishing*. New York, Crowell, 1949.

Hubbs, Carl L., and Lagler, Karl F., *Fishes of the Great Lakes Region*. Ann Arbor, University of Michigan Press, 1947.

Hunter, J. G., "The Arctic Char." Fisheries Fact Sheet Issued by the Information and Consumer Service Department of Fisheries of Canada, September 1966.

————, "Production of Arctic Char (*Salvelinus alpinus* Linnaeus) in a Small Arctic Lake." Fisheries Research Board of Canada, Technical Report No. 231 (1970).

————, "Arctic Char and Hydroelectric Power in the Sylvia Grinnell River." Fisheries Research Board of Canada, Report No. 1376 (1976).

Huntsman, A. G., "Why Did Ontario Salmon Disappear?" Transactions of the Royal Society of Canada, Vol. XXXVIII, Section V (May 1944), p. 83.

Janes, Edward C., *Salmon Fishing in the Northeast*. Lexington, Ma., Stone Wall Press 1973.

Jeppson, Paul, "Evaluation of Kokanee and Trout Spawning Areas in Pend Oreille Lane and Tributary Streams." Biological and Economic Survey of Fishery Resources in Lake Pend Oreille. Idaho Department of Fish and Game, Final Report, Federal Aid in Fisheries Restoration, Project F-3-R-10 (1960), pp. 43–66.

Johnson, Les, "Fishing the Sea-Run Cutthroat Trout." Portland, *Salmon Trout Steelheader*, 1971.

Jones, D. E., "Life History Study of Sea-Run Cutthroat Trout and Steelhead Trout in Southeast Alaska." Alaska Department of Fish and Game, Federal Aid in Fisheries Restoration, Annual Report of Progress, 1971–1972, Vol. 13.

————, "Life History of Sea-Run Cutthroat Trout in Southeast Alaska." Alaska Department of Fish and Game, Anadromous Fish Studies, Annual Report of Progress, 1973–1974 and 1974–1975.

Jones, J. W., *The Salmon*. New York, Harper & Row, 1959.

Jordan, David Starr, "Trout and Salmon of the Pacific Coast." Nineteenth Biennial Report of the California Board of Fish Commissioners, 1905–1906.

Kendall, William Converse, *The Fishes of New England—The Salmon Family*. Part I—*The Trout or Charrs*. Memoirs of the Boston Society of Natural History, Vol. 8, No. 1. Boston, 1914.

Krieder, Claude, *Steelhead*. New York, G. P. Putnam's Sons, 1948.

Lagler, K. F., Bardach, J. E. and Miller, R. R., *Ichthyology, the Study of Fishes*. New York, Wiley, 1962.

Lowry, G. R., 1965. "Movement of Cutthroat Trout, *Salmo clarki clarki*: Richardson, in Three Oregon Coastal Streams." Transactions of the American Fisheries Society, Vol. 94, pp. 334–338.

Luch, Bill, "Steelhead Drift Fishing." Portland, *Salmon Trout Steel-header*, 1976.

MacCrimmon, Hugh R., and Gots, Barra L., *Rainbow Trout in the Great Lakes*, Ontario Ministry of Natural Resources, 1972.

MacDowell, S., *Western Trout*. New York, Knopf, 1948.

MacKay, H. H., *Fishes of Ontario*. Toronto, Bryant Press, 1963.

Malloch, P. D., *Life History and Habits of the Salmon, Sea Trout, and Other Freshwater Fish*. London, Adam and Charles Black, 1910.

Marshall, Mel, *Steelhead*. New York, Winchester Press, 1973.

Menzies, W. J. M., *Sea Trout and Trout*. London, Edward Arnold and Co., 1936.

Nall, G. Herbert, *The Life of the Sea Trout Especially in Scottish Waters with Chapters On the Reading and Measuring of Scales*. London, Seeley Service, 1930.

Needham, Paul, *Trout Streams*. Ithaca, N.Y., Comstock Publishing Co., 1938.

———, "Observations on the Natural Spawning of Eastern Brook Trout" California Fish and Game Bulletin, Vol. 47, No. 1 (1961), pp. 27–40.

———, "Observations on Spawning of Steelhead Trout." Transactions of the American Fisheries Society, Vol. 64 (1934), pp. 332–339.

Needham, P. R., and Vaughn, T. M., "Spawning of Dolly Varden in Twin Creek, Idaho" *Copeia*, No. 3 (1952), pp. 197–199.

Netboy, Anthony, *The Atlantic Salmon—A Vanishing Species?* Boston, Houghton Mifflin Co., 1968.

Niemuth, Wallace, "A Study of Migratory Lake-Run Trout in the Brule River, Wisconsin." Fish Management Report No. 12 (1967). (One of twelve papers about the 1940 Brule River study bound under the title *The Brule River—Douglas County*, published by the Wisconsin Conservation Department, 1954.)

Powers, E. B., "Chemical Factors Affecting the Migratory Movements of Pacific Salmon. The Migration and Conservation of Salmon." Publication of the American Association of Advanced Science, Vol. 8 (1941), pp. 72–85.

Proceedings of the 1971 symposium of Salmonid Communities in Oligotrophic Lakes (SCOL). *Journal, Fisheries Research Board of Canada*, Vol. 29, No. 6 (June 1972).

Reed, Roger J., "Observations of Fishes Associated with Spawning Salmon." Transactions of the American Fisheries Society, Vol. 96, No. 1 (1967), pp. 62–67.

Richey, David, Steelheading for Everybody. Harrisburg, Pa., Stackpole, 1976.

Russell, Jack, Jill and I and the Salmon. Boston, Little, Brown & Co., 1950.

Schultz, Leonard P., and students, "The Breeding Activities of Little Redfish, Oncorhynchus nerka, a land-locked form of the Sockeye Salmon." Journal of the Pan-Pacific Research Institution, Vol. 10, No. 1, pp. 67–76.

Schultz, Leonard P., "The Breeding Habits of Salmon and Trout." Annual Report, Smithsonian Institution, 1937, pp. 365–376.

Schwiebert, Ernest G., Salmon of the World. New York, Winchester Press, 1970.

Scott, W. B., and Crossman, E. J., Freshwater Fishes of Canada. Fisheries Research Board of Canada, Bulletin No. 184, Ottawa, 1973.

Shapovalov, Leo, and Taft, Alan C., "The Life History of the Steelhead Rainbow Trout, Salmo gairdneri gairdneri, and Silver Salmon, Oncorhynchus kisutch, with Special Reference to Waddell Creek." California Department of Fish and Game, Bulletin No. 98, 1954.

Smith, Osgood R., "The Spawning Habits of Cutthroat and Eastern Brook Trouts." Journal of Wildlife Management, Vol. 5, No. 4 (October 1941), pp. 461–471.

Sprules, Wm. M., "The Arctic Char of the West Coast of Hudson Bay." Transactions of the Fisheries Research Board of Canada.

Stauffer, Thomas M., "Age, Growth, and Downstream Migration of Juvenile Rainbow Trout in a Lake Michigan Tributary." Transactions of the American Fisheries Society, Vol. 101, pp. 18–28.

Sumner, F. H., "Migrations of Salmonids in Sand Creek, Oregon." Transactions of the American Fisheries Society, Vol. 82, pp. 139–150 (1953).

Sutterlin, A. M., and Sutterlin, N., "Electrical Responses of the Olfactory Epithelium of Atlantic Salmon (Salmo salar)." Journal, Fisheries Research Board of Canada, Vol. 28, No. 4 (1971).

Swift, D. R., "Effect of Temperature on Mortality and Rate of Development of the Eggs of the Windermere Char, Salvelinus alpinus." Journal, Fisheries Research Board of Canada, Vol. 22, No. 4 (1965), pp. 913–917.

Tody, Wayne H., and Tanner, Howard A., "Coho Salmon for the Great Lakes." Michigan Department of Conservation, Fish Division, Report No. 1, 1966.

Vesey-FitzGerald, Brian, *The World of Fishes*. London, Pelham Books, 1968.

White, H. C., "Some Observations of the Eastern Brook Trout, *S. fontinalis*, of Prince Edward Island." Transactions of the American Fisheries Society, Vol. 60, pp. 101–109.

————, "Migrating Behavior of Sea-Running *Salvelinus fontinalis*." *Journal, Fisheries Research Board of Canada*, Vol. 5, No. 3 (1941), pp. 258–264.

————, "Life History of Sea-Running Brook Trout, *Salvelinus fontinalis*, of Moser River, N.S." *Journal, Fisheries Research Board of Canada*, Vol. 5, No. 2 (1940), pp. 176–186.

————, "Sea Life of the Brook Trout, *Salvelinus fontinalis*."

Wilder, D. G., "A Comparative Study of Anadromous and Freshwater Populations of Brook Trout, *Salvelinus fontinalis* (Mitchill). *Journal, Fisheries Research Board of Canada*, Vol. 9, No. 4 (1952), pp. 169–203.

Withler, I. L., "Variability in Life History Characteristics of Steelhead Along the Pacific Coast." *Journal, Fisheries Research Board of Canada*, Vol. 23 (1966), pp. 365–393.

Wulff, Lee, *The Atlantic Salmon*. Cranbury, N.J., A. S. Barnes, 1958.

Yoshihara, Harvey T., "Some Life History Aspects of Arctic Char." Part A of "Monitoring and Evaluation of Arctic Waters with Emphasis on the North Slope Drainages." Project No. F-9-5, Study No. GIII, Vol. 14 (Study Period: July 1972–June 1973).

Younger, John, *On River Angling for Salmon and Trout*. New York, Abercrombie & Fitch, 1967 (original edition published in 1840 by William Blackwood & Sons, Edinburgh, Scotland).

Index

(Boldface numbers refer to illustrations)

A

L

Lake trout, **236, 238**

Lamphrey, 1, 32

Lateral line, 24, 32-33

Lievense, Stan, **165, 167, 204, 210**

Life of the Sea Trout, The (G. Herbert Nell), 57, 59

Little Manistee (fly), 92

Loftus, K. H., 195

Lures, *see* Exciter lures; Flies

M

MacLeon, David, **170**

Male fish, 20, 21

Mating, *see* Spawning time

Michigan, fishing, 160-177, **161**; Chocolay River, 172-174; Muskegon River, 174-176; salmon, 176, 177; streams and geography, 166-172; trout, 177

Migration-spawning factors, 37-40; calendar, 40-43

Miller, Kent, **175**

Minnesota, fishing, 178-180; Kimball Creek, 179-180

N

Nall, G. Herbert, *Life of the Sea Trout*, 57, 59

Needham, Paul R., *Trout Streams*, 58

T